T0290812

U.S. Airport Infrastructure Funding and Financing

Issues and Policy Options Pursuant to Section 122 of the 2018 Federal Aviation Administration Reauthorization Act

BENJAMIN M. MILLER, DEBRA KNOPMAN, LIISA ECOLA, BRIAN PHILLIPS, MOON KIM, NATHANIEL EDENFIELD, DANIEL SCHWAM, DIOGO PROSDOCIMI

Prepared for the U.S. Congress and the Secretary of Transportation

SOCIAL AND ECONOMIC WELL-BEING

For more information on this publication, visit www.rand.org/t/RR3175

Library of Congress Cataloging-in-Publication Data is available for this publication.
ISBN: 978-1-9774-0427-5

Support RAND
Make a tax-deductible charitable contribution at
www.rand.org/giving/contribute

www.rand.org

Preface

Passenger air travel is at an all-time high. In 2018, passengers boarded (enplaned) domestic flights more than 780 million times at the nation's 506 *commercial service airports*, which are publicly owned airports that serve at least 2,500 enplanements per year and receive scheduled passenger service. Demand for air travel has increased over time, and projections suggest that trend will continue. In response, commercial service airports have been investing in the infrastructure required to meet future demand for air travel. A key question for Congress is whether current levels of spending will be sufficient under existing federal policies to enable commercial service airports to make appropriate and timely infrastructure investments to meet future demand.

Congress authorized a study of commercial service airports' infrastructure needs and existing financial resources in the Federal Aviation Administration (FAA) Reauthorization Act of 2018. Section 122 of the Act directed the FAA to engage an independent research organization to consider these issues, as well as related concerns, and to "make recommendations on the actions needed to upgrade the national aviation infrastructure system to meet the growing and shifting demands of the 21st century." RAND, a nonprofit and nonpartisan policy research organization, was selected by the FAA through a competitive qualifications-based process to conduct this study. This report, like all RAND reports, is published independently by the RAND Corporation and does not require the consent or approval of the FAA or any other government agency.

The RAND research team commenced the study in late December 2018. Throughout the study period, we gathered and analyzed data, reports, and other materials relevant to funding, financing, and infrastructure conditions at U.S. airports. As required in Section 122(b) of the Act, we convened a panel of national experts drawn from a variety of stakeholder perspectives. The first meeting of this panel occurred in March 2019, and a second meeting occurred in August 2019. We also sought the perspectives of additional experts in the field. This report is the product of these research activities and fulfills the mandate of Section 122 that the independent organization (RAND) submit a report of its findings directly to Congress and the Secretary of Transportation by January 2020.

The primary audience for this report is members of Congress and their staffs as well as officials in the U.S. Department of Transportation, which includes the FAA. However, this report has been written to make this important but complex topic accessible to a broader audience. To this end, the purposes of this report are to explain how airports in the United States currently fund and finance their infrastructure needs, assess the adequacy of those mechanisms for maintaining a well-functioning aviation system, and present findings and recommendations to policymakers. In support of these purposes, we describe airports' planning and business processes; examine airports' interactions with the airline industry, local and state governments, and other stakeholders; and describe the federal government's role in funding, regulating, and otherwise affecting the decisionmaking behind airport infrastructure investment.

RAND Social and Economic Well-Being

RAND Social and Economic Well-Being (SEW), a division of the RAND Corporation, seeks to actively improve the health, social, and economic well-being of populations and communities throughout the world. This work has been managed within SEW's Community Health and Environmental Policy program, which focuses on such topics as infrastructure, science and technology, community design, community health promotion, migration and population dynamics, transportation, energy, and climate and the environment, as well as other policy concerns that are influenced by the natural and built environment, technology, and community organizations and institutions that affect well-being. For more information, email chep@ rand.org.

Contents

ONLINE APPENDIXES

Available for download at www.rand.org/t/RR3175

Figures

Tables

Summary

Section 122 of the Federal Aviation Administration (FAA) Reauthorization Act of 2018 directed the FAA to contract with an independent research organization to address questions and provide recommendations related to infrastructure funding and financing at commercial service airports. These airports are publicly owned, serve at least 2,500 passenger boardings per year, and receive scheduled passenger service. They provide the physical infrastructure—runways, terminals, gates, and other facilities—used by commercial airlines, travelers, and other air service providers.

This summary presents the report's core findings, recommendations, and answers to the questions listed in Section 122. As context and justification for these answers and recommendations, we provide in Chapters One through Eight a comprehensive review of the role of the federal government and an analysis of the status and trends in airport infrastructure funding and financing. In Chapter Nine, we present our findings and recommendations in greater detail.

The Nation's Airports

Commercial service airports are categorized by the FAA as "large hub," "medium hub," "small hub," "non-hub," or "nonprimary commercial service," according to the number of *enplanements* (passenger boardings) that occur at the airport, as shown in Table S.1. The National Plan of Integrated Airport Systems (NPIAS), developed and managed by the FAA, identifies airports that are eligible to receive federal airport infrastructure funding. The NPIAS includes all 506 commercial service airports, 2,815 general aviation (GA) airports, and seven proposed airports that are anticipated to open or be under development in the next five years. GA airports serve operations—i.e., the take-off or landing of an aircraft at an airport—beyond commercial passenger transportation, including flight training, agricultural services, aerial law enforcement, and recreational flying. Some GA airports are designated as *relievers* because they help reduce congestion at nearby commercial service airports.

Key Findings

Finding 1: The Color—and Control—of Money Matters

Airports draw revenue from a wide variety of sources, each of which comes with different rules and restrictions on how funds can be spent, as well as different conditions regarding which

Table S.1
Characteristics of National Plan of Integrated Airport Systems Airports, 2018

Airport Classification		Common Name	Criterion for Determining Common Name	Percentage of Total Enplanements	Total Enplanements	Number of Airports
Commercial service: At least 2,500 annual enplanements and scheduled passenger service	Primary: More than 10,000 annual enplanements	Large hub	Airport accounts for 1 percent or more of total enplanements	67.88	534,507,475	30
		Medium hub	At least 0.25 percent but less than 1 percent	18.75	147,624,888	31
		Small hub	At least 0.05 percent but less than 0.25 percent	9.54	75,150,646	72
		Non-hub	More than 10,000, but less than 0.05 percent	3.67	28,874,664	247
	Nonprimary: No more than 10,000 annual enplanements	Nonprimary commercial service	At least 2,500 and no more than 10,000	0.10	813,688	126
Noncommercial service: Less than 2,500 annual enplanements		General aviation	Less than 2,500	0.05	378,858	2,549
		Reliever	Designated to relieve congestion at commercial service airports	0.01	107,503	261

SOURCE: RAND analysis of T-100 segment data (Bureau of Transportation Statistics, 2019c) and FAA, 2017c.
NOTE: Enplanements are for domestic flights only. Domestic flights begin and end in the United States.

entities must approve the spending. As a consequence, airport operators consider more than whether sufficient dollars are available to fund an infrastructure project. They also carefully consider whether and how much funding can come from different sources. Control of funding decisions is an important determinant in an airport's funding preferences. Depending on the "color of money," airports also are required to line up approvals from the appropriate combination of federal regulators, local and state governments, and airlines before proceeding to make capital investments in airport infrastructure.

Finding 2: If You've Seen One Airport, You've Seen One Airport

Although airports across the nation face many of the same challenges, the financial capabilities and local context of each airport can vary widely. All commercial service airports face the same broad industry trends, such as growing demand for air travel, increasing plane sizes, and vulnerability of airport business models to disruptive technologies, such as ride-hailing services (e.g., Uber and Lyft), self-driving vehicles, and the use of drones. Airports also face the same federal rules and regulations on funding, safety, security, and other issues. Most airports have managed to sustain sufficient investment in runways, terminals, and other services while maintaining strong credit ratings.

However, other factors affecting airports' financial capacities vary widely from airport to airport. Some airports appear better-positioned financially to manage future growth than others. The prospect of growth in demand is closely tied to local economic conditions, which can inject a significant amount of uncertainty into airports' financial plans. Further, how financial risks are distributed between airports and airlines depends on the particulars of use-and-lease agreements between individual airports and their tenant airlines. Differences in local governance arrangements and physical assets shape airports' opportunities for raising capital. Airports also have widely varying amounts of cash reserves, airline competition, and infrastructure-related delays, some of which reflect limitations on land availability or disagreements over local land-use policy and public priorities.

Finding 3: There Are Known Areas in Which Infrastructure Investment Is Needed

Airport runways are generally in good repair. This reflects the priority given to airside infrastructure—i.e., infrastructure for the operation of aircraft—in federal grants provided under the Airport Improvement Program (AIP) and the effectiveness of funding from all sources to meet airside needs. However, terminals and control towers are widely viewed as being in need of modernization, repair, or replacement. The growth in the number of enplanements has led to more crowded terminals at some airports, and many aging control towers and other air traffic control facilities require rehabilitation and upgrading. Smaller airports, which are almost wholly reliant on federal grants, struggle to generate sufficient revenues for spending on landside infrastructure for ground transportation vehicles, the processing of passengers, and other purposes.

These infrastructure limitations are one of several factors contributing to delays in the National Airspace System (NAS), and these infrastructure-related delays are thus not spread evenly across the system. Rather, a small number of capacity-constrained airports and airport pairs appear to be responsible for delays that could be partially (but not fully) addressed by sound infrastructure investment. Twenty airports (19 large hubs and one reliever) accounted for 96 percent of delays measured by the FAA's Operations Network in 2018. The top five airports alone, three of which are operated by the Port Authority of New York and New Jersey (LaGuardia Airport, John F. Kennedy International Airport, and Newark Liberty International Airport), accounted for 61 percent of delays. These delays propagate through the NAS: A flight delayed in arriving at its initial destination might be late departing for its next destination. Some of this congestion could be addressed in part through sound investments in reconfiguring or expanding infrastructure on both the airside and the landside.

Finding 4: Easing Revenue Restrictions on the Passenger Facility Charge Would Reduce Airports' Borrowing Costs but Likely Would Increase Ticket Prices

Airports will need to make significant investments in the coming years to sustain existing capacity and services and to accommodate growth in enplanements and commercial operations. The larger commercial service airports are likely to find ways to make the investments they deem to be critical, but increased access to higher revenue streams in the near term would enable these airports to complete approved priority projects sooner and at lower borrowing costs.

One proposed method for allowing commercial service airports to raise additional revenue is to change the cap on the fee that passengers are charged for their use of airport infrastructure at airports that choose to participate in the federally authorized passenger facility charge (PFC) program. With reference to the color of money in Finding 1, airlines cannot veto FAA-approved PFC-funded projects. The cap on PFCs has been set at $4.50 per passenger since the 2000 FAA Reauthorization Act. Since that time, the purchasing power of a dollar of PFC revenues has eroded because of inflation; each dollar of PFC revenue buys only 60 percent of the construction materials it did in 2000. Increasing enplanements have increased capital investment needs at many airports. It is also true that aggregate PFC revenues have grown because of increases in nationwide enplanements, increases in the number of airports using PFCs, and the increase of the PFC cap from $3.00 to $4.50.

Increasing the PFC cap above the current level of $4.50 would enable those airports that seek additional PFC revenue to initiate their approved projects sooner and pay them off more quickly, lowering costs. In the aggregate, costs for some passengers are likely to increase as a consequence of the higher PFC. However, the impacts of a PFC increase on ticket prices at a particular airport may vary depending on both airport and airline decisions.

Finding 5: Smaller Airports in Small Markets Have Limited Opportunities for Revenue Generation and Rely Primarily on Grants

Smaller airports by definition have a smaller user base that offers fewer opportunities for raising revenue and are therefore more reliant on federal (and to a much lesser extent, state) grants than larger airports for paying the high fixed costs related to runways, taxiways, aprons, safety, and security. GA airports are not eligible to collect PFCs, a mechanism that Congress authorized exclusively for use by commercial service airports, nor do GA airports have sufficient passenger volume to support such a user fee. Instead, GA and nonprimary commercial service airports rely on AIP funding, which is redistributive by design; smaller airports receive a larger share of AIP dollars than they generate in excise tax revenues to the Airport and Airway Trust Fund (AATF), which funds the AIP and many other FAA programs. Airports must be included in the NPIAS to be eligible to receive AIP funds.

There are two general types of AIP grants: entitlements and discretionary. The FAA uses discretionary grants to target specific projects at individual airports according to need and benefit to the system as a whole. The FAA awards entitlement grants to most airports in the NPIAS, although airports that receive approval for PFC-funded projects forgo a portion of their entitlement. Under current congressionally mandated funding formulas, GA and nonprimary commercial service airports are each eligible to receive entitlement grants of up to $150,000 per year, an amount too small to support airport construction of any consequence. Airports, however, are permitted to defer their annual entitlements over several years to accumulate sufficient funds to undertake a project.

Finding 6: The Airport and Airway Trust Fund Has a Large and Growing Uncommitted Balance

The AATF, which funds many FAA programs (including the AIP), took in $750 million more in excise tax revenues than it spent in FY 2018, ending the year with an uncommitted balance of $6.1 billion. An uncommitted balance refers to funds that have not yet been obligated for spending. The AATF's uncommitted balance is projected to grow to $18.8 billion by the end of FY 2023, assuming passenger enplanements (and associated excise tax revenues) continue to rise. Several of the excise taxes that fund the AATF are pegged to inflation, and all of them relate to the volume of air infrastructure utilization.

Congress has the authority to obligate AATF funds for AIP grants to airports and a wide array of other underfunded capital needs. Currently, the FAA Reauthorization Act of 2018 holds the authorized level of AATF-funded AIP grants constant at $3.35 billion over the

FY 2019 to FY 2023 period, and outlays from the AATF for other FAA purposes are assumed to grow only with inflation.

Finding 7: Revenue Diversion Is Still an Issue

Revenue diversion is the use of airport operating revenues for expenditures that are either not on airport property or do not directly serve aviation purposes. Revenue diversion comes in two forms that are treated differently in policy. Both are problematic. In the first form, 12 airport sponsors—i.e., the cities or other public entities that own one or more airports—were grandfathered in when Congress mandated an end to such revenue diversion practices in 1982. Airports operated by these airport sponsors are legally allowed to divert airport operating revenue, up to a statutory limit. The second form encompasses revenue diversion by any other airport sponsor, which most frequently takes the form of state or local governments diverting revenue from aviation fuel taxes to nonaviation purposes.

The argument for grandfathering was that accounting and spending practices at these airports made a clean separation of revenue between airport and nonairport uses difficult. Correcting this challenge is not impossible because the grandfathering provision has been removed for three of the 12 airport sponsors. The amount of funds being diverted is not trivial, as a 2018 U.S. Department of Transportation (USDOT) Inspector General's report found that "[f]rom 1995 to 2015, grandfathered sponsors have reported over $10 billion in grandfathered payments in 2015 inflation-adjusted dollars, including over $1.2 billion in 2015" (USDOT, Office of Inspector General, 2018, pp. 1–2). The full extent of revenue collected and diverted is difficult to quantify by outside observers, including the FAA. The FAA has effective enforcement options available for discouraging the second form of revenue diversion, but the FAA's existing enforcement mechanisms are largely unable to prevent grandfathered airports from exceeding their statutory limit.

Recommendations

We recommend a portfolio of complementary changes in the PFC program, the AIP, the AATF, and in policies and procedures regarding revenue diversion. The interrelated nature of these funding programs and policies makes it important to consider these recommendations as a whole rather than in isolation. As with any proposed changes in policy, the benefits and costs of the proposed changes could result in some stakeholders being better off and others worse off, in reality or perception. In shaping our recommendations, we were guided by our findings and a vision of what funding and financing policies in support of an effective NAS should look like, informed by our analysis and consultations with experts and stakeholders. In our vision of a well-functioning system of funding and finance,

- airports are able to draw on sufficient and stable sources of revenue, in conjunction with funding from capital markets, to maintain existing capacity, accommodate growth, and support a safe and sustainable NAS in the coming decades
- federal funding is effectively, efficiently, and flexibly deployed to address needs in the NAS that are of national significance and benefit
- airports of all sizes run safe, efficient, and sustainable operations for the betterment of their communities and the NAS as a whole.

This vision and the findings discussed above provide the basis for our recommendations. Table S.2 shows how our recommendations are connected to the preceding findings. Our findings are in turn supported by the details presented in this report.

Changes to the PFC Program

Congress has several options regarding changes to the PFC program. We present and discuss four policy options in Chapter Nine: (1) index the current cap to inflation, (2) increase the flexibility of airport revenue but do not increase cumulative revenue other than indexing the cap to inflation, (3) raise but do not remove the PFC cap and index the cap to inflation thereafter, and (4) remove the PFC cap entirely.

We recommend that Congress pursue the third option of increasing, but not removing, the PFC cap, with subsequent indexing. This option would improve airports' abilities to make timely and efficient capital investments to meet growing future demand, while leaving in place FAA oversight of project justification and costs on passengers. Specifically, we recommend that Congress

- raise the current PFC cap of $4.50 to approximately $7.50 for passengers at their point of origin only
- index the new PFC cap to inflation
- eliminate 100 percent of AIP primary entitlements for medium- and large-hub airports that choose to raise their PFC above $4.50.

We are not aware of compelling evidence or data justifying a particular level for a new cap. Any number could be chosen, but we note that if the $4.50 cap had been indexed to inflation in 2000 using the Producer Price Index for construction materials, it would now be set at $7.44. For this reason, we suggest that the cap in this option be around this value, perhaps

Table S.2
Connection Between Recommendations and Findings

Finding	Changes to the PFC	Changes to the AIP	Changes to the AATF	Changes to revenue diversion
Finding 1: The color—and control—of money matters.	■			■
Finding 2: If you've seen one airport, you've seen one airport.	■			■
Finding 3: There are known areas in which infrastructure investment is needed.	■			
Finding 4: Easing revenue restrictions on the PFC would reduce airports' borrowing costs but likely would increase ticket prices.	■	■		
Finding 5: Small airports in small markets have limited opportunities for revenue generation and rely primarily on grants.		■	■	
Finding 6: The AATF has a large and growing uncommitted balance.			■	
Finding 7: Revenue diversion is still an issue.				■

NOTE: Shaded boxes identify the findings that provide evidentiary support for the recommendation.

rounded up to $7.50, although other levels could be chosen. Although an increase in the PFC cap would likely result in higher ticket prices for passengers traveling through airports that raised their PFC collections, there remains in place a set of guardrails to weigh the public benefits of PFC-funded projects relative to the costs imposed on passengers. Airports will continue to be required to justify the net benefits of projects proposed for PFC funding to the FAA, and the FAA retains its discretion to approve or disapprove applications for these projects. Further, airports will still need to be responsive to comments from airlines and other stakeholders when requesting a PFC increase.

To ensure that airports have sufficient and stable sources of revenue commensurate with present and future capital needs, the PFC cap should be indexed to inflation, regardless of whether the PFC cap is otherwise changed. Indexing the PFC to a construction index, such as the Producer Price Index for construction materials, would stabilize the parity of purchasing power at the current cap or a new cap set by Congress for airports making infrastructure investments. In contrast, indexing to the Consumer Price Index would hold constant the impact of PFC increases on passenger ticket prices. PFC collections in the aggregate have increased without indexing because of increases in nationwide enplanements, increases in the number of airports using PFCs, and the increase in the PFC cap from $3.00 to $4.50. Increases in enplanements and operations place demands on infrastructure.

Not all airports will choose to seek an immediate or longer-term PFC increase. To increase transparency regarding the intentions of airports in maintaining cash reserves beyond those required by bond rating agencies, we suggest that the FAA consider an airport's cash reserves and broader financial status when determining whether to approve an airport's request for an increase in its PFC.

We further recommend that large- and medium-hub airports that raise their PFC above $4.50, indexed to inflation, should forgo their AIP primary entitlements dollar-for-dollar for each dollar of PFCs they collect, up to 100 percent of these entitlements. Instead, that money could more efficiently achieve the redistributive purpose of the AIP either by being focused on needs of national significance among smaller airports or by being directed to other priorities affecting the safety and sustainability of the NAS. Airports that raise their PFC above $4.50 would remain eligible for other categories of AIP funding, including discretionary grants and cargo entitlements.

Under current law, passengers with one or more layovers must pay two PFCs: one to the origin airport and one to the first layover airport. Because an airport's PFC applies to these layover passengers, an increase in the PFC could reduce demand for flights that have layovers at that airport. This could be particularly problematic for small airports, where almost all routes go through one or two larger "feeder" airports to connect their community to the national and international system. For this reason, we recommend that any increase in the PFC cap beyond $4.50 apply only to passengers that originate at the airport raising its PFC, while the PFC for layover passengers remains capped at $4.50, indexed to inflation. The rationale for restricting future PFC increases to only passengers originating at that airport is to ensure that airports that increase their PFCs to meet their own capital needs do not impose costs on other airports in the process. Origin passengers represent the majority of passengers at most airports, with the notable exception of three large hubs, and layover passengers could still be charged PFCs of up to $4.50, indexed to inflation.

Changes to the Airport Improvement Program
Congress Should Remove the Automatic Doubling of Airport Improvement Program Primary Entitlements

Under current law, whenever Congress appropriates at least $3.2 billion to the AIP, primary entitlements per passenger double (subject to a cap), with those increases resulting in less money available for other AIP funds, including discretionary grants. As a consequence of this policy, annual AIP funding is spread across all primary airports according to their enplanements, and the FAA has less discretion to effectively direct funds to current high-priority projects at specific airports.

We recommend that Congress remove the triggered primary entitlement increase that occurs when Congress appropriates at least at $3.2 billion to the AIP. Those airports not voluntarily forgoing AIP entitlements in return for the ability to collect PFCs could still receive comparable levels of AIP funding over time, but the timing and magnitude of annual grants would be better aligned with the timing and magnitude of needs. Airports could compete to receive more funds in the form of larger grants from the pool of discretionary funding, when needed, but would receive fewer guaranteed funds in the form of annual entitlements.

Congress Should Consider Removing Nonprimary Entitlements

As with primary entitlements, under current law, whenever Congress appropriates at least $3.2 billion to the AIP, each nonprimary airport in the NPIAS receives an entitlement of up to $150,000 instead of those funds going to more-flexible state apportionments for nonprimary airports. This amount is insufficient for major construction projects, and the existing state apportionment mechanism is both better suited to meet nonprimary airports' needs and has sufficient oversight mechanisms in place. We recommend that Congress eliminate nonprimary entitlements that occur under current law when the AIP appropriation is at least $3.2 billion. As with the previous recommendation, airports could still compete to receive comparable levels of funding over time, but the timing and magnitude of individual distributions would be better aligned with the timing and magnitude of needs.

Changes to the Airport and Airway Trust Fund
Congress Should Avoid the Accumulation of Large Uncommitted Airport and Airway Trust Fund Balances While Still Maintaining a "Rainy Day" Reserve Fund

Existing spending guarantee mechanisms in statute are designed to prevent the accumulation of a large uncommitted balance in the AATF and to ensure excise tax revenues are spent on aviation system priorities. In practice, the enforcement mechanism is weak and is regularly ignored by Congress. Under excise tax levels set in current law, a large uncommitted balance is projected to materialize. Congress should take advantage of the existing uncommitted balance to establish and maintain a "rainy day" fund to ensure funding levels can remain stable over time. In years that experience unusually low demand for air travel, such as 2002 and 2009, actual revenues to the AATF can fall approximately $2 billion below projected revenues. A rainy day fund containing $4 billion to $6 billion would be sufficient to ensure that AATF outflows, for all purposes, can remain stable even in the face of two to three years of severe revenue shortfalls. However, after seeding the rainy day fund, additional revenues should be appropriated to meet clearly identified needs, as determined by the FAA.

Congress Should Include Ancillary Fees in the Domestic Passenger Ticket Tax

Ancillary fees are charges for airline-provided services or products that some airlines sell separately from tickets, such as checked baggage, advance seat assignments, and priority boarding. These fees are excluded from the 7.5 percent Domestic Passenger Ticket Tax that helps fund the AATF. This policy favors airlines that separate ancillary fees from their base ticket price over those that do not. Airlines should be free to separate ancillary fees if they wish, but the Domestic Passenger Ticket Tax should not incentivize one business model over another by taxing ancillary services differently than bundled ticket prices. However, Congress should not be collecting additional AATF revenue without a commitment to spend it, as noted in the preceding recommendation. For this reason, we recommend that Congress ask the FAA to help determine the level of reduction in the Domestic Passenger Ticket Tax that would make the taxation of ancillary fees revenue-neutral.

Changes to Enforcement of Prohibitions on Revenue Diversion
The FAA Should Increase Enforcement of Existing Rules

Revenue diversion refers to the practice of airport sponsors spending aviation-related revenue on nonaviation purposes, a practice generally prohibited by law. Revenue diversion remains a significant problem, even though the FAA has sought to clarify its rules regarding the disposition of state-based fuel taxes in recent years. Generally, the pressure to divert revenue comes from other local interests and not airport management, which has every interest in retaining the revenues generated by airport operations. Thus, withholding AIP grants as a punishment for revenue diversion is not a well-targeted deterrence strategy. Under current law, the USDOT, if triggered by FAA enforcement action, has the authority to withhold other USDOT grants from airport sponsors (as opposed to withholding FAA grants from airport management) that remain out of compliance with revenue diversion rules. This withholding rarely occurs, but the FAA should pursue this path when compliance is not swift.

Congress Should Phase Out Grandfathering

Twelve airport sponsors were originally granted waivers in 1982 from prohibitions on revenue diversion because of their particularly complicated arrangements for mingling revenues and expenditures across multiple public assets under their jurisdiction. The grandfathering provision has already been removed for three of these airport sponsors, proving that ending this exception is possible. Ending this exception also is important for supporting good governance at the local level.

Issues for Further Analysis

Many Airports and Routes Lack a Healthy Level of Competition

Lack of competition can affect passengers in several ways. We highlight two cases here. First, many airports, cities, and routes are served by only one or two airlines. Lack of competition among airlines at a given airport can result in higher costs for travelers. In practice, PFC projects provide airports with a means of accommodating new entrants without a veto by legacy carriers, but competition cannot be enhanced solely through changes in infrastructure finance policy. Second, passengers also can be affected by lack of competition among airports in a given region. Under current law, airport sponsors that manage multiple airports can use PFC funds collected at one of their airports to pay for projects at another of their airports. This does not occur often, but when it does, it challenges the notion that PFCs are a user fee. In both cases, broader regional economic issues and trade-offs are in play that require a more comprehensive assessment.

Impacts of Regulations and Requirements Are Uncertain

As previously noted, airports draw revenue from a wide variety of sources, each of which comes with its own rules and restrictions on how funds can be spent and who has approval authority. Many anecdotes have accumulated over the years about individual projects being delayed or stopped entirely as a consequence of local opposition, whether because of cost, noise, or encroachment into neighboring communities. But projects being halted or delayed by regulations or requirements is not necessarily inappropriate; impacts on other stakeholders are important considerations. This long-standing question in public policy remains a topic ripe for independent, objective, and rigorous analysis to provide Congress and other decisionmakers with clearer direction on how regulations can be harmonized and streamlined to increase their effectiveness and enhance their efficiency.

Revenue-Neutral Alternatives to Fuel Taxes Will Eventually Be Needed

Fuel taxes are not the largest portion of AATF revenue. Nonetheless, progress on developing and deploying electric planes could eventually lead to declines in fuel-based tax revenues while leaving the electric planes using the same or new infrastructure untaxed (a comparable situation applies to the gas tax supporting the Highway Trust Fund). To ensure stability and equity of funding, Congress should authorize the FAA to conduct a study that considers transitional or alternative tax structures, such as weight-based or operations-based taxes, including alternatives that would be revenue-neutral relative to revenues generated by the current levels of fuel-based taxes.

Inventory Existing Infrastructure and Assess Infrastructure Capacity and Physical Condition

Existing inventories and assessments of airport infrastructure have significant shortcomings. There is a need for an objective and analytically rigorous national inventory of existing airport infrastructure, air traffic control towers, and other air traffic facilities, and there is a need for an assessment of their current capacity, functionality, and physical condition. An up-to-date inventory and assessment of infrastructure conditions would provide a valuable foundation for Congress to make more-informed choices in the future about the levels of investment required across the different infrastructure types.

Summary of Findings on Section 122 Issues

To ease the tracking of issues in Section 122, Table S.3 provides a guide to the Section 122 findings and their locations within the report.

Table S.3
Summary of Responses to Section 122 Issues

Subsection of Section 122	Issue	Summary of Findings	Chapter in Report
All Commercial Service Airports			
(c)(1)	Ability of airport infrastructure to meet current and projected passenger volumes	Twenty airports (19 large hubs and one reliever) account for 96 percent of delays measured by the FAA's Operations Network (OPSNET). Delays at most of these airports, as well as the National Airspace System (NAS) as a whole, had been declining since 2009 but have been increasing over the past three years as enplanements have increased. Some of these delays could be partially reduced by appropriate infrastructure investments.	Chapter Eight
(c)(2)	Available financial tools and resources for airports of different sizes	Airports of all sizes draw on multiple sources of funding. Larger airports tend to generate most of their revenues from their operations and take advantage of the municipal bond market. In contrast, smaller airports rely on Airport Improvement Program (AIP) and other grants for funding and have limited access to the bond market.	Chapters Four and Seven
(c)(3)	Available financing tools and resources for airports in rural areas	Rural airports, which are predominantly smaller airports, rely heavily on AIP and other grants as their major source of revenue, with these grants accounting for more than 50 percent of their revenue on average. Rural airports are less likely to participate in the bond market.	Chapter Four
(c)(4)	Current debt held by airports and its impact on future construction and capacity needs	Over the last ten years, large-hub airports have increased their debt by 34 percent, to $73.6 billion in 2017, but their debt-to-revenue ratio has remained relatively stable. Debt and debt-to-revenue ratios across commercial service airports of all other sizes have generally held steady over the past two decades. Airports' ability to finance future construction and capacity needs will depend on their financial status, regional and local economic conditions, and other factors.	Chapter Seven
(c)(5)	Impact of capacity constraints on passengers and ticket prices	As noted in (c)(1), 20 airports account for 96 percent of delays measured by the FAA's OPSNET. These airports create delays for passengers that propagate throughout the NAS.	Chapter Eight
		Separately, the average inflation-adjusted domestic ticket price fell from $630 in 1993 to $432 in 2018. Competition and market conditions are the primary determinants of ticket prices. We do not find evidence that capacity-enhancing projects significantly affect ticket prices.	Chapters Two and Six
(c)(6)	Purchasing power of the passenger facility charge (PFC) from the last increase in 2000 to the year of enactment of this Act	The purchasing power of the maximum per-enplanement PFC has declined, from $4.50 in 2000 to $2.72 in 2018, expressed in year 2000 dollars indexed to construction prices.	Chapter Six
(c)(7)	Impact to passengers and airports of indexing the PFC for inflation	If the $4.50 PFC cap had been indexed to inflation in construction prices in 2000, the current cap on passengers would be $7.44. If the cap were indexed to inflation moving forward, this would prevent further erosion of its purchasing power. According to historical precedent, airports' adoption of higher PFCs likely would become widespread over time.	Chapter Six
(c)(8)	How long airports are constrained with current PFC collections	PFC revenues at all large-hub airports but one are fully committed to FAA-approved projects through 2022. Eighteen of 30 large hubs have fully committed their PFC revenues until at least 2030, and six are committed until at least 2040. Among the 31 medium hubs, ten have fully committed their PFC revenues until at least 2030, while 14 will have new revenues available by 2025.	Chapter Six

Table S.3—Continued

Subsection of Section 122	Issue	Summary of Findings	Chapter in Report
(c)(9)	Impact of PFCs on promoting competition	Analysis of existing data does not provide conclusive evidence of whether individual PFC projects have had impacts on competition. Facilities funded with PFCs may not be leased on an exclusive-use basis, and that policy element of the PFC program might support competition. Airline hubbing decisions and local economic conditions are more likely to drive significant changes in competition.	Chapter Six
(c)(10)	Additional resources or options to fund terminal construction projects	Airports typically combine funds from multiple sources to fund terminal construction projects. Many funds come from airport revenue. PFC funds can be used for non–revenue-generating portions of terminals, while AIP grants are generally focused on airside infrastructure. Expanding airports' revenue bases to include the taxing of nonairport local businesses and residents is unattractive to local governments and would increase the cost of local goods and services unrelated to air travel. Privatization is possible but rarely pursued; the Airport Investment Partnership Program, established in 1997, allows airports to explore privatization but has had few takers.	Chapters Four through Seven
(c)(11)	Resources eligible for use toward noise reduction and emission reduction projects	AIP grants and PFCs can be applied to noise reduction and emission reduction projects. We found no evidence that resources for these purposes are insufficient to meet current noise and emissions requirements.	Chapter Three
(c)(12)	Gap between the cost of projects eligible for the AIP and the annual federal funding provided	Airports consult with FAA regional staff to determine which AIP-eligible projects to submit, given program funds and priorities. This consultation process makes identifying the magnitude of a funding gap difficult in practice. The FAA's list of AIP-eligible projects exceeds annual AIP funding, but airports can and do use other funds to pay for AIP-eligible projects.	Chapters Five and Eight
(c)(13)	Impact of regulatory requirements on airport infrastructure financing needs	Airports draw revenue from a wide variety of sources, each of which comes with its own rules and restrictions on how funds can be spent and who has approval authority. A benefit of regulatory processes is that they provide an opportunity for the public to voice concerns or support for specific projects. Effects on project completion timelines and cost are likely to vary depending on local context. We were unable to estimate cumulative impacts.	Chapters Three and Four
(c)(14)	Airline competition	Over the past few decades, mergers and bankruptcies in the airline industry have led to fewer overall airlines, with four airlines currently responsible for 73 percent of available seat miles and 80 percent of enplanements. National average fares have fallen 36 percent since 1993, but fares on individual routes fluctuate. Markets with fewer passengers are likely to be served by fewer airlines.	Chapter Two
(c)(15)	Airline ancillary fees and their impact on ticket pricing and taxable revenue	Some airlines have separated ancillary fees, such as fees for baggage and reserved seats, from their base fares. Ancillary fees that have been separated from base fares are exempt from the 7.5 percent excise tax that helps fund the Airport and Airway Trust Fund (AATF). If the $4.9 billion in baggage fees collected by airlines in 2018 had been subject to the 7.5 percent tax, AATF revenues would have been about $367 million higher, all other factors being equal.	Chapter Five
(c)(16)	Ability of airports to finance necessary safety, security, and capacity projects	To date, airports have been able to finance necessary safety, security, capacity, and environmental projects identified in capital improvement plans. Their financial ability to continue doing so in a timely manner varies. Policy changes that increase revenue would enable some airports to initiate projects sooner and at a lower borrowing cost than they could otherwise but would likely increase passenger ticket prices.	Chapter Eight

Table S.3—Continued

Subsection of Section 122	Issue	Summary of Findings	Chapter in Report
Large-Hub Airports			
(d)(1)	Analyze the current and future capacity constraints of large-hub airports	Nineteen large-hub airports account for 94 percent of delays measured by FAA's OPSNET. Delays at most of these airports, as well as the NAS as a whole, had been declining since 2009 but have been increasing over the past three years as enplanements have increased. Some of these delays could be partially reduced by appropriate infrastructure investments.	Chapter Eight
(d)(2)	Quantify large-hub airports' infrastructure requirements, including terminal, landside, and airside infrastructure	Infrastructure at large-hub airports served 534,507,475 domestic commercial enplanements and 11,893,110 operations in 2018. As noted in (d)(3), this use of airport infrastructure is expected to grow. We cannot say how to convert these activity levels to credible estimates of specific infrastructure requirements, because this depends largely on the flexibility of airports' current configuration, local context, market forces, and changes in technology.	Chapter Two
(d)(3)	Quantify the percentage growth in infrastructure requirements of the large-hub airports relative to other commercial service airports	The FAA's Terminal Area Forecast suggests that large-hub airports' operations will increase by 19 percent and enplanements will increase by 30 percent from 2018 to 2030. Over the same period, operations at medium hubs are forecast to grow by 17 percent, small hubs by 10 percent, and non-hubs by 6 percent. This growth will likely lead to increased infrastructure requirements, but local circumstances will determine whether changes are required and, if so, their associated costs.	Chapter Eight
(d)(4)	Analyze how much funding from the AIP has gone to meet the requirements of large-hub airports over the past ten years	In total, large hubs received about $6 billion in AIP grants from FYs 2009 to 2018. This was 17 percent of all AIP grant dollars over that period. The percentage of large hubs' capital expenditures that comes from AIP grants has declined, down to 5 percent in FY 2018 from approximately 10 percent to 15 percent between FYs 2009 and 2015. Under present policies, large- and medium-hub airports forgo much of their AIP primary entitlement grants when imposing PFCs but retain access to other AIP grants.	Chapter Five
(d)(5)	Project how much AIP funding would be available to meet the requirements of large-hub airports in the next five years if funding levels are held constant	If appropriations, statutory entitlements, and the distribution of discretionary funds that goes to large hubs were all to remain the same as they have over the past ten years, then about $3 billion of AIP funding would be available for large hubs over the next five years. This would represent 17 percent of the total AIP funding that would be available over this five-year period.	Chapter Five

Acknowledgments

As a part of Section 122 of the FAA Reauthorization Act of 2018, the RAND research team was required to convene an expert panel representing a specified range of stakeholder perspectives. We were more than happy to do so. We therefore would like to begin by expressing our deep appreciation to each of the members of the expert panel. Panel members were generous with their time and responsive to our requests for information. They provided us with much-needed context and detail about the workings of the airport sector and the perspectives of their organizations. Together, they represent a wealth of experience and insight that could not easily have been acquired through other means. However, we emphasize that the findings and recommendations made in this report are attributed to the authors and not the panel. Participation on the panel does not represent an endorsement of the report by the individual panel members nor the organizations they represent, and at no point was the panel tasked with providing consensus recommendations. Panel members, listed alphabetically by last name, were

- Jim Coon, Senior Vice President, Government Affairs and Advocacy, Aircraft Owners and Pilots Association
- Shane Downey, Vice President of Government Relations, Global Business Travel Association
- Bryant Francis, Director of Aviation at the Port of Oakland
- Trish Gilbert, Executive Vice President of the National Air Traffic Controllers Association
- Adam Giombetti, Deputy CFO at Denver International Airport
- Erik Hansen, Vice President of Government Relations at the U.S. Travel Association
- Arlene Juracek, Mayor of Mount Prospect, Illinois, and Chair of the O'Hare Noise Compatibility Commission
- Charles Leocha, President of Travelers United
- Candace McGraw, CEO of Cincinnati/Northern Kentucky International Airport and Chair of the Airports Council International–North America Executive Committee
- Scott McMahon, Executive Director, Morristown Municipal Airport and Chair of the AAAE General Aviation Airports Committee
- Jeffrey Northgraves, Manager of Knox County Regional Airport
- Sharon Pinkerton, Senior Vice President, Legislative and Regulatory Policy, Airlines for America
- Chris Poinsatte, CFO at Dallas/Fort Worth International Airport
- Mark Rodrigues, Assistant Director, Airport Development, Regional APCS Division, International Air Transport Association
- Brian Sprenger, Airport Director of Bozeman Yellowstone International Airport
- John Strong, CSX Professor of Business Administration at William and Mary.

In addition to panel members, we wish to thank other experts who made themselves available to the RAND team for in-person and phone interviews. These include, in alphabetical order, representatives from Airlines for America, Airports Council International–North America, Airports Council International–World, Cincinnati/Northern Kentucky International Airport, Frasca & Associates, International Air Transport Association, Landrum and Brown, LoneStar Airport Holdings LLC, the National Business Aviation Administration, United Airlines, and a retired airline executive. We wish to express particular gratitude to Ken Cushine for his generosity in ensuring we correctly understood the airport bond market.

Many experts from the FAA were crucial to our ability to acquire data from numerous FAA databases, to understand the details of the Airport Improvement Program and the Airport and Airway Trust Fund, and to learn about other aspects of FAA programs relevant to airport infrastructure. We particularly wish to thank Elliott Black, Christina Nutting, Michael Hines, Neil Kumar, Rebecca Didio, Roger Schaufele, Jr., Chia-Mei Liu, Li Ding, Peter Leboff, Jeffrey Wharff, David Duchow, Kevin Willis, Jim Brown, Scott Mitchell, Joe Manges, Beth Newman, and many others we have failed to mention, all of whom were unfailingly responsive and helpful throughout the study process, enabling us to conduct our independent assessment.

Finally, we wish to thank our RAND colleagues, Frank Camm and Lauri Rohn, for their timely and constructive reviews of our work throughout the study period as part of the RAND quality assurance process. We thank John Strong for wearing a second hat as an external reviewer in addition to being a member of our expert panel. Jessie Coe helped review our econometric methodology. Anita Chandra and Ben Preston provided us with superb management support all along the way. Kristin Leuschner and Dori Walker contributed their prodigious skills in communications and graphics to the project, for which we are grateful. Brian Dau provided exceptional and timely copyediting, and Babitha Balan provided expert oversight to the production process. And finally, we express immense gratitude to our RAND colleague, Chanel Skinner, who assisted us with meeting planning and all manner of administrative details and generally made the impossible somehow come together anyway.

Abbreviations

A4A	Airlines for America
AAIA	Airport and Airway Improvement Act of 1982
AATF	Airport and Airway Trust Fund
ACRP	Airport Cooperative Research Program
ACI	Airports Council International
ACI-NA	Airports Council International–North America
AIP	Airport Improvement Program
AIR-21	Wendell H. Ford Aviation Investment and Reform Act for the 21st Century
AMT	alternative minimum tax
ARTCC	Air Route Traffic Control Center
ASCE	American Society of Civil Engineers
ASM	available seat miles
ASQP	Airline Service Quality Performance
ATL	Hartsfield-Jackson Atlanta International Airport
BTS	Bureau of Transportation Statistics
CAB	Civil Aeronautics Board
CATS	Certification Activity Tracking System
CFC	customer facility charge
CFR	Code of Federal Regulations
CLT	Charlotte Douglas International Airport
CPI	Consumer Price Index
DB1B	Airline Origin and Destination Survey

DCA	Ronald Reagan Washington National Airport
DSCR	debt service coverage ratio
EMMA	Electronic Municipal Market Access
EWR	Newark Liberty International Airport
FAA	Federal Aviation Administration
FAA/OST	Federal Aviation Administration/Office of the Secretary of Transportation
FACT	Future Airport Capacity Task
FY	fiscal year
GA	general aviation
GAO	Government Accountability Office
GARB	general airport revenue bond
GO	general obligation
HHI	Herfindahl-Hirschman Index
IATA	International Air Transportation Association
ICAO	International Civil Aviation Organization
IRS	Internal Revenue Service
JCT	Joint Committee on Taxation
JFK	John F. Kennedy International Airport (New York City)
LAX	Los Angeles International Airport
LCC	low-cost carrier
LGA	LaGuardia Airport (New York City)
LOI	Letter of Intent
MII	majority-in-interest
MSRB	Municipal Securities Rulemaking Board
NAS	National Airspace System

NAS delay	national aviation system delay[1]
NPIAS	National Plan of Integrated Airport Systems
NPR	National Priority Rating
NPS	National Priority System
O&D	origin and destination
OMB	Office of Management and Budget
OPSNET	Operations Network
ORD	O'Hare International Airport
PFC	passenger facility charge
PHX	Phoenix Sky Harbor International Airport
PIT	Pittsburgh International Airport
SEA	Seattle-Tacoma International Airport
SFO	San Francisco International Airport
TAF	Terminal Area Forecast
TRACON	Terminal Radar Approach Control
TSA	Transportation Security Administration
ULCC	ultra-low-cost carrier
USDOT	U.S. Department of Transportation

---

[1] The Bureau of Transportation Statistics uses the term *national aviation system* as a general category of delays that are attributable to a broad set of conditions, such as nonextreme weather, airport operations, heavy traffic volume, and air traffic control (U.S. Department of Transportation, 2002). The term *NAS delay* is distinct from the FAA's definition of the *National Airspace System*.

Glossary

Aeronautical revenue	Revenue generated from users of airside operations (such as landing fees).
Airport sponsor	A state government, local government, regional authority, or other entity that owns one or more airports, distinct from airport management responsible for day-to-day operations at an airport.
Airside	The portion of an airport that contains the facilities necessary for the operation of aircraft.
Ancillary fee	Any fee associated with an airline-provided service or product previously included in the price of an airline ticket that is now sold separately, such as checked baggage, advance seat assignments, and priority boarding.
Based aircraft	Aircraft that are operational, airworthy, and based at an airport for a majority of the year.
Compensatory	An arrangement in which airports charge airlines based exclusively on their use of services.
Commercial service airport	A publicly owned airport that serves at least 2,500 commercial passenger boardings per year and receives scheduled passenger service.
Common use	Facilities that are available to any airport user, such as restrooms.
Debt	Funds borrowed by an airport from a bank or in the bond market that require payback of principal with interest within a specified time.
Enplanement	Boarding of an aircraft by a commercial passenger.
Exclusive use	Facilities that can only be used by one airline according to contractual arrangements.
Financing	Process of obtaining funding for a transaction, often through borrowing from a bank or in the bond market.
Focus city	A city at which an airline has concentrated a large number of flights but which does not operate as a hub in a hub-and-spoke system.

Fortress hub	An airport at which 70 percent or more of flights are controlled by one airline.
Funding	Sources of money for a project, such as a grant, passenger facility charge, or revenues from airport operations.
General aviation	Civil aviation operations other than scheduled air services and nonscheduled air transport operations for remuneration or hire.
Hub-and-spoke system	A system of organizing airline routes in which passengers flying from their origin transfer at a "hub" airport to reach their final destination.
Hybrid	An arrangement between an airport and airlines that combines elements of the residual and compensatory models.
Joint use	Facilities that airports can allocate to any airline as needed and that are paid for according to usage, such as baggage handling.
Landside	The portion of an airport that provides the facilities necessary for the processing of passengers, cargo, freight, and ground transportation vehicles.
Majority-in-interest provision	A clause in an airport-airline use-and-lease agreement that gives signatory airlines some degree of control over airport capital investments.
Non-aeronautical revenue	Airport revenue from sources other than airside operations, such as parking garages and terminal concessions.
Operation	Take-off or landing of an aircraft at an airport.
Passenger facility charge	A federally authorized user fee paid by passengers at the time of ticket purchase and remitted to the airport at which the passenger boards.
Preferential use	Facilities for which one "preferred" airline has first access but that can be used by other airlines when the preferred airline is not using them.
Reliever airport	Airports designated by the FAA to relieve congestion at commercial service airports and to provide improved general aviation access to the overall community. These may be publicly or privately owned.
Residual	An agreement between an airport and airlines in which signatory airlines agree to cover an airport's operating expenses irrespective of actual use.
Revenue	Funding that is collected from user fees, provision of services, operations, grants, and other sources.
Signatory airline	An airline that has signed a use-and-lease agreement with an airport.
Use-and-lease agreement	A formal agreement between an airport and tenant airline that sets rates and charges paid by the airline to the airport and specifies the responsibilities of both parties.

CHAPTER ONE

Introduction

Throughout the 100-year history of commercial air travel in the United States, airports have stood at a distinct intersection of public and private interests. At this intersection, airports and airlines have had a complicated relationship, marked by a desire for independence in running their businesses and an imperative to work collaboratively. U.S. commercial service airports are publicly owned airports that have at least 2,500 passenger boardings (enplanements) a year and that receive scheduled passenger service. There are currently 506 commercial service airports, and these airports handled 99.9 percent of annual enplanements in 2018 (Federal Aviation Administration [FAA], 2018a). *Enplanements* is the industry's term for the number of passengers boarding aircraft at an airport. These airports are owned (with only one exception) by state and local governments or regional authorities, which essentially operate their airports as independent, nonprofit enterprises. Commercial passenger airlines are entirely in private ownership and are for-profit enterprises.[1] Airport operations and capital investments are governed by federal, state, and local laws and regulations but also are fully exposed to competitive forces of the market. Congress deregulated the economic side of the airline industry in the late 1970s (Pub. L. 95-504, 1978), although airlines are still subject to safety, environmental, and other regulations.

Airports and airlines both aim to serve the same traveling public with safe and efficient air travel, and both are essential components of our national network of air-based passenger transport. Airports and airlines generally agree on airport infrastructure investment decisions. Both desire safe and efficient operations, and airlines have invested significant amounts of money in infrastructure at airports around the country. However, given their markedly different business models, their interests can sometimes diverge in important ways. For example, airports have long favored user fees on passengers as a mechanism to fund major renovations for terminals and other infrastructure and are often looking for ways to attract new airlines to their airport. Airlines have had long-standing concerns about adding fees or taxes that increase fares, subsidizing overly ambitious local airport expansion plans, supporting plans that might open the way toward more competition, or enabling jurisdictions to divert airport-generated revenue for nonaviation public priorities.

A divergence of perspectives is not surprising. Airports are anchored to specific locations; airlines must go to where their customers are, but in doing so, they have some flexibility about where to locate hubs and which routes to serve. Airports' capital investments require long plan-

---

[1] Consistent with the language of Section 122 of the FAA Reauthorization Act of 2018 (Pub. L. 115-254), this report focuses on passenger air travel through commercial service airports, but does not address issues concerning freight transport and related infrastructure needs.

ning horizons. Airlines also must plan years ahead when investing in aircraft and maintenance facilities, but they can shift aircraft from airport to airport as business conditions change. Airports could seek to expand their capacity to stimulate regional economic development, but with one principal exception in the era of deregulation: Neither the FAA nor the airports can compel airlines to use an airport.[2]

In this chapter, we explain the study's purpose and approach and provide an overview of the composition of commercial service airports in the United States and demand for their services. At the end of the chapter, we offer a road map to guide the reader through the remainder of the report.

Purpose of Study and Approach to Analysis

The condition and capacity of U.S. commercial service airports have long been concerns of the federal government; this study is the most recent in a long line of studies authorized or instigated by Congress to inform its deliberations on policy and future investment. The Section 122 language of the FAA Reauthorization Act of 2018, reproduced in Appendix A, enumerates 21 issues or questions that the authors of this report are directed to consider. Although many of these issues have been the subject of one or more past studies by the Government Accountability Office (GAO) and other research organizations, Congress intended the Section 122 study to take a comprehensive approach to examining these issues, using the most-current data available. Section 122 also directs the authors of this report to "make recommendations on the actions needed to upgrade the national aviation infrastructure system to meet the growing and shifting demands of the 21st century."

Section 122 is placed within the title of the FAA Reauthorization Act of 2018 that addresses the passenger facility charge (PFC) , a federally authorized user fee paid by passengers at the time of ticket purchase and remitted to the airport at which the passenger boards a plane. This placement suggests congressional interest in this study is closely tied to understanding impacts of potential changes in the PFC program on airports, airlines, and passengers before commencing further legislative action. In Chapter Six of this report, we discuss the PFC program in detail, but because PFCs are only one of many interrelated infrastructure funding and financing tools available to airports, we take a comprehensive view of airport infrastructure finance approach, as requested by Congress. This approach will enable Congress to consider questions regarding PFCs in the larger context of funding and financing issues faced by airports.

The 21 issues enumerated for study in Section 122 do not follow a particular thematic order or structure. To organize our analysis, we considered five broad themes raised in the legislation:

- trends in supply and demand for airport capacity
- competitive environment among airlines and airports
- business of airports, including agreements with airlines

---

[2]   This exception is when the U.S. Department of Transportation (USDOT) contracts with carriers to operate at "essential air service" airports (USDOT, 2017).

- funding and financing, including the Airport Improvement Program (AIP), PFC program, and borrowing in bond markets
- future demand and capacity constraints.

We organized our analytical approach around these general themes and then sought to structure a narrative that would give readers the requisite background and context for assessing the facts and accompanying analysis. In each thematic area, we initiated a literature review, conducted interviews with experts, and identified appropriate data sets related to expenses, revenue, capital investment, debt, enplanements, operations, system delays, and other metrics associated with infrastructure. The synthesis of information from these sources informed our analyses of the issues raised in Section 122.

Composition of the Airport Sector

There are more than 19,000 landing areas within the United States of varying size and type, 5,099 of which are considered public-use airports (FAA, 2018a). A *public-use airport* is defined as being (1) publicly owned, (2) privately owned but designated by the FAA as a "reliever" for congestion at commercial service airports, or (3) privately owned but having scheduled service and at least 2,500 annual enplanements. The FAA includes 3,321 public-use airports in the National Plan of Integrated Airport Systems (NPIAS), which is an FAA-managed plan to develop an integrated system of public-use airports and identify priorities for federal airport infrastructure funding (FAA, 2018a). Notably, an airport must be included in the NPIAS to receive federal grants. To assist with decisionmaking and organization within the NPIAS, airports are grouped into several categories based on an airport's annual number of enplanements, number of based aircraft, and role within the national airport system.

Table 1.1 presents the various airport categories and subcategories, along with their definitions and relevant statistics. The FAA aggregates airports as either commercial service airports or noncommercial airports, the latter of which is broken down into general aviation (GA) airports and reliever airports.

GA and reliever airports serve multiple purposes, including reducing congestion at commercial service airports by handling aircraft that do not have enplanements or passengers who require a terminal. GA airports make up approximately 76 percent of NPIAS airports (but handle only 0.05 percent of annual enplanements).[3] These airports serve a wide variety of users (typically, small noncommercial transport of people, cargo, or mail) and support emergency preparedness and response, local economic activity, and access for local or remote areas, as well as provide a "safety net" for the National Airspace System (NAS) (FAA, 2012a). Reliever airports make up 8 percent of NPIAS airports and 0.01 percent of enplanements and are defined by the FAA as public or private airports designated to relieve congestion at commercial service airports.

The FAA further categorizes airports as either primary or nonprimary to distinguish those airports that handle the most passengers within the NPIAS. Formally, primary airports are airports that have 10,000 or more enplanements per year. Primary airports are further

---

[3]   The International Civil Aviation Organization (ICAO) defines *general aviation* as "an aircraft operation other than a commercial air transport operation or an aerial work operation" (ICAO, 2010, pp. 1–5).

Table 1.1
Characteristics of National Plan of Integrated Airport Systems Airports, 2018

Airport Classification		Common Name	Criterion for Determining Common Name	Percentage of Total Enplanements	Total Enplanements	Number of Airports
Commercial service: At least 2,500 annual enplanements and scheduled passenger service	Primary: More than 10,000 annual enplanements	Large hub	Airport accounts for 1 percent or more of total enplanements	67.88	534,507,475	30
		Medium hub	At least 0.25 percent but less than 1 percent	18.75	147,624,888	31
		Small hub	At least 0.05 percent but less than 0.25 percent	9.54	75,150,646	72
		Non-hub	More than 10,000, but less than 0.05 percent	3.67	28,874,664	247
	Nonprimary: No more than 10,000 annual enplanements	Nonprimary commercial service	At least 2,500 and no more than 10,000	0.10	813,688	126
Noncommercial service: Less than 2,500 annual enplanements		General aviation	Less than 2,500	0.05	378,858	2,549
		Reliever	Designated to relieve congestion at commercial service airports	0.01	107,503	261

SOURCE: RAND analysis of T-100 segment data (Bureau of Transportation Statistics [BTS], 2019c) and FAA, 2017c.
NOTE: Enplanements are for domestic flights only. Domestic flights begin and end in the United States.

grouped as either large-, medium-, small-, or non-hub airports based on the airport's number of annual enplanements.[4] Airports within the NPIAS that have no more than 10,000 enplanements, including all GA and reliever airports, are considered nonprimary airports. As of 2017, there were 380 primary airports and 2,941 nonprimary airports within the NPIAS, as well as two proposed new primary airports and five proposed new nonprimary airports (FAA, 2018a).

Definition of Airport Infrastructure

Airport infrastructure is typically distinguished by the categories of airside and landside, as shown in Figure 1.1. *Airside* refers to "[t]he portion of an airport that contains the facilities necessary for the operation of aircraft" (FAA Advisory Circular 150/5360-13A, 2018). *Airside development* is defined as "the areas accessible to aircraft including runways, taxiways, aprons, and aircraft gates and the land adjacent to these facilities required by current FAA standards" (FAA Order 5100.38D, 2019). *Landside* refers to "[t]he portion of an airport that provides the facilities necessary for the processing of passengers, cargo, freight, and ground transportation vehicles" (FAA Advisory Circular 150/5360-13A, 2018). *Landside development* is defined

---

[4]   Although these numbers are generally stable, airports can change hub categories if enplanement numbers increase or decrease.

Figure 1.1
Categorization of Airport Infrastructure

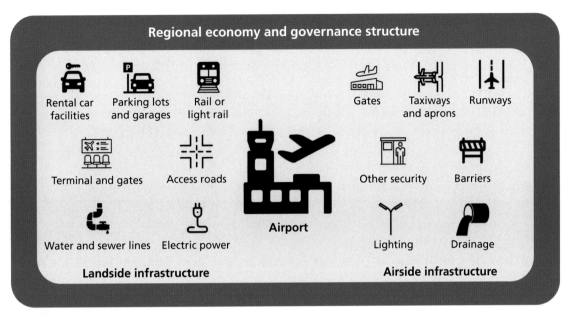

SOURCE: RAND, using icons from Noun Project by Adrien Coquet, Anniken & Andreas, Ahock, Ayi Prasetyo, Geogiana Ionescu, Graphic Tigers, Lili Gareeva, Logan, Made, Nikita Tcherednekov, ProSymbols, Putu Kharismayadi, Srnivas Agra, and Thomas Knopp.

as "[a]ll development on airport property that does not meet the definition of airside needs/development" (FAA Order 5100.38D, 2019). In more-explicit terms, landside infrastructure includes airport terminals, the terminal side of gates, parking lots and garages, transportation access roads and rails, rental car facilities, and other facilities on the landside of airport property.

The official definitions of airside and landside infrastructure do not explicitly address the ambiguity that exists in the categorization of gates that serve both landside and airside activities. Further, the definition of landside refers to "all development on airport property" that is not airside. This definition excludes transit and other surface transportation links connecting from outside the airport to the airport, enabling passengers to access the airport's services. This exclusion can be problematic for funding and finance at some airports and jurisdictions, as will be discussed further in Chapter Three.

Figure 1.1 also is intended to place the airport in the context of its larger regional economy and airport governance structure. Airports can be engines of economic vitality and growth in a region, and they can be sensitive to changing regional economic and demographic changes. Further, as discussed in Chapters Two and Three in greater detail, airport operations and capital flows for infrastructure can be fully or partially controlled by local governments. Under any governance arrangement, airports are a part of the fabric of adjacent communities, which might experience both the convenience of air mobility and the nuisance of noise and traffic.

Air traffic control infrastructure includes towers and other vital facilities that are not owned or operated by airports, and not all of which are located on airport property. Congressional staff made clear to us that the Section 122 study was not intended to address the infrastructure needs of the more than 300 air traffic control facilities operated by the FAA. For that reason, this issue was not included within the scope of this study. However, we note that the

FAA has a substantial backlog of maintenance and repairs, although we do not have data on the precise magnitude of the problem. According to September 2019 congressional testimony by the Executive Vice President of the National Air Traffic Controllers Association,

> [t]he FAA's 20 Air Route Traffic Control Centers (ARTCCs) located in the continental United States were built in the 1960s and are more than 50 years old. The FAA's large, stand-alone Terminal Radar Approach Control facilities (TRACONs) are, on average, 25 years old. In addition, the FAA has 132 combined TRACON/Towers, which on average are approximately 35 years old. Finally, the FAA has another 131 stand-alone towers, which average approximately 30 years old; the oldest is over 75 years old (Gilbert, 2019, p. 12).

Gilbert also noted in her testimony that although the FAA has been addressing its asset management priorities, "that process has been slow and hampered by the stop-and-go funding stream" of congressional appropriations in recent years (Gilbert, 2019, p. 12).

Snapshot of Conditions of Airport Infrastructure and Related Flight Delays

There is a view among some stakeholders that U.S. airport infrastructure is in poor condition. This view, however, is not supported by survey data on passenger satisfaction. For example, J. D. Power, 2017, reports all-time highs in passenger satisfaction across airports of all sizes since beginning the survey in 2005. Nor is this view supported in the latest edition of the American Society of Civil Engineers (ASCE) Infrastructure Report Card, which states,

> The FAA's set performance goal is that no less than 93% of runways at NPIAS airports are in excellent, good or fair condition. In 2013, 97.5% of NPIAS runways were rated excellent, good, or fair; at commercial service airports 98% of runways are rated excellent, good, or fair. The condition of existing runways is not an issue, rather the overall capacity of the busiest airports, as well as other airport facilities for handling passengers, cargo, security, and related functions (ASCE, 2017).

The ASCE's "D" grade for airports is not based on condition but on anticipated capacity constraints, the fact that only 78.5 percent of flights arrive on time (BTS, 2019a), and delays in implementing the NextGen system.[5] Understanding capacity constraints and the role that infrastructure might play in causing delays and travel disruption is thus a key concern of this study.

Delays Related to Infrastructure Capacity Constraints

As described in the ASCE's report, "While most of the nation's airports have adequate airport capacity and little or no delay, a small number of larger airports experience chronic capacity constraints and delays regularly occur, frequently impacting the entire air transportation system" (ASCE, 2017). The USDOT and FAA compile information on delays and break out the delays by cause, such as weather, security, and other factors related to capacity constraints at airports (USDOT, 2019; FAA, undated f). We expand this discussion in Chapter Eight

---

[5]   NextGen is the name of the FAA's major effort to modernize air transportation and "make flying even safer, more efficient, and more predictable" (FAA, 2019i).

to gain some insight into trends in delays, where most delays occur, and the interdependencies within the network that can cause a delay at one airport to lead to delays throughout the system.

How This Report Is Organized

In Chapter Two, we describe the competitive environment affecting airlines and airports and highlight the high degree of variability among airports and routes. Understanding this variability is the source of a well-known but still apt cliché among airport experts: "If you've seen one airport, you've seen one airport." Competition, or lack thereof, is key to understanding the ability of airports to negotiate mutually favorable agreements with airlines that in turn help to shape airports' capital planning and financing. In Chapter Three, we explain the business models of airports and airlines in broad terms in the context of existing legislative and regulatory requirements and constraints. Understanding the various forms of airport-airline agreements helps explain variations in revenues, expenditures, and financing mechanisms among airports. In Chapter Four, we provide an overview of the economics of airport operations, including aeronautical and non-aeronautical expenditures and revenue, federal and state grants, and other sources of capital.

In Chapters Five and Six, we take a closer look at two important funding mechanisms administered by the FAA: the AIP, funded by the federal Airport and Airway Trust Fund (AATF), and the PFC. In Chapter Seven, we provide an overview of the bond market for airport capital improvement projects, another vital source of investment capital for many airports. In Chapter Eight, we consider how growth in demand affects current and future infrastructure needs and capacity constraints, what it means for the NAS to meet demand, and whether infrastructure is keeping pace with changes. In Chapter Nine, we review and synthesize the key findings of this report and present a portfolio of policy recommendations to help airports of all sizes maintain safe, efficient, and sustainable operations. Twelve appendixes to this report are available for download at www.rand.org/t/RR3175.[6]

Table 1.2 lists the chapters of the report that are relevant to each of the issues identified in Section 122 of the FAA Reauthorization Act of 2018.

---

[6] Appendix A reproduces verbatim the statutory language authorizing this study. Appendix B provides an overview of our approach to the research and analysis underlying this report. Appendix C provides further detail on airport ownership and configuration. Appendix D provides additional details about airport revenues, expenses, and debt activities for 2017. Appendix E provides the legislative time line that led to current funding and regulatory arrangements governing the FAA and its administration and oversight of airport infrastructure funding and operations. Appendix F summarizes the airport master planning process. Appendix G provides additional details on the AIP. Appendix H provides additional details on the distribution of PFC dollars. Appendix I includes additional information on airport revenues and expenses. Appendix J includes notes on allowable uses of funding sources. Appendix K describes the details of our statistical analyses. Appendix L provides further detail on approaches to measuring airside and landside capacity constraints.

Table 1.2
Crosswalk Between Section 122 Issues and Their Location in the Report

Subsection of Section 122	Issue	Chapter in Report
All Commercial Service Airports		
(c)(1)	Ability of airport infrastructure to meet current and projected passenger volumes	Chapter Eight
(c)(2)	Available financing tools and resources for airports of different sizes	Chapters Four and Seven
(c)(3)	Available financing tools and resources for airports in rural areas	Chapter Four
(c)(4)	Current debt held by airports, and its impact on future construction and capacity needs	Chapter Seven
(c)(5)	Impact of capacity constraints on passengers and ticket prices	Chapters Two, Six, and Eight
(c)(6)	Purchasing power of the PFC from the last increase in 2000 to the year of enactment of this Act	Chapter Six
(c)(7)	Impact to passengers and airports of indexing the PFC for inflation	Chapter Six
(c)(8)	How long airports are constrained with current PFC collections	Chapter Six
(c)(9)	Impact of PFCs on promoting competition	Chapter Six
(c)(10)	Additional resources or options to fund terminal construction projects	Chapters Four through Seven
(c)(11)	Resources eligible for use toward noise reduction and emission reduction projects	Chapter Three
(c)(12)	Gap between the cost of projects eligible for the airport improvement program and the annual federal funding provided	Chapters Five and Eight
(c)(13)	Impact of regulatory requirements on airport infrastructure financing needs	Chapters Three and Four
(c)(14)	Airline competition	Chapter Two
(c)(15)	Airline ancillary fees and their impact on ticket pricing and taxable revenue	Chapter Five
(c)(16)	Ability of airports to finance necessary safety, security, capacity, and environmental projects identified in capital improvement plans	Chapter Eight
Large-Hub Airports		
(d)(1)	Analyze the current and future capacity constraints of large-hub airports	Chapter Eight
(d)(2)	Quantify large-hub airports' infrastructure requirements, including terminal, landside, and airside infrastructure	Chapter Two
(d)(3)	Quantify the percentage growth in infrastructure requirements of the large-hub airports relative to other commercial service airports	Chapter Eight
(d)(4)	Analyze how much funding from the AIP has gone to meet the requirements of large hub airports over the past ten years	Chapter Five
(d)(5)	Project how much AIP funding would be available to meet the requirements of large-hub airports in the next five years if funding levels are held constant	Chapter Five

CHAPTER TWO

Historical Context and Trends in Air Travel

In this chapter, we provide some historical background and perspective on the current status of airline competition at airports. The level of competition among airlines at a given airport can have a significant impact on airline ticket prices and therefore affects passenger demand and revenue generation at the airport (Federal Aviation Administration/Office of the Secretary of Transportation [FAA/OST] Task Force, 1999; Kwoka and Shumilkina, 2010). Competition among airlines also affects the relative bargaining power between airports and airlines. In this chapter, we provide some historical background on how airline competition changed following deregulation, introduce some of the key measures of competition among airports and airlines, analyze competition from a variety of perspectives, and discuss broad trends in enplanement and prices.

Conditions Before and After Airline Deregulation in 1978

The aviation industry literally got off the ground in the 1910s when the U.S. Post Office began encouraging mail delivery via air.[1] The main legislation regulating commercial flight passed in 1938 and was patterned on trucking regulation, which in turn had grown from concerns rooted in the monopoly power of some railroads. The Civil Aeronautics Act of 1938 created the regulatory authority that came to be known as the Civil Aeronautics Board (CAB). The CAB had the authority to regulate airline market entry, routes, and fares; it also oversaw safety regulation until the FAA was created in 1958. New entrants were rarely allowed.

By 1978, the 16 airlines that had been grandfathered in as trunk carriers (airlines that were allowed to serve long-distance routes) in 1938 were reduced to 11, and they accounted for 94 percent of scheduled flights. It was difficult for airlines to obtain CAB permission to add new routes or drop unprofitable routes. Unofficially, the number of airlines in specific markets was limited. Fare increases had to be approved by the CAB, and airlines could seldom compete on price, although airlines could discount fares in some circumstances. The CAB essentially protected airlines from failing.

The process of deregulating the airline industry began in 1975, when reforms affecting the CAB gave airlines more flexibility to discount their prices and serve new markets. The Airline Deregulation Act of 1978 (Pub. L. 95-504) ended the CAB's authority over routes and fares and dissolved the CAB by the end of 1985. By mid-1979, airlines were allowed to fly any

---

[1] Much of the discussion of the period of regulation and early deregulation is drawn from Transportation Research Board, 1991.

route at almost any fare. The Act also created subsidies to support essential air service to small communities.

The main goals of deregulation were to promote competition through lower fares and to create a more efficient market. Both directly and indirectly, deregulation greatly changed the airline market and the relationships between airports and airlines. In the early years following deregulation, airline competition increased as airlines that had previously flown within states went national, new airlines entered the market, and the market share of the 11 main airlines that were operating under regulation decreased from 94 percent to 77 percent. Airlines could also compete by offering new routes; for example, an airline that previously had flown mostly north-south routes could add east-west routes.

Since 1978, the deregulated market has been volatile in terms of entry and exit of airlines. In 1979, the year following deregulation, 22 new airlines went into service, but the rate slowed considerably after a decade; only three new airlines entered the market in 1988. From 2000 to 2008, the industry saw two major mergers and at least nine airlines that ceased to operate (Goetz and Vowles, 2009). Since 2008, another six major airlines have been acquired by other airlines:

- Midwest, acquired by Republic Airlines, 2009
- Northwest, acquired by Delta Air Lines, 2009
- Continental, acquired by United Airlines, 2010
- AirTran, acquired by Southwest Airlines, 2011
- USAir, acquired by American Airlines, 2013
- Virgin America, acquired by Alaska Airlines, 2016 (Airlines for America [A4A], undated).

Only one new major airline from the past nearly two decades, JetBlue, is still in service (Ostrower, 2018). Mergers and bankruptcies might eliminate weak performers, but in doing so, their effect is to reduce competition. Further, mergers do not always result in stable airlines, either; some of these merged companies have also ceased to operate. This trend was noted in a 1991 review (Transportation Research Board, 1991) and has remained true. For example, USAir merged with America West in 2005 and was later acquired by American in 2013.

Other disruptions in the airline industry have included two major declines in air travel (beginning in 2001 and 2008), swings in fuel prices, and the advent of new business models: low-cost carriers (LCCs) and ultra-low-cost carriers (ULCCs), as well as the advent of regional affiliated carriers. None of these new models are precisely defined, either by industry or by the FAA, but LCCs are generally those that entered the deregulated market with lower operating costs than regulation-era "legacy" carriers. ULCCs have taken this model even further, emphasizing à la carte pricing for many passenger amenities that were previously bundled in the ticket price. LCCs and ULCCs have different operating profiles from legacy carriers, such as faster turnaround times per gate. This model has created a demand for more flexibility from airports, as well as a preference for lower charges (Graham, 2013). Regional carriers tend to fly between large- or medium-hub airports to small hubs or non-hubs, generally under contract to larger carriers. Some are wholly owned subsidiaries of larger airlines, and some fly for multiple airlines.[2] Figure 2.1 shows the growth in the four currently largest airlines (American, Delta,

---

[2]   For example, according to the Regional Airline Association, American Airlines has partnerships with nine regional carriers, three of which are wholly owned subsidiaries (Envoy Air, Piedmont Airlines, and PSA Airlines). Some regional airlines

Figure 2.1
Market Share by the Four Largest Carriers and Other Airline Types, 1990–2018

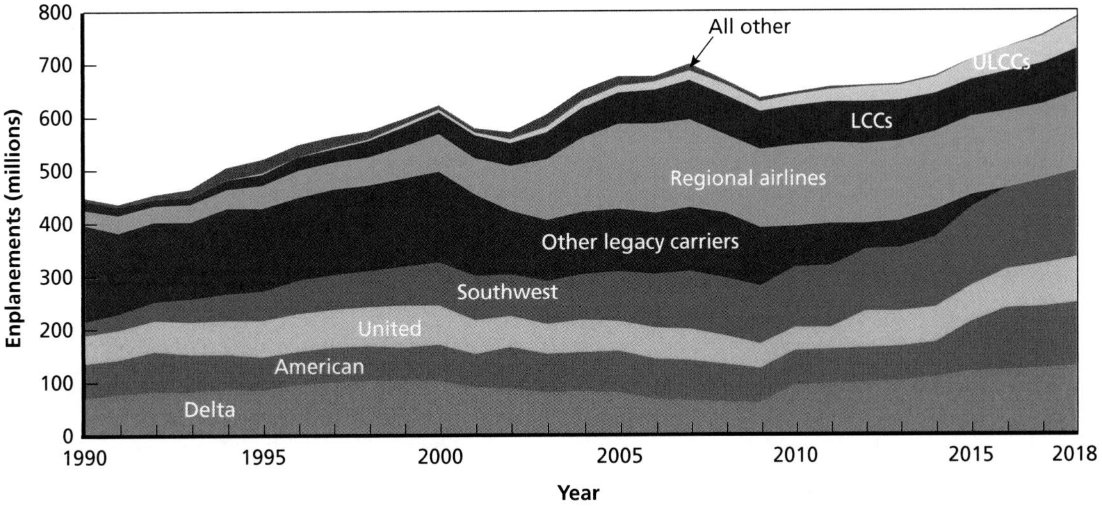

SOURCE: T-100 segment data (BTS, 2019c), domestic enplanements only.
NOTE: The "other legacy carriers" category includes Continental, Eastern, Pan Am, Northwest, TWA, and USAir, all of which have merged with other airlines or ceased operating as of 2018. The "LCCs" category includes AirTran, Alaska, ATA, Hawaiian, JetBlue, Midway, Sun Country, Vanguard, and Virgin America. The "ULCCs" category includes Allegiant, Frontier, and Spirit. "All other" includes enplanements of foreign-flag, charter, and cargo carriers. Although most of the regional carriers serve marketing carriers (such as American, United, and Delta), this data set does not match their enplanements to the individual marketing carriers. For this reason, they are included as a separate category.

Southwest, and United), the decline in legacy carriers (those that existed under regulation), and the growth in regional airlines, LCCs, and ULCCs.

In addition to responding to the changing competitive landscape within the airline industry, airports have had to make several major changes in their operations over the past two decades for other reasons. One was new security mandates that emerged following the terrorist attacks on four commercial flights in September 2001. The attacks led to the federalization of airport security under the newly formed Transportation Security Administration (TSA; now part of the Department of Homeland Security following that agency's creation in 2002). In addition to the increased needs for screening space, security requirements changed the way passengers access and use airports. For example, only ticketed passengers are allowed to go to gates. Technologies have also changed the amount of space needed for various functions. For example, check-in kiosks have reduced the need for check-in space, while ride-hailing companies (such as Uber and Lyft) and smartphones have increased the need for passenger pick-up and drop-off space.

operate flights under their own name, while others primarily or exclusively fly under the brand name of a larger airline (the "marketing carrier"). See Forbes and Lederman, 2006, and Regional Airline Association, 2019. More information on various airline industry characterizations is provided in Appendix C.

Measuring the Extent of Competition

Given the importance of competition as one of the major motivators of federal policy intervention, it is important to have some way to track changes in competitiveness over time. One well-accepted (and simple) way to measure competitiveness is the Herfindahl-Hirschman Index (HHI), which measures the concentration of firms in a given market. The HHI is calculated by adding the squares of the market share (in terms of percentage) of the largest firms in a market. If one firm controls an entire market, the HHI would be $(100)^2$, or 10,000; if 100 firms each had 1 percent of market share, the HHI would be 100 times $(1)^2$, or 100.[3] More-concentrated markets have higher HHI. The Department of Justice considers a market or industry HHI of 1,500 to 2,500 to be moderately concentrated and anything above 2,500 to be highly concentrated (U.S. Department of Justice, 2018). The HHI is a widely accepted measure, and we adopt it for our purposes here.[4]

Competition in the Airline Industry as a Whole

We calculated the HHI of the airline industry using three metrics of market share: *available seat miles* (ASM), defined as the total number of available seats, adjusted for the length of the flights; total enplanements; and marketing carrier enplanements (the marketing carrier is the airline from which a passenger purchases a ticket).[5] We begin by considering the HHI for the NAS as a whole. As Figure 2.2 shows, the HHI using ASM for the aviation system as a whole reached a low in the 700s within the first decade after deregulation, increased rapidly to the 1300s in the early 1990s as the wave of new entrants shook out, declined again through the Great Recession, and has been increasing since around 2010.

As of 2018, the four largest airlines accounted for 73 percent of ASM—down from 74 percent the previous two years, which was the highest point over the 40-year period for which data are readily available.[6] However, the HHI remains just below what would be considered moderately concentrated.

Market share based on total enplanements is lower, although it follows the same general trends. The difference between the two is likely due to longer flight distances on some airlines than others. However, the ASM and total enplanement figures include the regional airlines as independent entities, since the data sources for ASM and total enplanements do not distinguish the marketing carrier from the operating carrier (the airline that actually operates the flight, which, in some cases, is a regional carrier).[7] The gray line in Figure 2.2 shows how the HHI changes when enplanements flown by regional operating carriers are combined and "assigned"

---

[3]   These calculations represent two extreme examples. A more typical calculation would be a scenario in which the top three firms had 35, 30, and 15 percent of the market: $(35)^2 + (30)^2 + (15)^2 = 2,350$. Although this hypothetical example represents only 80 percent of the market, firms with very low shares of the market (e.g., 5 percent or less) would not substantially increase the HHI.

[4]   As a general matter, many other factors related to market structure and industry characteristics beyond the HHI are considered in disputes over anticompetitive practices and antitrust litigation.

[5]   More detail on individual data sources for these and other commonly used metrics and data sources is available in Appendix B.

[6]   Authors' analysis of BTS, 2019b.

[7]   Although data on marketing and operating carriers are available in the Airline Origin and Destination Survey (DB1B) data set, those data do not include ASM or revenue passenger miles, so we could not recalculate the HHI for ASM and revenue passenger miles to include operating carriers as part of the marketing carriers.

Figure 2.2
Herfindahl-Hirschman Index for Three Airline Industry Metrics, 1974–2018

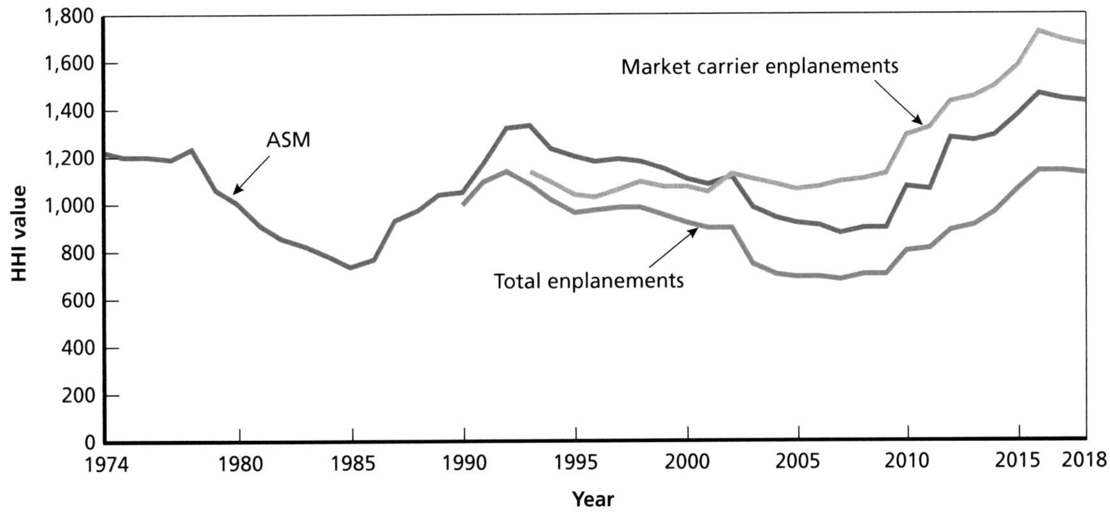

SOURCES: ASM: authors' analysis of BTS, 2019a; total enplanements: authors' analysis of BTS, BTS, 2019c; market carrier enplanements: authors' analysis of BTS, 2019d.
NOTE: ASM includes international flights but only on U.S.-based carriers. Total enplanements include all segments but only on domestic flights.

to the marketing carrier. The two lines were relatively close before 1995, but the HHI using only the marketing carriers has risen substantially since then. This suggests that, from a passenger's point of view, the number of airlines offering tickets for purchase has declined; the industry has become more concentrated.

For enplanements, we can calculate the proportion of passengers on each type of carrier, which can shed some light on current competition.[8] Table 2.1 shows 2018 enplanements by carrier type, using T-100 domestic segment data and DB1B ticketing data (BTS, 2019d).[9] The total of the four largest carriers plus that of the regionals who fly for them accounts for more than 80 percent of enplanements. Based on DB1B data, the 15 regional carriers who work with one or more marketing carriers operate almost exclusively for those marketing carriers.[10]

Competition at the Individual Airport and Market Level

The HHI also can be used to gauge the extent to which airlines have a monopoly on flights into and out of individual airports. If an airport has only one or two tenant airlines, those airlines might be able to negotiate an agreement that gives them more control over the airport's infrastructure investment decisions. It is important to emphasize that, in some cases, airport and airline incentives are aligned in support of airport infrastructure investment. Both desire

[8] The T-100 database contains hundreds of airlines below the somewhat arbitrary 2 percent threshold over the past several decades. Many of these are international, commuter, or small regional carriers, and more than 375 of the approximately 550 airlines in the T-100 database for 1990 to 2018 showed zero passengers in 2018.

[9] T-100 data can include all flights or only domestic flights, and all segments (which counts each leg of a trip with a transfer as a separate enplanement) or only markets (in which one trip equals one enplanement, regardless of the number of legs). More information on T-100 and other data sources is provided in Appendix B.

[10] The only exception is Peninsula Air; 89 percent of its enplanements were for Alaska Air and 11 percent were under its own name in 2018.

Table 2.1
Proportion of Enplanements, by Airline Category, 2018

Carrier Type	Percentage of Enplanements
Four largest airlines, including all enplanements with their respective operating carriers (American, Southwest, Delta, United)	80.2
LCCs (Alaska, JetBlue, Hawaiian, Sun Country, Virgin America)	11.5
ULCCs (Allegiant, Frontier, and Spirit)	7.6
Regional carriers that fly under their own name	0.5
Charters and unknown	0.1

SOURCE: Authors' analysis of T-100 domestic segment data (BTS, 2019c) and DB1B data (BTS, 2019d).
NOTE: Of the four largest airlines, only Southwest does not work with any regional operating carriers. The four largest airlines have hardly changed since 1995, when Southwest reached fourth place over USAir. Percentages do not sum to 100 because of rounding.

safe and efficient operations, and airlines have invested in infrastructure at airports around the country, occasionally through direct investments but more often through payment of rates and charges that support capital projects (in the same way drivers who pay tolls support highway infrastructure). Disagreements, however, might arise over investments aimed at increasing airline competition, and insufficient competition could result in higher prices for travelers.

The number of passenger seats provided by airlines at any given airport can reveal whether one or two airlines are dominant and whether, as a consequence, other airlines would have difficulty entering that airport. A 2015 analysis of flight data concluded that "[a]t 40 of the 100 largest U.S. airports, a single airline controls a majority of the market, as measured by the number of seats for sale, up from 34 airports a decade earlier. At 93 of the top 100, one or two airlines control a majority of the seats, an increase from 78 airports" (Koenig and Mayerowitz, 2015).

According to the HHI for large and medium hubs, a majority of airports would be considered highly concentrated, with an HHI of more than 2,500 (Figure 2.3). According to DB1B data (BTS, 2019d), which include the operating carriers as part of the marketing carriers' tickets, all airports have HHI scores above 1,500, which is the threshold for moderately concentrated. At four airports—Chicago's Midway International Airport, Houston's William P. Hobby Airport, Dallas Love Field Airport, and Charlotte Douglas International (CLT)—almost all inbound and outbound flights are controlled by a single airline.

The picture changes when we consider all airports in a given geographic area as one market, designated by the name of that market's largest city. Using USDOT classifications of airports by market,[11] we identified 12 markets served by more than one hub airport (Table 2.2). As Figure 2.4 shows, those multi-hub markets are less concentrated, meaning that passengers in those markets have a greater choice of ticketing carriers to choose from. Three of the four most highly concentrated airports (Midway, Hobby, and Love) are in multi-hub markets. The

[11] Airports are assigned to city markets by the USDOT to identify a geographical area that is serviced by specific airports. For example, San Francisco International, Oakland International, and Mineta San Jose International all service the San Francisco Bay Area, as do other, smaller regional airports. The USDOT categorizes airports as serving 378 distinct markets. Of these markets, more than 200 are located in Alaska.

Figure 2.3
Herfindahl-Hirschman Index According to Enplanements at Large- and Medium-Hub Airports, 2018

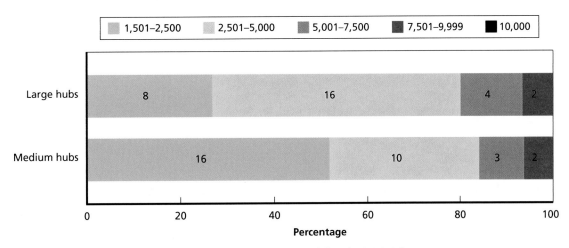

SOURCE: DB1B data, using a straight average of four quarters of data (BTS, 2019d).
NOTE: The number of airports within each hub and HHI category is noted inside each bar.

Table 2.2
Multi-Hub Markets

Market	Number of Hubs by Size		
	Large	Medium	Small
Boston	1		1
Chicago	2		
Cleveland		1	1
Dallas	1	1	
Houston	1	1	
Los Angeles	1	3	1
Miami	2		
New York	3	2	
Phoenix	1		1
San Francisco	1	2	
Tampa	1		1
Washington, D.C.	3		

SOURCE: NPIAS data (FAA, 2018a, Appendix A).

Figure 2.4
Herfindahl-Hirschman Index According to Enplanements at Large-, Medium-, Small-, and Non-Hub and Nonprimary Markets, 2018

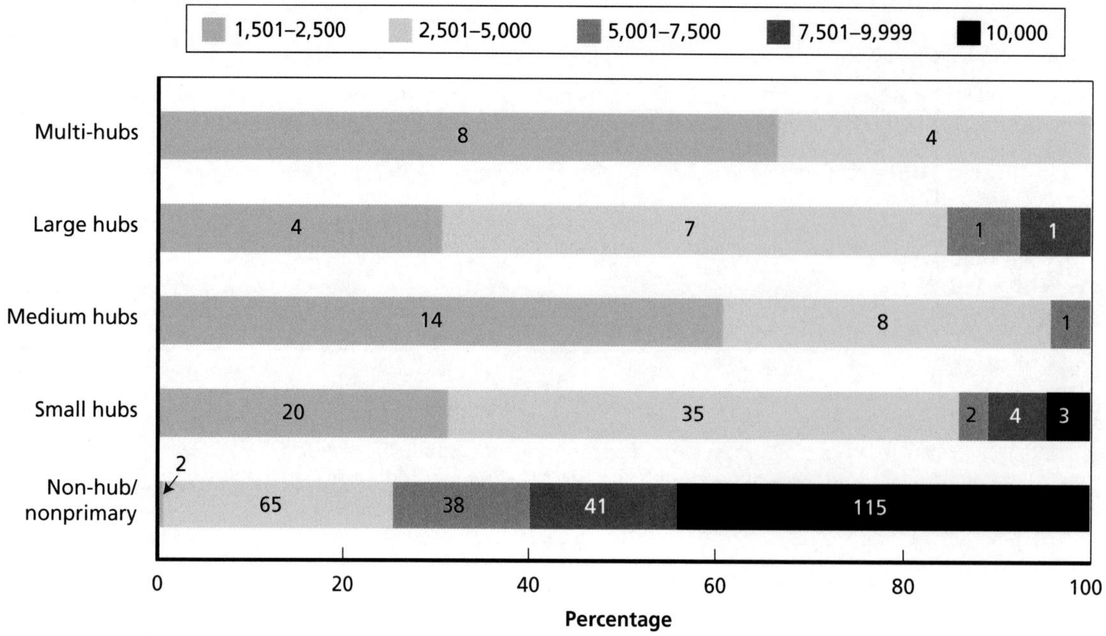

SOURCES: RAND analysis of 2018 DB1B data (BTS, 2019d) and NPIAS data (FAA, 2012a, Appendix A).
NOTE: With the exception of multi-hub markets, market size is defined by the size of the largest airport in that market. If the largest airport in a market is a small hub, we consider it a small-hub market.

only large- or medium-hub airport outside of a multi-hub market that has an HHI over 7,500 is CLT.

Competition at the Individual Route Level

For cases in which multiple airports serve the same city, a single monopolistic airport does not necessarily mean the market for flights into or out of that city is monopolistic. For example, although almost all flights in and out of Midway International Airport are operated by Southwest, customers can choose to purchase flights from other airlines at O'Hare International Airport (ORD). Competition matters to individual travelers in terms of the number of options they have when flying between two markets. Air travel is not a single national market but a collection of many individual markets; a flight from Detroit to Las Vegas is not a substitute for a flight from Milwaukee to New Orleans.

Figure 2.5 shows the distribution of HHI for flights between pairs of markets with hub airports,[12] accounting for direct flights as well as flights with one or two layovers. We looked at round-trip itineraries between two markets, and each market pair is included twice, once with one city being the origin and a second time with that city as the destination (so HHI is calculated separately for Chicago-Phoenix-Chicago and Phoenix-Chicago-Phoenix). Markets are divided into four categories according to the largest market size (so "multi-hub" includes

---

[12]   Unlike the analysis shown in Figure 2.4, this analysis does not include non-hubs or nonprimary airports. With 378 individual markets, this would have meant analyzing over 140,000 market pairs. Many of these markets only have flights to one or two other airports.

Figure 2.5
Herfindahl-Hirschman Index Between Market Pairs According to Enplanements, 2018

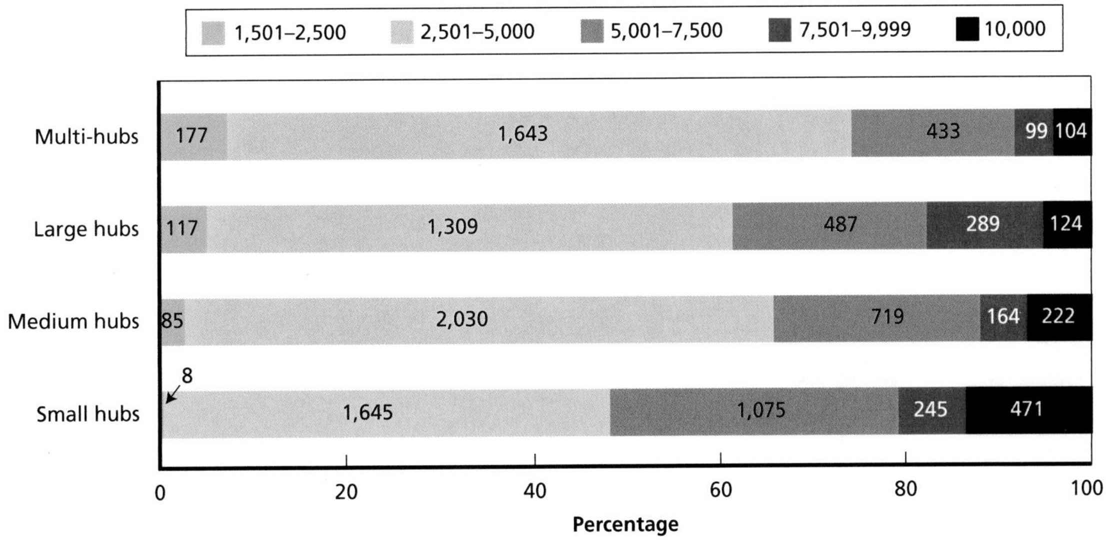

SOURCE: RAND analysis of 2018 DB1B data (BTS, 2019d).
NOTE: The number of market pairs within each airport and HHI category is noted within the bar. Non-hub and nonprimary pairs are not included.

market pairs with other multi-hub markets, large markets, medium markets, and small markets). The vast majority of markets for flights between two cities meet the Department of Justice's definition of "highly concentrated" because they have an HHI of greater than 2,500 (U.S. Department of Justice, 2018). Not surprisingly, the multi-hub group is the most competitive, with only 4 percent of market pairs having no competition, and the majority of these are pairs of multi-hubs and small hubs.

Trends in Fares and Passenger Traffic

Overall, average round-trip fares nationwide decreased during the period following deregulation,[13] although this effect has not been a steady pattern or shown the same decrease for all flight types. In the first decade of deregulation, fares fell the most on long-distance routes (more than 1,500 miles), while fares on the shortest routes (less than 750 miles) generally increased (Transportation Research Board, 1991, Table 3.3). According to more-recent data from the BTS (DB1B), inflation-adjusted domestic ticket prices fell over the 25-year period from 1993 through 2018, from $630 (average over four quarters) in 1993 to $432 (average over four quarters) in 2018 (BTS, 2019d). These changes are driven by a wide variety of factors, including but not limited to competition. However, these prices do not include bag fees, which amounted to $5 billion in airline revenue in 2018.[14] The recent trend among air-

---

[13]   This average is based on all fares nationwide and is not adjusted for trip distance. Flights to and from the noncontiguous United States are excluded.

[14]   Although airlines are required to report change and baggage fees to the USDOT, other fees are exempted from reporting (GAO, 2014a). Bag fee collections increased substantially beginning in 2008, when they grew by almost 150 percent (BTS, 2019e).

lines of unbundling fares into a base fare and separate ancillary fees (e.g., for baggage, preferred seating) makes it difficult to compare current airfares with bundled airfares under regulation (Brancatelli, 2014).

Although average fares have generally declined, Figure 2.6 shows substantial volatility on individual market routes. We selected five routes to compare so that the trip distance would not change over time, as the national average trip distance might. Even on a major route between two of the largest markets in the country—New York to Los Angeles, each of which is served by multiple hub airports—fares fluctuate considerably and have even changed in a single quarter by as much as 60 percent, as shown by the green line in Figure 2.6. Although the national inflation-adjusted average fare has declined by 36 percent over this period (shown by the black line), other routes have declined by as little as 16 percent (Houston-Pittsburgh, shown by the blue line) and as much as 55 percent (Cincinnati-St. Louis, shown by the gray line).

Over the last 30 years, demand for air travel in the United States has grown. Figure 2.7 shows the growth of annual U.S. enplanements over time. Total enplanements have increased since 1990. The increase over the past 30 or so years has been fairly gradual. The sharp declines around 2002 and 2009 are generally attributed to the terrorist attacks in September 2001 and the Great Recession, respectively. Air travel rebounded each time.

Growth in enplanements can be broadly attributed to three factors:

- an increase in population over this period, from approximately 250 million to 325 million
- an increase in enplanements per capita, from 1.8 in 1990 to 2.4 in 2018 (an increase of one-third)

Figure 2.6
Quarterly Inflation-Adjusted Round-Trip Fares, National Average and Five Market Pairs, 1993–2018

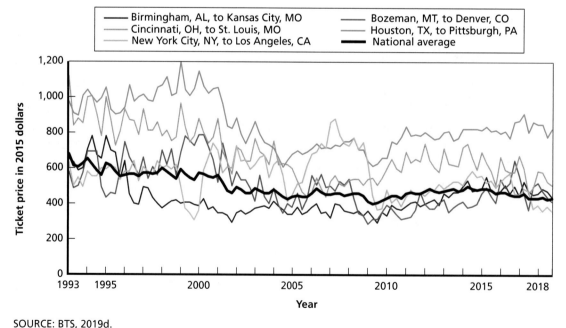

SOURCE: BTS, 2019d.
NOTE: Routes were selected for geographic, trip-distance, and hub-size diversity. Fares are quarterly and represent round-trip tickets from the first city of each pair to the second. The national average includes round-trip flights between markets within the contiguous United States. Costs do not include ancillary fees.

Figure 2.7
Total U.S. Enplanements and Enplanements per Capita, 1990–2018

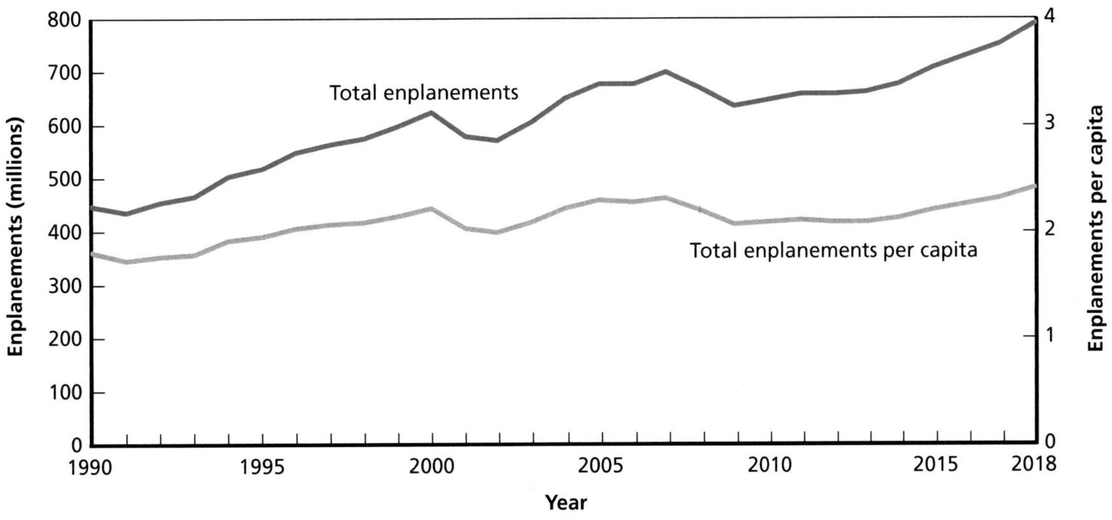

SOURCE: BTS, 2019b.

- changes in flight routing (because of the hub-and-spoke system, flights that were previously point-to-point might now involve transfers, although we were unable to locate data on the magnitude of this change).

Figure 2.8 shows trends in enplanements by airport size. Total enplanements increased by roughly 75 percent between 1990 and 2018. Most of this growth has been at large-hub airports. Small- and medium-hub enplanements have increased over this period, but their market share relative to the large hubs has not changed significantly. Overall, enplanement trends have generally tracked trends in broad economic conditions, declining during recessions and rising during periods of economic growth.

Other Trends in Airline and Airport Operations

Other factors besides deregulation and demographic trends have proven to be highly influential over the past several decades in shaping the use of airports.

Transition to Hub-and-Spoke Operations
Hub-and-spoke networks of flights became widespread following deregulation, although a few networks did exist previously.[15] A *hub-and-spoke network* is generally defined as a pattern in which passengers travel to one city, change aircraft, and then continue to their final destination, instead of a network of direct point-to-point flights between many cities. This is advantageous to airlines because fewer flights are needed to serve the same number of cities. Hub-and-spoke networks also allow airlines to serve cities that might not have sufficient demand

---

[15]   The word *hub* is used both by the FAA to characterize airports by size—large, medium, small, and non-hub—and within the industry to designate hubs in a hub-and-spoke system.

Figure 2.8
Domestic Enplanements Across Airport Categories, 1990–2018

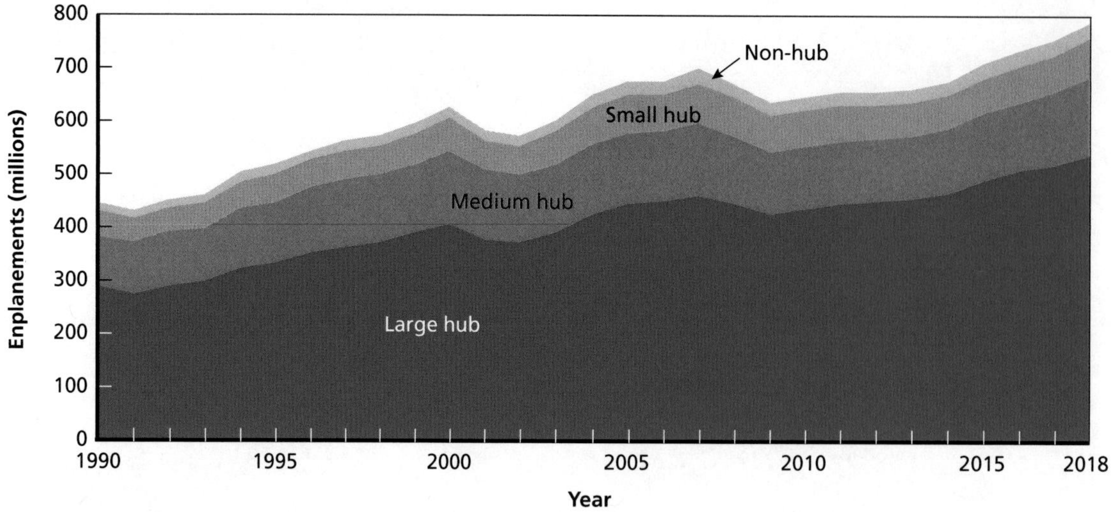

SOURCE: BTS, 2019c.
NOTE: Nonprimary enplanements are not shown; they are a small fraction (less than one-tenth of 1 percent) of all domestic commercial enplanements.

for point-to-point flights and to meet passenger demand to travel on one airline between many cities (Transportation Research Board, 1991).

More-Efficient Use of Aircraft

Deregulation provided incentives to airlines to achieve greater efficiency. Almost immediately after deregulation, airlines began flying their aircraft, on average, one more hour per day (Transportation Research Board, 1991) and, in some cases, increased the number of seats per aircraft as a way to compete more on price than quality. LCCs continue to seek out airports that enable quick turnaround times at gates, since using aircraft efficiently continues to be an important element of their business model (Graham, 2013).

As the demand for aviation has increased, airlines and airports have adapted their infrastructure, operations, and aircraft mix to increase their capacity. For instance, from 2000 to 2015, 18 runways were constructed at commercial service airports, 15 of which were at large-hub airports.[16] Airlines have increased the size of their aircraft, allowing them to carry more passengers and cargo with fewer aircraft. From 1995 to 2018, the average number of seats per commercial aircraft increased from 166 to 179 (Massachusetts Institute of Technology, undated).[17] Depending on the existing airport infrastructure, larger aircraft might create new infrastructure needs, such as longer runways, wider concourses, and larger gates.

---

[16]   FAA Office of Airports staff, personal communication with study team, August 2019.

[17]   In general, the physical size of the aircraft, as measured in length and wingspan, and its seating capacity are correlated with the number of seats: Larger aircraft accommodate more passengers. However, because aircraft of the same wingspan can be built with several different seat configurations, there is not an exact correlation between the two metrics. For example, Poirier, Rakas, and Perry, 2007, p. 11, Figure 7, shows that aircraft with a wingspan of approximately 200 feet generally seat between 200 to 400 passengers. Figure 2.9 suggests that the number of passengers per aircraft has increased, but this could be because seat configurations have changed, aircraft are becoming larger, or both.

The switch to larger aircraft has meant that the overall number of airport operations (take-offs and landings) at commercial service airports has grown more slowly than the number of enplanements. The recent relationship between increasing enplanements and the flat number of operations is illustrated in Figure 2.9. Sixty percent (11,893,110) of all operations occurred at large-hub airports in 2018.

Summary of Findings

Competitive markets for air travel have been difficult to sustain in the United States since the era of deregulation began in 1978. This is true when considering the U.S. market as a whole or when looking at individual airports or individual origin-destination pairs. Lowering air fares is the primary motivation for government intervention to increase competition. Round-trip domestic air fares have declined from 1993 through 2018.

Enplanements are an insufficient measure of demand for airport infrastructure. The number of flights (operations), relative to aircraft size and noncommercial passenger air services, is another critical indicator. The evidence shows that, as enplanements have risen over the past three decades, the number of operations rose at a slower pace and has declined over the past 15 years.

Forecasting airport trends too far into the future is risky because industry-wide changes have often required airports to reconfigure their future plans. Capacity projections based solely on enplanements in the 1990s, although using the best information available at the time, would have likely overestimated the need for increased airport runway and gate capacity in the aggregate but not necessarily for terminal and other landside infrastructure. The

Figure 2.9
Trends in Airport Operations Compared with Enplanements at Commercial Service Airports, 1990–2018

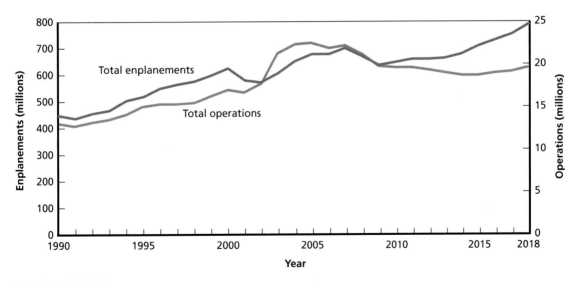

SOURCE: BTS, 2019c.
NOTE: The increase in the early 2000s reflects a reporting change: As of October 2002, small certificated and commuter air carriers began reporting operations as well (see BTS, 2002). We define operations as departures and arrivals. BTS, 2019c, provides the number of departures, and we assume there is an arrival associated with each departure.

September 11, 2001, terrorist attacks radically altered the infrastructure needs associated with airport security. Similarly, there is no reason to conclude that the current trend of airlines using larger aircraft will continue indefinitely. Ride-hailing technology is currently changing landside infrastructure needs and parking revenue. Electric planes could eventually force changes to infrastructure and policies involving fuel. The ideal airport of 2030 might look quite different from that of 2020.

CHAPTER THREE

The Business of Airports

Keeping in mind the national trends in airline competition, demand for commercial passenger service, and implications for airport utilization summarized in Chapter Two, we turn in this chapter to the ways in which individual airports function as businesses in this larger environment. This discussion includes an overview of airport ownership and governance, customers and stakeholders, revenues, expenditures, factors affecting the relationship between airports and airlines, and airports' approach to planning. Airports are complex entities, and their operations are influenced by many factors: agreements with airlines, federal regulations, and formal and informal relationships with states, localities, and other stakeholders. This chapter reviews these agreements, regulations, and relationships and highlights the issues most relevant to the ability of airports to fund infrastructure projects.

Ownership and Governance

Almost all commercial service airports in the United States are publicly owned, and our focus in this chapter is on commercial service airports. Among large- and medium-hub airports, almost all are owned by cities, counties, or independent authorities established by a city or county, with a small number owned by states. Although most airports are operated by the same entity that owns them, that is not universally true. (A list of all large- and medium-hub airports, along with their owners and operators, is provided in Appendix C, Table C.1.[1])

Within metropolitan areas with multiple hubs, airports are sometimes owned or operated by the same entity. For example, the Port Authority of New York and New Jersey operates all three large hubs in the New York area; the Metropolitan Washington Airports Authority operates both Dulles Washington International Airport and Ronald Reagan Washington National Airport (DCA) in the Washington, D.C., area. In other cases, multiple entities are involved. For example, the three San Francisco Bay Area airports are owned and operated by three different city sponsors. Occasionally, governance structures are even more complex. Dallas/Fort Worth International is jointly owned by both cities, while Love Field is owned only by the City of Dallas.[2] Although private operation and even partial ownership by private firms is common in other countries, only one hub airport (the Luis Muñoz Marín International Airport in San Juan) is currently operated by a private firm, although its ownership remains public. Privatization is discussed in more detail later in this chapter.

---

[1] In FAA terminology, *airport sponsors* are the entities that operate the airport and accept AIP grants.

[2] On the further complication of the relationship between these two airports, see Smith, 2019.

Basic Operational Model

Although airports are publicly owned and operated, they function in many ways as businesses. To the extent practicable, they are obligated to generate sufficient revenues to cover their costs of operations, maintenance, and construction of infrastructure and facilities. Although not in business to make a profit, airports are not supported by tax revenues as most public entities are. Revenues flow directly and indirectly to airports from several sources and in different forms. Passengers purchase goods and services from airlines (e.g., tickets, baggage handling), and individuals purchase goods and services from other airport tenants (e.g., food, car rental, sundries). These purchases generate revenue for the airlines and tenants, which enables them to pay leases and fees to use an airport's infrastructure. Businesses other than airlines (such as fixed-base operators) provide services that generate revenue for airports as well. Passengers also pay for airport infrastructure through a PFC, discussed at length in Chapter Six.

Not all revenues, however, can be used to cover all expenses. The color of money matters. Revenue use is governed by a system of statutory-based "grant assurances," which are administered by the FAA and restrict airports' abilities to raise and spend revenues in specific ways.[3] Further, many airlines and airports enter into use-and-lease agreements that stipulate, among other terms, whether airlines have some degree of control over how airports spend revenues provided by airlines. Details regarding grant assurances and use-and-lease agreements are discussed later in this chapter.

To understand the rationale (in part) for the rules governing revenue use and spending on operations and infrastructure, it helps to categorize airport infrastructure, facilities, and services as airside or landside, with terminals in between, as represented in Figure 1.1. This simple categorization guides most rules, regulations, and decisions about how infrastructure should be paid for and who makes those decisions. For example, fees collected from airlines are generally applied to airside operations, maintenance, infrastructure, and related costs for which the airlines derive the most direct benefits of those capital investments. Rent and fees paid by other airport tenants might be allocated to a different mix of operating and capital expenditures.

Although publicly owned, airports compete both with each other and with other transportation modes for business. However, this competition is mediated by several factors. First, every metropolitan area is served by a small and essentially fixed number of airports, so new entrants to the market are extremely rare, and passengers living in a particular geographic area have a limited number of options.[4] Second, although airports can compete for transfer passengers, transfers are, generally speaking, influenced by geography (most airlines would not want to "flow" passengers through Minneapolis if they are traveling from Boston to Miami). Finally, airports have very different catchment areas, especially for longer-haul flights. For example, passengers on the eastern seaboard can compare multiple direct flights to Europe from Washington, D.C., Baltimore, Philadelphia, and New York. Although passengers in western states might have fewer options to Europe, they might have more options to Asia.

---

[3] For example, grant assurance 23 restricts sponsors from allowing a business to have an exclusive right to operate at that airport. Grant assurances are discussed further in the "Promotion of Competition" section later in this chapter. Grant assurances apply to all airports that have ever received federal AIP funds.

[4] Only one new large-hub airport, in Denver, has been built in the past four decades, and it replaced an existing large-hub airport, which is no longer in service (Morrison and Winston, 2008).

How airlines choose to use an individual airport (for example, in either an origin-destination or hub mode) can affect the finances of the airport, its access to certain types of revenue sources, and its leverage in negotiations with incumbent airlines and new entrants. The next section looks in more detail at relationships between airports and their primary tenants, airlines.

Airport and Airline Use-and-Lease Agreements

Airports and airlines have a symbiotic relationship; in most cases, their interests align and they work together effectively to provide passengers with transportation services. Airports charge airlines a variety of fees for use of their facilities. Airlines need well-functioning airports to support their core business. Both value safe and efficient transportation of travelers. However, their interests might not always align, such as when making decisions that affect airline competition.

Airlines and airports have long used formal use-and-lease agreements to spell out fees, services, and responsibilities.[5] Agreements define such issues as

- how rates paid by airlines to airports are set
- which facilities an airline can use at an airport, and on what conditions
- whether airlines have any degree of control over airport investments and expenses
- who bears responsibility for such issues as insurance and environmental compliance (Faulhaber et al., 2010, p. 7).

The details of agreements between airports and airlines can vary significantly from airport to airport, and no two airports share the same circumstances.

This section describes the nature and variety of these agreements, how these agreements affect the relationships between airports and airlines, and other ways that airports and airlines interact today. This assessment is limited because there is no central repository of agreements and no requirement that they be made public. For this reason, we did not attempt to systematically collect use-and-lease agreements, and therefore we are unable to make any claims about the extent to which examples from specific airports are representative. We emphasize our understanding that relations between airports and airlines vary significantly from airport to airport. Despite this variability, the structure of the relationships between airports and airlines is important. It affects airports' revenue streams, their degree of autonomy in capital planning, and perceptions of whether airports or airlines have the "upper hand" when their desires are in conflict.

Rate-Setting Methods
One issue that is foremost in agreements is the arrangement they describe regarding payments from airlines for airport expenses. According to the FAA Rates and Charges Policy (FAA, 2013), airports can use any reasonable method for charging rates, but rates generally fall into two groups, residual and compensatory, with a variety of possible combinations of the two.

---

[5] We will simply refer to these as *agreements*. Although not every airport signs such agreements with its incumbent airlines, the large majority do (Faulhaber et al., 2010). Agreements are discussed in more detail later in this chapter.

These methods can greatly influence the relationship between the airport and the tenant airlines because they represent different ways of trading off risks and rewards.[6] Agreements are developed in the context of particular funding sources, such as AIP grants and PFCs, discussed later in this chapter.

In a residual arrangement, the airlines essentially act as the financial backers of the airport. They agree to pay operating costs that are not covered by concessions or other revenues. Residual agreements must be voluntarily negotiated between the airport and the tenant airlines; an airport cannot unilaterally impose a residual agreement (Wu, 2015b). Under residual agreements, which were more common prior to deregulation, airlines were ultimately responsible for the airport's operating and capital costs (Faulhaber et al., 2010, p. 14).

In a compensatory arrangement, the airport develops rental rates for facilities and fees for the use of specific services. Airlines then pay for the facilities and services they use. This means that the airport bears more financial risk: If revenues from the airlines do not cover the costs of providing these facilities and services, the airport will lose money.

Many airports use a *hybrid arrangement*, which combines elements of both residual and compensatory arrangements. For example, airfield fees could be assessed on a residual basis, while terminal fees could be set on a compensatory basis. These arrangements can be further complicated by the fact that airports can also establish "safety net" and revenue-sharing policies, by which airlines might provide an emergency financial backstop or receive a share of concession revenue to be credited against their other payments (Wu, 2015b). Airports Council International–North America (ACI-NA) further divides hybrid approaches into hybrid-residual and hybrid-compensatory based on revenue-sharing arrangements, as illustrated in Figure 3.1 (Starostina and Wu, 2018).

These arrangements have major effects on how airports operate and manage their finances. For example, a Moody's study found that residual-based airports had an average of 354 days'

Figure 3.1
Schematic of Residual, Compensatory, and Hybrid Rate-Setting Methods

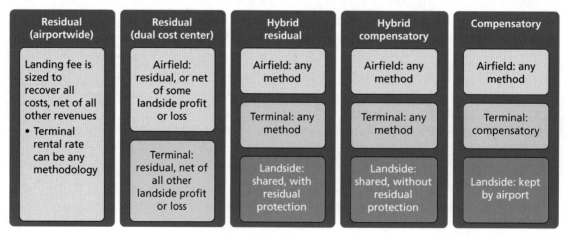

SOURCE: Starostina and Wu, 2018, slide 7.

---

[6]   This section is largely based on Wu, 2015a; Wu, 2015b; and Faulhaber et al., 2010.

worth of expenses in cash reserves, compared with 394 days at hybrid and compensatory airports (Faulhaber et al., 2010, p. 83).[7] Table 3.1 shows some key differences.

Prior to deregulation, many airports operated on residual agreements with 30-year terms that were aligned with 30-year bond issuances. Credit rating agencies generally assumed that the financial health of the airport was directly tied to the strength of its incumbent airlines. Under deregulation, more airports began adopting compensatory and hybrid arrangements with shorter terms, sometimes only five years (Faulhaber et al., 2010). A recent airport survey found that, of 27 large-hub airports, four had agreements of less than five years, five had agreements of five to seven years, ten had ten-year agreements, and eight had agreements of more than ten years (Starostina and Wu, 2018).[8] No one model predominates; of the 30 large-hub airports, eight are considered residual, seven hybrid, and 15 compensatory. Medium-hub airports also show a variety of types: eight residual, 12 hybrid, and six compensatory (Wu, 2017).[9] Appendix C provides details for large- and medium-hub airports.

Signatory Status

At airports that use agreements, airlines can choose whether they sign this agreement, hence the term *signatory airlines*. In exchange for signing the agreement, which could obligate them to a residual arrangement (depending on the airport), signatory airlines might enjoy exclusive or preferential access to gates (FAA/OST Task Force, 1999),[10] some degree of influence over airport capital planning, lower rates and charges, or revenue sharing. However, the recent trend

Table 3.1
Effects of Residual and Compensatory Arrangements on Airlines and Airports

	Residual Model	Hybrid Model	Compensatory Model
	⟵———————————————————————————⟶		
Financial risk is primarily borne by	Airlines	Shared	Airports
Airport motivation to maximize other revenue sources is	Lower	Medium	Higher
Degree of airline oversight of capital projects is	High	Medium	Low
Cash reserves held by airport are	Lower	Medium	Higher

SOURCE: RAND analysis, based on Faulhaber et al., 2010.

---

[7]   Because of the way the Certification Activity Tracking System (CATS) data are structured, there are no distinctions between truly unrestricted funds and those set aside for specific projects or operations and maintenance reserves. Therefore, days of cash reserves may not necessarily be available for all purposes, and CATS may not accurately reflect the money available to airports for capital projects.

[8]   Comparable data on medium hubs were not provided.

[9]   Wu notes that his categorizations differ slightly from the FAA; however, he also notes that "there are no consistent definitions of the types of rate methodologies" (Wu, 2015a, p. 1). Wu's data indicated five airports for which information was not available.

[10]   Access to airport facilities is generally provided on four bases: exclusive (for one airline only), preferential (with preference for one airline, but can be used by other airlines when the preferred airline is not using it), joint (can be allocated to any airline as needed, and is paid for according to usage, such as baggage handling), and common (this generally refers to facilities that are available to any user, such as restrooms). See Kaplan and Smith, 2014.

has been away from exclusive gates and toward preferential and common-use gates (Faulhaber et al., 2010).

Majority-in-Interest Provisions

Airports with agreements might include majority-in-interest (MII) provisions for signatory airlines. These provisions collectively give airlines some formal authority to approve or disapprove of capital plan projects. The agreement governs which airlines can participate in the process and the type of authority they have.[11]

Threshold provisions govern how many "votes" are needed to approve or disapprove a project. The threshold required to approve or disapprove a project might vary by activity level (by percentage of landed weight) or by the percentage of all airlines (e.g., 50 percent of those airlines that collectively account for 60 percent of landed weight). Threshold provisions might also be cost-center specific, meaning that thresholds to approve or disapprove a project might differ depending on the level of airline activity (e.g., they could vary with the amount that an airline uses an airfield versus the number of gates they use).

MII provision types can be either positive (the airlines that constitute the threshold must affirmatively agree that the airport can pursue a specific project) or negative (airports can proceed unless a certain percentage of airlines vote no).

Types of control can include absolute disapproval (the airport cannot proceed at all), rate-based disapproval (the airport cannot use airline rates and charges to fund the project), and deferral (the airport must wait a certain period before proceeding with the project). The degree and type of control is closely linked with the sharing—or bearing—of risk among the parties.

Importantly, MII provisions apply only to projects funded with fees paid by airlines to airports. If projects are funded entirely with other sources of funding, they would generally not be subject to airline review. Projects funded with PFCs, which were introduced in 1990, require airports to consult with airlines and other stakeholders and to obtain FAA approval, but they do not require airline approval. These issues are discussed in greater detail in Chapter Six.

Gate Control and New Market Entrants

One common point of contention between airports and airlines is the ability of carriers to enter a new airport. At airports where airlines have a high degree of control over specific gates, some airlines have been able to effectively bar new carriers—their potential competition—from entering a market, often by leaving their gates underused or unused. This practice was one factor in the introduction of PFCs, designed to reduce over time the number of exclusive gates. In contrast, it is advantageous to airports for gates be fully used, since many of their revenue sources depend on spending by passengers and operations fees paid by airlines.

Even though the trend has been away from exclusive-use gates, airlines at some airports are still able to block potential competitors. For example, Virgin America was unable to obtain gates at Chicago's ORD for three years because two legacy carriers controlled most of the gates.[12] It is difficult to say how common this situation is, since negotiations take place between airlines and airports and might not necessarily become public. The industry term for

---

[11] Discussion based on Faulhaber et al., 2010.

[12] Only when the airport used PFC revenue to purchase the lease for a concourse—which was previously operated by another airline—was Virgin able to begin flights (Mouawad, 2012).

an airport that is dominated by one airline is *fortress hub*, suggesting the ability of an airline to protect its market share at that airport.[13]

Two other issues directly related to gate control affect the ability of an airline to discourage its competitors. First, some agreements restrict the amount that airlines can charge to sublease their gates, which is a typical way for new airlines to enter a market (Ciliberto and Williams, 2010). Second, airlines at a few airports have built and now operate their own terminals, which allows an airline to control its terminal's use.[14] The effects of these provisions on competition at individual markets is discussed in Chapter Two.

Hubbing

Hub-and-spoke networks can affect the relationship between airlines and airports. A hub airport tends to have a higher proportion of flights from the hub carriers. In contrast, other airports might have a larger number of airlines and be less dependent on any one airline to supply their passenger base. The greater the dependence on one airline, the greater the risk to an airport of that airline suddenly reducing its presence because of market forces, mergers, or bankruptcy. For example, both Lambert-St. Louis and Pittsburgh International airports saw enplanements decline substantially when their main respective tenants reduced their hub operations.[15] However, the fact that an airline uses an airport as a hub does not mean it has a majority of passengers and operations at that airport; an airport might serve as a hub for more than one airline.[16]

Another issue is that hub airports might have a higher proportion of passengers who are transiting the airport. This can have financial implications to the airport because those passengers would not generate parking or rental car revenue, since they do not require ground transportation. These are substantial sources of revenue for many airports. Hub status can also affect passenger spending on concessions, such as food, beverage, and retail, but in varying ways. One study found that dwell time tends to increase spending, since passengers spend more time in the airport; that airports with high international connection volumes tend to have higher per-passenger spending; and that connecting passengers spend only 70 percent of what originating passengers spend because they are time-constrained (LeighFisher and Exstare Federal Services Group, 2011).

Of the 61 large and medium hubs, about 40 are designated by airlines as their hubs or *focus cities* (airports that are not necessarily hubs in a hub-and-spoke system but that are locations where an airline has concentrated many of its flights). Of these 40 hubs, 25 are hubs for

---

[13] Although there is no formal definition of *fortress hub*, it is generally thought of as an airport where 70 percent or more of flights are by one airline. See, for example, Mathews, 1999.

[14] In extreme cases, airlines cannot move aircraft between terminals even in an emergency; see Rabinowitz, 2018, for an account of the difficulty of recovering from a snowstorm at John F. Kennedy International Airport (JFK) in New York City because of such restrictions.

[15] For a brief case study of Lambert and the loss of TWA and later American Airlines operations, see Kincaid et al., 2012. For a review of Pittsburgh's dehubbing and its impact, see Belko, 2012. Dehubbing can result from airline mergers and subsequent decisions to reduce hubs (for example, St. Louis' dehubbing followed the merger of American and TWA), or simply from operational changes at an airline (such as when USAir reduced operations in Pittsburgh) (Rupp and Tan, 2019). Other dehubbed airports since 2000 include Las Vegas, Cleveland, Memphis, Baltimore-Washington International, Dallas/Fort Worth, Cincinnati, Orlando, and Luis Muñoz Marín (San Juan). Roughly half of these were due to mergers, and half were due to other airline operational changes (Rupp and Tan, 2019; Redondi, Malighetti, and Paleari, 2012).

[16] Table C.1. in Appendix C shows the number of airlines that consider each airport a hub or focus city.

only one airline; these are airports where that airline might exercise more power than at airports with zero or multiple hub airlines. All but one of the large-hub airports serve as a hub or focus city for at least one airline. Specifics are shown in Table 3.2.

Market Size and Demand

Larger airports with high demand should be in a better position to negotiate with airlines, since other airlines could be readily available to take up landing slots because of overall strong demand for air travel. This could be especially true when that metropolitan area is served by only one airport or if all large-hub airports in the area are operated by the same entity. For example, Newark Liberty International Airport (EWR) has been accused of assessing unusually high fares that airlines cannot avoid by moving to another New York–area airport.[17]

Smaller airports have suggested to the FAA that they have less influence than airlines in negotiations, especially when one airline is dominant in a region (FAA, 2014). This could explain why smaller airports are far less likely to designate PFC funds for use on competition enhancement, as discussed further in Chapter Six. Smaller airports are also more likely to be dependent on fewer carriers. Although large and medium hubs have, on average, three to four competitors for each city pair, small hubs and non-hubs have only one or two (Kasper and Lee, 2017). This is consistent with a pattern of lower demand in smaller markets than larger ones.

Revenues, Expenditures, and Governing Regulations

In this section, we discuss the types of revenues that airports can generate, how they categorize their expenses, and the federal regulations that affect their ability to raise and spend revenues. Although this section introduces the main types of revenues, three types are covered in more detail in subsequent chapters: AIP grants (Chapter Five), PFCs (Chapter Six), and bonds (Chapter Seven).

Table 3.2
Airports Operating as Hubs or Focus Cities for Airlines

Airport Hub Size	Total Number of Airports	How Many Are Considered Hubs or Focus Cities by at Least One Airline	How Many Are Considered Hubs or Focus Cities by Two or More Airlines	Fortress Hubs
Large	30	29	15	14
Medium	31	12	0	2

SOURCE: Authors' review of airline websites as of May 2019.
NOTE: Although Southwest Airlines calls its airports with concentrations of flights "focus cities" and not hubs, we have classified these airports as fortress hubs if Southwest has more than 70 percent of the flights at those airports because the airline does not operate on a conventional hub-and-spoke system.

---

[17] See United's successful complaint to the FAA about rates at EWR. Because all three New York metropolitan airports are operated by the Port Authority of New York and New Jersey, United could not easily switch its flights to another airport with lower fees (United Airlines, Inc. v. The Port Authority of New York and New Jersey, 2015).

Airport Revenues and Other Funding Sources

Airports report their revenues and expenditures to the FAA using its CATS database, which contains a standard categorization of revenues and other funding sources as well as individual items in each category. CATS distinguishes between two types of operating revenues: aeronautical (those generated by airside and aviation-related activities) and non-aeronautical (those generated by landside activities). PFCs and AIP grants are typically included as subcategories of non-operating revenue in CATS, but for the purposes of this study, we list them as separate, high-level categories to make it easier to distinguish differences in usage and impacts across classes of airports. Bond proceeds are not revenues; they are essentially a loan. Airports borrow funds from investors today to pay for large expenses and repay that amount, along with interest, over time. Table 3.3 lists funding categories and associated items.

The following sections describe the broad revenue categories. Detailed definitions of operating revenue categories can be found in Appendix D. Chapters Five, Six, and Seven provide in-depth analysis of AIP, PFCs, and bonds.

Operating and Non-Operating Revenue Sources

Airports as a whole make the largest proportion of their aeronautical operating revenue from terminal fees (paid by airlines) and the largest proportion of their non-aeronautical operating

Table 3.3
Revenue and Other Funding Sources in CATS

Funding Category	Items
Operating Revenues	
Aeronautical operating revenue	• Apron charges and tie downs • Aviation fuel tax retained for airport use • Cargo and hangar rentals • Federal inspection fees • Fixed-base operator revenue • Fuel sales net profit/loss or fuel flowage fees • Landing fees • Landing fees from cargo • Landing fees from GA and military • Other aeronautical fees • Security reimbursement from federal government • Terminal rentals (aero)
Non-aeronautical operating revenue	• Hotel • Land and nonterminal facility leases and revenues • Other non-aeronautical fees • Parking • Rental car • Terminal services and other • Terminal: food and beverage • Terminal: retail stores and duty free
Other Funding Sources	
Non-operating revenue	• Capital contributions • Interest revenue • Other non-operating • Special non-operating items
AIP and state grants	• AIP and other grants
PFCs	• PFC

SOURCE: CATS (FAA, undated c).

revenues from parking and ground transportation (categorized separately from rental cars). Ground transportation includes revenues from shuttle services, taxis, and ride-hailing services (such as Uber and Lyft).

In addition to operating revenues generated from aeronautical and non-aeronautical users, airports draw on several sources of funding that are collectively categorized in CATS as "non-operating revenues." These sources include interest earnings and capital contributions by airport sponsors and others,[18] as well as federal and state grant programs and the PFC program. Generally, these non-operating revenues might not be used for operating expenses of the airport, and as a result, are especially important as sources of funding for infrastructure projects.

Airport Improvement Program Grants and Other Grants

AIP grants represent the largest, most direct involvement of the federal government in funding airport infrastructure. The predecessor grant program to the AIP was established in 1970 in tandem with the creation of the AATF, a federal trust fund that receives excise tax revenues from passenger and cargo travel and fuel purchases and that is used exclusively to fund aviation-related activities.[19] When the AATF was created, there was some debate over the best way to collect fees, since there were and still are few avenues available to efficiently attach and collect revenues from sources other than ticket sales and taxes. Congress intended for the AIP to fund airports across the system for the good of the system as a whole, even if it meant that some airports would contribute more funds than they would receive. Details about the AATF and AIP are provided in Chapter Five.

The annual AIP funding appropriation limitation is set by Congress.[20] AIP grants are distributed to public-use airports listed in the NPIAS via a complex set of apportionment formulas and percentage set-asides. As a result of the mechanism for the collection of the fees, there is a deliberate allocation that results in a distribution of funds from the airports responsible for the most passenger and cargo traffic (and therefore for generating the most revenues to the AATF) to the needs of the air system more broadly. This results in smaller airports receiving more funds than they contribute because they are critical to the functioning of the overall system but have far more limited means of generating revenues. Large- and medium-hub airports receive only about one-quarter of AIP dollars, while accounting for about 90 percent of all enplanements.

Although the AIP is the largest federal grant program for airports, other grant programs also provide funding to airports. For example, the TSA uses other transaction agreements[21] to

---

[18]   An *airport sponsor* is the legal owner of an airport, usually a state government, local government, regional authority, or other entity that owns one or more airports. Airport sponsors are distinct from *airport management*, which is responsible for day-to-day operations at an airport.

[19]   The federal government began making grants to airports in 1946, as authorized by the Federal Airport Act. In 1970, the Airport and Airway Development Act created two grant programs, the Planning Grant Program and the Airport Development Aid Program, which were funded by the newly created AATF. In 1982, these programs were consolidated into the AIP in the Airport and Airway Improvement Act of 1982 (AAIA). See FAA, 2017c.

[20]   The appropriation limitation also includes four other funding categories: Small Community Fund, Administrative Expenses, Airport Technology Research, and Airport Cooperative Research (FAA staff, personal communication with the authors, September 24, 2019).

[21]   An *other transaction agreement* is an alternative mechanism through which some federal agencies distribute funding (i.e., other than a grant or a traditional contract). Other transaction agreements are exempt from certain federal regulations under the Federal Acquisition Regulation. See GAO, 2017b.

provide funding for checked baggage systems through its Electronic Baggage Screening Program (TSA, undated). States also often offer grants to support airports and grants that help fund airport infrastructure. These grants can include providing a portion or all of the local match to AIP grants, as well as separate grant programs established by the state (National Association of State Aviation Officials, 2015). Funding for these state-level programs varies by state and comes from an array of state excise taxes and from general revenues.

Passenger Facility Charges

The PFC program was established in 1990 as a complement to the AIP at a time of concern both about the adequacy of existing resources to fund airport infrastructure and about the federal budget. It is the only authorized exception to the Anti-Head Tax Act,[22] which prohibits airports from charging per-passenger fees. Eligible airports seek approval from the FAA to impose a PFC on departing passengers in tandem with requesting approval for eligible projects toward which revenue from the PFC would go.[23] The maximum allowable PFC is currently $4.50, effective April 2001. Currently, all medium- and large-hub airports impose a PFC, and all but one in each of these hub size categories charge the maximum allowable rate. This is despite a requirement that these airports forgo 50 percent or 75 percent of their AIP entitlement grants, depending on the PFC collection rate, as discussed in Chapter Six.

PFC revenues can be applied by airports to a wider range of projects than AIP grants, including borrowing costs. About two-thirds of approved PFC collections over time have gone or are expected to go toward paying bond principal and interest. PFC-funded projects are largely focused on landside projects, but one explicit category of PFC-eligible projects is competition. Indeed, one of the goals of Congress in establishing the PFC program was to make resources available to airports that could be used to enhance airline competition (e.g., by expanding terminals and offering gate slots to new entrants). We explore this issue in some detail in Chapter Six.

Capital Financing

Along with various revenue categories, airports separately categorize their debt activities, which occur primarily through the municipal bond market. Bond proceeds are inflows of capital. Repayment of borrowed capital and interest payments associated with the debt incurred, collectively called *debt service*, is counted as a non-operating expense.

Four major types of bonds are used to finance airport infrastructure: general airport revenue bonds (GARBs), PFC bonds, general obligation (GO) bonds, and special facility bonds. Airport bonds are usually considered investment-grade bonds by the major credit rating agencies. This means that the airports are at low risk of defaulting on their bonds and thus produce a safe and stable return on investment for bond buyers. These types of bonds are described in greater detail in Chapter Seven.

The issuer and the purpose of the bond depend on the type of bond. Airport sponsors generally issue GARBs and PFC bonds. Because these bonds are backed by various revenue streams and PFCs generated by the airports commensurate with their enplanements, larger

---

[22] This is the common name for the provision of the Airport Development Acceleration Act of 1973 that federally preempts local governments from levying taxes that would restrict interstate commerce.

[23] Current statutory requirements for eligibility are that airports be publicly owned, provide scheduled air carrier service, and have more than 2,500 annual enplanements.

airports can more easily access the bond market than can smaller airports with lower revenues. Smaller airports therefore tend to rely on their local and state governments to issue GO bonds on their behalf to fund airport infrastructure projects. GO bonds are backed by the taxing power of a local or state government and therefore are considered to have near-zero risk of default. Special facility bonds are issued by third-party agents, such as development corporations and finance authorities, to fund such projects as parking lots and leased facilities (e.g., hangers or car rental centers). The issuers of special facility bonds use the revenue generated from such facilities to repay their debt.

Most airports also have the option of borrowing directly from banks rather than entering the bond market. Bank lending might be more attractive for smaller airports for which the transaction costs of bonds are too high, although smaller airports might also be hindered if the only collateral is the airport itself or revenues are insufficient to repay loans.

Airport Expenses and Expenditures

Airports report their expenses to CATS using a standard three-part categorization of operating expenses, non-operating expenses, and capital expenditures, as summarized in Table 3.4. Detailed definitions of these categories can be found in Appendix D.

One important consideration is that certain expenditures can be made only with certain types of funds. The following section on federal regulations touches on some of these restrictions, and the results of these and revenue-specific restrictions are shown in Tables 3.5 and 3.6 at the end of that section.

Federal Regulation Affecting Revenues and Expenditures

In this section, we discuss some key issues that affect how airports can generate and spend revenue. A listing of major federal authorizing legislation can be found in Table E.1 in Appendix E. Guidance on FAA policies for airports is codified in the *FAA Airport Compliance Manual* (FAA Order 5190.6B, 2009).

Airport operating revenues include nearly every type of revenue generated on airport property, including all concessionaire rentals, air carrier charges, proceeds from the sales or rental of airport property, and state and local aviation fuel taxes. The main exception is local

Table 3.4
Categorization of Airport Expenses in CATS

Category	Items
Operating expenses	• Communications and utilities • Contractual services • Insurance claims and settlements • Other operating expenses • Personnel compensation and benefits • Supplies and materials
Non-operating expenses	• Interest expense
Capital expenditures	• Airfield • Parking • Roadways, rail, and transit • Terminal • Other capital and construction expenses

SOURCE: CATS (FAA, undated c).

sales taxes. Although they are collected from concessionaires on airport property, they do not constitute airport revenue (Dempsey, 2008).

Self-Sustainability

The AAIA requires that airports be as self-sustaining as possible "under the circumstances at that airport" (Pub. L. 97-248, 1982). Airports are not allowed to raise fees to a level that would generate a revenue surplus, although fees may be used to facilitate financing and cover contingencies. However, should accumulations of fees reach a level that could be considered a surplus, the FAA can investigate (FAA Order 5190.6B, 2009, Chapter 17).

The implementation of this requirement varies based on the type of charge. Charges for aeronautical uses must be set in such a way that they reflect the actual cost of services provided (regardless of fair market value). Charges for non-aeronautical uses must be set at fair market value, with some exceptions for community uses, non-profit aviation organizations, some ground transportation services, and military units with aeronautical missions (FAA Order 5190.6B, 2009, Chapter 17).

Airline Fees and Charges: Nondiscriminatory and Reasonable

The AAIA also establishes that airports must charge "reasonable" fees to airlines, and that "air carriers making similar use of the airport will be subject to substantially comparable charges" (Pub. L. 97-248, 1982). The FAA published guidance in 2013, the *Policy Regarding Airport Rates and Charges*,[24] which established that the method for setting rates must be consistent and "may not exceed the costs allocated to that user or user group under a cost allocation methodology adopted by the airport proprietor that is consistent with this guidance" (FAA, 2013, Section 3.1). This policy allows for fees to vary between signatory and nonsignatory airlines, but it does not provide any guidance for determining whether fees are reasonable (Goldberg, 2007).

Revenue Diversion

One important set of regulations relates to limits on revenue diversion.[25] *Revenue diversion* is the use of airport operating revenues for expenditures that are either not on airport property or do not directly serve aviation purposes.[26] Limits on revenue diversion were first promulgated by the AAIA, with a mandate that airport operators "use all revenues generated by the airport for the capital or operating costs of the airport, the local airport system, or other local facilities which are owned or operated by the owner or operator of the airport and directly related to the actual transportation of passengers or property" (Pub. L. 97-248, 1982). The goal of this provision is to prevent local governments from using airport-generated revenues for nonairport purposes, such as education.

This law has evolved since 1982. In 1987, the law changed "directly related to transportation" to "substantially related" (Pub. L. 100-223, 1987). In 1994, airports were required to report airport revenues and payments to other levels of government as a way of strengthening FAA oversight (Pub. L. 103-305, 1994). In 1996, the law was applied to all airports that receive

---

[24] The FAA's policy is similar to that of ICAO, which establishes international recommendations for airport charging. See ICAO, 2012.

[25] Much of this discussion is based on Coogan, MarketSense Consulting LLC, and Jacobs Consultancy, 2008.

[26] Although often described simply as "airport revenues," these provisions do not specifically apply to the AIP, PFCs, or other types of revenues because those are governed by other statutes. However, those statutes incorporate similar restrictions on the nonairport use of those funding sources.

federal assistance and included a provision that the USDOT could withhold other types of transportation funding as a sanction (Pub. L. 104-264, 1996). Even if an airport later chooses to forgo AIP funds, it remains subject to revenue diversion rules as long as it functions as an airport (Dempsey, 2008).

Although the FAA does not review or approve uses of airport revenues, it can audit airports to ensure they are in compliance with revenue diversion regulations (Karaskiewicz, 2018). Past audits have found numerous instances of revenue diversion, ranging from construction on nonairport projects to payments to cities (Dempsey, 2008).

If the federal government transfers potentially revenue-generating property to an airport, the airport must use those revenues for airport purposes (FAA Order 5190.6B, 2009, Chapter 3). Although airports can raise revenue by selling airport property, the FAA must approve any sales. Approval requires that the airport establish the property's fair market value with an independent appraisal (Dempsey, 2008).

Sponsors that are found to be diverting revenues can face several sanctions. Many cases are resolved through an FAA notice of investigation that informs the sponsor that they are not in compliance. Should diversion continue, the FAA can withhold approval of new PFC collections (existing collections can continue) and can consider the sponsor's noncompliant status as a factor in making discretionary grants. If further enforcement mechanisms are needed, a sponsor's other USDOT funding (e.g., Federal Highway or Federal Transit Administration funds) could be legally withheld, although cases that reach this point are extremely rare. The FAA can also bring legal remedies against cities or counties that use aviation fuel tax collections for nonaviation purposes,[27] with sponsors potentially being subject to damages of three times the amount of diverted revenue.

The AAIA grandfathered 12 airport sponsors to continue using airport revenues for nonairport purposes where arrangements pre-dated the AAIA (FAA Order 5190.6B, 2009, Chapter 15).[28] Currently, nine airports are still allowed to exercise their grandfathered status to divert revenue up to a maximum cap annually.[29] Airports that are allowed to divert revenue sometimes exceed their cap; the FAA calls this particular type of revenue diversion *excess revenue*. When a grandfathered airport diverts more revenue than allowed by its cap, the FAA can and does use the airport's noncompliant status as a factor in determining whether to grant discretionary funds. The FAA can also deny future PFC applications once it has made a finding of noncompliance, which is rare.[30] However, the FAA cannot withhold PFC funds that have already been approved. Unlike other forms of revenue diversion, the FAA cannot withhold USDOT funding from grandfathered airports with excess revenue, and sponsors are not

---

[27]   FAA Office of Compliance staff, conference call with the authors, September 4, 2019.

[28]   Sponsors, not airports, are grandfathered, so the number of airports exceeds 12. A subsequent list of 11 sponsors excludes the Port of San Diego (FAA, 2018c).

[29]   The nine currently grandfathered sponsors are the Maryland Aviation Authority, the Massachusetts Port Authority, the City of Chicago, the City and County of San Francisco, the state of Hawaii, the City and County of Denver, the City of St. Louis, the Niagara Frontier Transportation Authority, and the Port Authority of New York and New Jersey (USDOT, Office of Inspector General, 2018). Grandfathering provisions for the City and Borough of Juneau and the Texarkana Airport Authority have expired (FAA, 2018c). San Diego's grandfathering authority was eliminated when the airport was transferred to a new and independent authority. The cap was set independently for each airport and increases annually according to inflation (USDOT, Office of Inspector General, 2018).

[30]   FAA staff told us they have issued only one finding of noncompliance in the past 15 years (personal communication with FAA staff, October 12, 2019).

subject to financial damages.[31] A 2018 USDOT Office of Inspector General report found that four of eight sponsors reviewed were incorrectly reporting their grandfathered payments (USDOT, Office of Inspector General, 2018).[32] One airport sponsor has exceeded its revenue diversion cap by hundreds of millions of dollars, but because the airports receive no discretionary funds and PFC applications are already approved, the FAA has no mechanism to prevent this excess revenue.[33]

Revenue Diversion and Ground Transportation

Prohibitions on revenue diversion are important for ensuring that funds raised by airports are used for airport purposes. However, they can complicate paying for ground transportation projects that are related to the airport but outside airport property. The main tenet of revenue diversion is that airport revenues must be spent on projects "substantially related" to the transportation of passengers or property. However, this guidance can be complicated by circumstances at individual airports.[34] As one public transit example, Bay Area Rapid Transit (BART) heavy rail service to San Francisco International Airport (SFO) was provided in the form of a Y-shaped "spur" rather than in a more direct "through-track" manner to ensure that the project would not constitute revenue diversion. This design was more expensive and resulted in longer travel times than the through-track would have had (Karaskiewicz, 2018).[35]

A second challenge facing ground transportation investments is that airport sponsors must occasionally use multiple revenue sources, each with its own restrictions. For example, the $2 billion Miami Intermodal Center (which includes rental car facilities as well as public transit) used two federal Transportation Infrastructure Finance and Innovation Act loans; contributions from the county, metropolitan planning organization, and expressway authority; three state infrastructure bank loans; and airport revenues (Miami Intermodal Center, undated).

By law, the FAA is required to exercise due diligence in its review of all projects, and this can be particularly challenging for off-airport projects that require interpretation. Because off-airport uses are generally prohibited, airports might need to acquire rights-of-way for transit projects. To fund the construction of the eight-mile-long AirTrain to JFK in New York, the airport had to acquire a median strip in an existing expressway to make the project eligible (Gosling, Wei, and Freeman, 2012). The project was not approved by the FAA until after a seven-year legal case clarified the interpretation of "exclusive use" (Karaskiewicz, 2018).[36] In a more recent example, the FAA allowed the use of airport revenues to upgrade signalized intersections

---

[31] FAA Office of Compliance staff, conference call with the authors, September 4, 2019.

[32] The Office of Inspector General did not review revenue diversion at the Port Authority of New York and New Jersey (USDOT, Office of Inspector General, 2018, Exhibit D).

[33] FAA Office of Compliance staff, conference call with the authors, September 4, 2019.

[34] Of course, this is not always the case; one member of our expert panel noted that city-owned airports were less likely to experience problems when the city is the owner/operator of both the airport and the transit system.

[35] The FAA proposed a more expansive definition of how transit projects could be considered in a Proposed Policy Amendment issued May 3, 2016 (see FAA, 2016). At the time of this writing, this amendment had not been adopted.

[36] Although the legal challenges were to a PFC application and not the use of airport-generated revenues, one of the primary concerns was closely tied to revenue diversion in that the proposed rail line was not located on airport property at the time of the request (Karaskiewicz, 2018).

off airport property on the grounds that they would reduce airport congestion.[37] Because of this legal uncertainty, airports have experienced additional transaction costs in navigating the bounds of these restrictions that affect the timeliness of providing transit and other transportation options for passengers and employees to and from the airport.

Summary Findings on Revenue Use

Using the preceding analysis, we summarize in Tables 3.5 and 3.6 the allowable uses and restrictions on revenues. The first column of Table 3.5 lists seven general funding sources. The next two columns present who or what entity provides the resources for the funding source and what expenses each funding source can be used for. The third column lists the document or institution that governs what expenses the funding source is legally eligible to be used for,

Table 3.5
Funding Sources and Their Allowable Uses

Funding Sources	Who Pays?	What Can the Funding Source Be Used for?	Who Determines Eligibility Criteria?	Who Can Approve?
Aeronautical revenue	• Air carriers	• Capital, operating, and administrative costs	• FAA Revenue Use Policy, based on legislation	• Use-and-lease agreement (differs by airport)
Non-aeronautical revenue	• Tenants • Concessionaires • Air carriers	• Capital, operating, and administrative costs	• FAA Revenue Use Policy, based on legislation	• Use-and-lease agreement
Non-operating revenue	• Miscellaneous	• Capital, operating, and administrative costs	• FAA Revenue Use Policy, based on legislation	• Use-and-lease agreement
AIP grants	• AATF • User fees • Fuel taxes	• Airside development and planning • Select projects in non–revenue-generating areas	• FAA AIP Handbook, based on legislation	• FAA (subject to statutory guidelines)
PFC	• Passengers	• All AIP eligible projects • Projects in revenue-generating areas, with certain limitations • Debt service	• FAA, based on legislation	• FAA (subject to statutory guidelines)
Bond proceeds	• Investors purchase bonds and are repaid by airports	• Capital expenditures	• State laws and U.S. Securities and Exchange Commission regulations	• Investors through bond covenant • Use-and-lease agreement (in some cases)
Private investment	• Investors	• Capital, operating, and administrative costs	• USDOT-FAA Rates and Charges; FAA for airport privatization	• Use-and-lease agreement (in some cases)

---

[37] FAA Office of Compliance staff, conference call with the authors, September 4, 2019.

almost all of which are based on statute. The final column states what body can approve or refuse the use of a respective funding source for a project, even if the funding source is legally eligible to be used for the project.

Within each funding source, there is further nuance as to where the funds come from and how they can be spent. For example, within non-aeronautical funding sources, some funds are collected from the *customer facility charge* (CFC), a user fee on rental car users. State law generally restricts CFC-derived funds to use on consolidated rental car facilities. Likewise, agreements between the airport sponsor and rental car concessionaire typically give approval authority for CFC-funded projects to the concessionaire. Distinct funding types, such as the CFC, and nuanced regulation within each broad category make clear distinctions for each funding source difficult to represent.

Table 3.6 indicates the degree to which a funding source is eligible and likely to be approved for each type of expenditure, subject to particular constraints within a given airport-airline agreement. A green cell indicates that a funding source (column) can be used for the corresponding expenditure (row) with very few or no restrictions. A red cell indicates that the funding source cannot or is very unlikely to be used for the corresponding expenditure type.

Table 3.6
Summary of Allowable Uses of Funding

Expenditure Type	Expenditure Detail	Funding Sources						
		Operating Aero	Operating Non-Aero	Non-Operating	AIP	PFC	Bonds	Private Investment
Administrative	Planning and project administration							
	Other administrative							
Capital	Airfield							
	Noise							
	Emissions							
	Parking							
	Roadways, rail, and transit							
	Terminal: Non–revenue-producing areas							
	Terminal: Revenue-producing areas							
	Debt service							
	Rental car facilities							
Operating	Operating costs							

SOURCES: Operating (aeronautical and non-aeronautical) and non-operating funds: FAA Order 5190.6B, 2009; Faulhaber et al., 2010; AIP: Gentry, Duffy, and Swedish, 2014; FAA Order 5500.1, 2001.
NOTE: Green means that the funding source can be used for the expenditure type broadly; yellow means it can be used with some restrictions, and red means it cannot or would not be used. For more detailed information about the allowable uses of different funding sources, see Appendixes G and J.

Yellow cells denote restrictions on how a funding source may be applied to a corresponding expenditure type. Details on these restrictions are provided in Appendixes G and J.

Table 3.6 shows that almost all revenue sources can be used toward airside development and airport planning. Conversely, landside projects—such as parking, roadways, rail, and terminals—have more-nuanced restrictions on which funding source they can use. Many of these restrictions are associated with AIP and PFC funds. Although AIP and PFC project eligibility rules share some similarities, PFC funds can used for a wider variety of expenditure types, including debt service, and for a far wider variety of projects in revenue-producing areas of the terminal, with certain limitations. Consequently, PFCs give airports more freedom over their spending when compared with AIP funds. Likewise, application of PFC funds is not within the purview of use-and-lease agreements, which give airports greater flexibility in spending on landside projects than other revenue sources.

Other Federal Regulations That Affect Airport Operations

This section discusses other federal regulations that relate to promoting competition; slot controls and perimeter rules that impose operational limits at a few airports; other federal regulations pertaining to safety, security, emissions, and noise; and privatization.

Promotion of Competition

Although the airline industry is now deregulated, concerns about renewed consolidation among the major airlines has spurred new regulations that require airports to foster competition.[38] The Wendell H. Ford Aviation Investment and Reform Act for the 21st Century (AIR-21; Pub. L. 106-181, 2000) requires competition plans from large- and medium-hub airports where one or two carriers control more than 50 percent of enplanements. Among other items, plans must include information on the number of gates and their use provisions (exclusive, preferential, or common), a description of how the airport would accommodate a request for new or expanded services, a gate utilization and assignment policy, leasing and subleasing arrangements, and any access complaints by carriers. Plans must be approved by the FAA before airports can receive AIP grants or PFC approvals (FAA Order 5100.38D, 2019, Appendix W).

AIP grant assurances—conditions that airport sponsors must meet as a condition for having accepted past AIP grants—also include several assurances designed to foster competition, including the following:

- **Assurance 5, Rights and Powers:** Airport sponsors cannot relinquish their ability to satisfy the grant assurances. Even if they contract out some elements of airport operations, they must retain the ability to promote competition.
- **Assurance 22, Economic Nondiscrimination:** Airport sponsors must provide equal access to aeronautical businesses wishing to provide operations at an airport. Access must be reasonable and nondiscriminatory.
- **Assurance 23, Exclusive Rights:** Airport sponsors cannot grant a business an exclusive right to operate at the airport.

---

[38] Unless otherwise noted, this discussion is drawn from Smith, 2019.

- **Assurance 24, Fee and Rental Structure:** Fees and rates charged at airports should be assessed in a way that makes the airport self-sufficient.
- **Assurance 25, Airport Revenues:** Revenues collected by the airport sponsor must be spent on costs that are "directly and substantially related" to moving passengers and freight; they cannot be used to benefit a specific airport-based business.
- **Assurance 39, Competitive Access:** If an airport sponsor cannot accommodate a request for access, it must file a report with the FAA explaining the reason for the denial. Reports must be filed every six months until the request can be accommodated (Smith, 2019).

Finally, PFCs were enacted, in part, to foster competition. Airport sponsors can use competition as a basis for requesting the ability to collect a PFC. However, regardless of the objective of the project, facilities built with PFCs cannot provide exclusive rights to one business, and PFC-funded projects cannot be subject to MII provisions in agreements.

Slot Controls and Perimeter Rules

Slot controls and perimeter rules impose restrictions on the number and length of allowed flights from an airport and represent a form of demand management. A *slot* is an authorization to either take off or land at an airport on a specific day during a specified period. Slot controls are in place at three airports: JFK, LaGuardia Airport (LGA), and DCA. These airports are considered Level 3 airports under the FAA and International Air Transportation Association (IATA) Worldwide Slot Guidelines. Level 3 means that they do not possess adequate infrastructure nor have near-term plans to build enough infrastructure to meet demand, and they would consequently produce systematic delays without slot controls (FAA, 2019d).

To prevent or reduce delays throughout the system, the FAA has the authority to allocate and regulate the number of slots available, as well as the authority to mandate the minimum usage of slots at Level 3 airports. At DCA and LGA, which serve primarily domestic flights, slots are distributed to carriers on a rolling basis, largely based on the number of slots a carrier has historically owned and operated. At JFK, the large number of international flights has led the FAA to adopt the IATA's Worldwide Slot Guidelines slot allocation process, which is used to facilitate international operations worldwide and which assigns slots on a seasonal basis (FAA, 2019d). The FAA also sets the number of permitted schedule operations per hour, which varies by airport,[39] and mandates that a carrier must use its assigned slots at least 80 percent of the time. If a carrier fails to meet the minimum usage requirements outside of defined exceptions, the FAA can withdraw the slots for reallocation.[40]

The effectiveness of the current slot control system within the United States is debated and currently under review. After several studies in the 1990s and 2000s showed that the slot control system, called the High-Density Rule, restricted competition and new airline entrants, Congress phased out the High-Density Rule in 2007. However, frequent system delays throughout the year from Level 3 airports led the FAA, through congressional authority, to temporarily reinstate slot controls. These temporary controls have been extended several times, most recently through 2020, while the FAA assesses different demand management systems, such as congestion pricing and slot auctions (GAO, 2012b).

---

[39] This excludes DCA's exemptions, which are congressionally approved and included in the FAA's reauthorization bills.

[40] Codified in 14 CFR § 93.227, para. d, for DCA and FAA Orders for LGA and JFK (USDOT, 2018a; USDOT, 2018b).

In addition to slot restrictions, the perimeter rules can restrict scheduled operations at a given airport to reduce congestion. A perimeter rule limits the distance a nonstop flight can travel to or from an airport and is in effect at only two major U.S. airports: DCA and LGA (GAO, 2012b). At DCA, one of the reasons the perimeter rule was set statutorily in the 1960s was to mitigate noise from new jet planes, which were noisier than today's aircraft (GAO, 2012b, p. 28).[41] Since then, Congress has issued exemptions to the perimeter rule, currently allowing nonstop flights to and from ten cities beyond the perimeter (Metropolitan Washington Airports Authority, undated). At LGA, the Port Authority of New York and New Jersey instituted an informal (and later formal) perimeter rule in 1984 to reduce congestion and move long-haul traffic to nearby JFK or EWR (Transportation Research Board, 1999). Both improving technology and growing demand for nonstop flights through DCA and LGA have prompted discussion of whether the perimeter rule remains a necessary restriction.[42] Because no clear verdict has been reached, the perimeter rules remain in place at the time of this writing.

Environmental, Noise, Safety, and Security Regulations

Airports are subject to many federal regulations in four areas: environmental, noise, safety, and security. Airport infrastructure investments must go through a variety of reviews and approvals to ensure they are compliant with these regulations. This section does not assess the sufficiency or insufficiency of these regulations but briefly describes current requirements and how these affect airport infrastructure planning.

Airports are subject to federal environmental regulations, the main one of which is the National Environmental Policy Act. This law requires review in the form of environmental assessments or environmental impact statements when airport development could have significant environmental impact. Environmental review is generally triggered by large projects, such as new airports or runways in major metropolitan areas. The environmental assessments or environmental impact statements are meant to ensure that airport development meets environmental regulations across a variety of topic areas, including cultural resources under the National Historic Preservation Act of 1966, resources protected by the Fish and Wildlife Coordination Act, air quality under the Clean Air Act, water quality protected by the Clean Water Act, and so on. These regulations often require lengthy reviews that extend development efforts (FAA Order 5100.38D, 2019).

With regard to noise, local and state governments are the primary entities responsible for land-use planning, zoning, and regulation; the federal government does not have regulatory authority over land-use noise compatibility. However, if an airport voluntarily participates in the Airport Noise Compatibility Planning program (known as Part 150), the airport is eligible to receive AIP funds for noise mitigation and sound insulation projects. Part 150 plans must contain a noise exposure map that identifies an airport's noise patterns, through current and projected noise contour lines, and compatibility problems that are current or projected to exist.

---

[41] Another reason for the perimeter rule's application to DCA was to drive longer-haul flights to the new Dulles Washington International Airport and thus enable its financial prospects.

[42] LGA most recently considered lifting the perimeter rule in 2015–2016. See "Why You Can't Get There from LaGuardia," 2015. In 2018, different congressional representatives sought to prevent additional exemptions to the rule and to nullify the rule at DCA. See "Lawmakers Press to Protect Perimeter Rule at DCA from Further Encroachment," 2018, and Russell, 2018.

Airports must also have an approved Part 150 Noise Compatibility Program, which maps out noise mitigation actions.

With regard to safety regulations, commercial service airports must maintain a current FAA-approved Airport Certification Manual to show that current and planned infrastructure meet safety requirements under 14 CFR Part 139. These requirements are mainly focused on airside infrastructure (such as runway pavement, marking, lighting, and safety areas) as well as safety procedures (such as snow removal and emergency operations).

Security regulations have been tightened considerably since the September 11, 2001, terrorist attacks. Airports must have a TSA-approved Airport Security Program that contains the airport's procedures and measures for access control for select areas within the airport's boundaries, per regulations found in 49 CFR Part 1542. Airports must also meet TSA requirements for Security Screening Checkpoints, Checked Baggage Inspection Systems, and Perimeter Intrusion Detection Systems when seeking to expand or modify these systems or areas. Each component of the airport, depending on its classification and purpose, ultimately requires varying levels of identification, screening, and monitoring equipment to be installed and thus be compatible with new and old airport infrastructure (National Safe Skies Alliance, 2017).

Privatization of Airports and Other Components of the National Airspace System

U.S. airports have remained almost exclusively publicly owned and operated, in contrast with trends elsewhere. For example, many airports in Europe have moved in the direction of joint ownership, in which 51 percent of ownership is retained by a public agency and 49 percent is owned by private interests (ACI Europe, 2016). In this section, we look at the landscape for privatization in the United States and compare it with developments in Europe. We also touch briefly on the discussion around privatizing the air traffic control system and the FAA itself.

Pilot Program for Airport Privatization

The FAA Authorization Act of 1996 created a pilot program to allow five commercial service airports to be privatized (a number that was raised to ten in 2012) (Tang, 2019). As of this writing, only one airport—Luis Muñoz Marín International Airport in San Juan—has successfully completed the process and remains privately operated. Eleven others have applied;[43] of these, seven eventually withdrew, one was privatized but later reverted to public ownership,[44] and three have obtained preliminary approval, but final applications are pending (FAA, 2019j). The FAA Reauthorization Act of 2018 eliminated both the cap on the number of airports that could apply and provided funding for airports to undertake the required analysis.[45] However, it retained the provision that 65 percent of airlines (both the overall number and by landed weight) must approve privatization. All versions of this program define *privatization* as long-term leasing by private operators; commercial service airports would not be sold to private investors (Poole, 2018).[46]

---

[43] The pilot program allows for up to ten airports to be privatized, and applications have been staggered over several years.

[44] Stewart International Airport in Newburgh, N.Y., successfully completed the process in 2000 and was turned over to National Express Group for private operation. However, the operator reverted the airport to the Port Authority of New York and New Jersey in 2007 (GAO, 2014b).

[45] The FAA Reauthorization Act of 2018 also renamed this program the Airport Investment Partnership Program.

[46] Separately from this program, general aviation airports may be sold to private operators.

Although widely used in other countries, privatization has not proven popular in the United States for several reasons. A GAO report cited higher financing costs,[47] the possible lack of state and local property exemptions, the difficulty of the privatization process, changing market conditions that reduced expected benefits, and the ability of airport owners to find ways to benefit from private sector investments without full privatization as the main reasons (GAO, 2014b). In discussions with the authors, other experts have suggested that communities might wish to see airports remain public to ensure greater accountability to the public, and that motivations to privatize because of burdensome state or local regulations (such as procurement) can be resolved by other means, such as by transferring the airport to an independent authority. Given the short amount of time that has passed between the most recent reauthorization bill (November 2018) and the writing of this report, it is too soon to say whether the most recent version of the program will garner greater interest.

Privatization as defined above or as practiced in other countries has not been widespread, but there are other examples of private sector participation in airport development and operations. One airport (Branson Airport in Missouri) has been privately developed and operated outside of the FAA pilot program (GAO, 2014b). Individual terminals at an airport have been built and operated with substantial private participation, such as Terminal 5 at JFK[48] and the South Terminal at Austin-Bergstrom International Airport.[49] Finally, at publicly owned airports, private firms typically provide many services in addition to air travel, including fuel, maintenance, janitorial services, construction, ground transportation, hotels, and retail.

European Experience with Privatization

Airport privatization is far more common in other countries than in the United States. In Europe, for example, private involvement in airport ownership and operations has been increasing rapidly over the past decade. According to ACI Europe, the share of Europe's 500 airports that are fully public fell from 78 percent to 59 percent between 2010 and 2016. *Mixed-ownership* airports, which encompass various types of public-private partnerships, have doubled over the same period, from 13 percent to 25 percent. Full privatization or mixed ownership is more common at larger airports; although only 41 percent of airports have some private involvement, those airports handle about 75 percent of European enplanements. The trend has been driven by financial needs as well as demand for greater efficiency (ACI Europe, 2016).[50]

Privatization of Air Traffic Control

Privatizing the nation's air traffic control system has been suggested by many commentators and members of Congress over the years. The most recent proposal was made by the Trump administration in fall 2017, but the effort stalled in Congress in 2018; there is no current legislation on this topic. Proponents, chiefly the commercial airline industry, claim that privatization would allow for more-nimble adoption of new technology (including the long-delayed

---

[47] As discussed in Chapter Seven, airports can issue tax-exempt bonds as public entities, a situation that does not exist in many countries aside from the United States. Private investor bonds are subject to taxes, which may make it more expensive for private entities to borrow than public ones.

[48] Although the terminal construction was paid for with general obligation bonds, JetBlue will repay the Port Authority of New York and New Jersey for the work. JetBlue has a 30-year lease (Cho, 2008).

[49] Under a public-private partnership between the city and private firm Lonestar Airport Holdings, LLC, Lonestar operates the terminal on a 30-year lease; the terminal opened in 2017 (Goldenstein, 2017).

[50] For additional information on recent trends in privatization around the world, see Poole, 2017.

Next Generation system that would update a variety of technologies used in air traffic control) and remove air traffic control from political interference. Opponents, including the general aviation community and smaller airports, claim that privatization would focus resources on larger airports and airlines and remove government oversight.[51] As noted in Chapter One, a broader discussion of air traffic control privatization is beyond the scope of this report.

Master Planning Process

Prior to deregulation in 1978, neither airports nor airlines had a major incentive to be nimble, since the number and types of services provided changed relatively little, and their agreements often lasted 30 years (Faulhaber et al., 2010, p. 14). Now, however, a larger gap has appeared between their relative planning horizons. With the arrival of competition from new domestic and international market entrants, airlines tend to think about business planning in annual terms, with a five-year horizon being a long-term proposition.

However, airport planning cycles are much longer, with many long-term master plans looking out 20 years or more. Changes to the physical infrastructure at airports tend to require many years to plan, permit, and build. Airports are also subject to a variety of safety and environmental regulations that have evolved and generally increased over the years, along with both mandatory and informal coordination with regional stakeholders, including local elected officials and adjacent neighborhood groups. This mismatch makes it difficult for airports to respond quickly to changes in airline operations.

Airport master plans, which are maintained by most commercial airports, attempt to translate these changing demands into short-, medium-, and long-term development strategies. Master plans are typically reviewed every five to ten years (or more frequently) to account for changes in airport activity and context. Plans can also take into account uncertainty by establishing thresholds, or "triggers," for new development. Master plans generally translate demand forecasts into facility requirements, culminating in part with a schedule for development based on set demand thresholds and a continuously updated Airport Layout Plan to match anticipated development. The FAA's approval of an airport's demand forecast and Airport Layout Plan is required for the airport's proposed projects to be eligible for AIP funds (FAA Advisory Circular 150/5070-6B, 2015). Further details about airports' master planning processes are provided in Appendix F.

Role of State and Local Statutes and Regulations

In contrast with federal regulations, many airport projects involve local issues, such as traffic, land use, and noise. The FAA provides some guidance on these topics, such as the interim guidance on land use within the runway protection zone (FAA, 2012b). In addition, airports could also be subject to state and local statutes and regulations regarding these issues, although

---

[51] See Mark, 2017, and Nunes, 2017, for further discussion of the most recent privatization proposals.

many complexities exist, and the FAA's authority in some issues preempts that of state and local entities.[52]

Airports can also receive funding from state and local sources for certain types of projects, which could be subject to regulations from those entities, as well. For example, the Florida Department of Transportation requires airports in the state to use any state funds exclusively for airport purposes, mirroring the FAA's requirements (Florida Department of Transportation, 2008). State funding often supports complex projects, such as transit lines (Dulles Corridor Metrorail Project, undated) and ground transportation centers (Miami Intermodal Center, undated).

Roles and Interests of Other Stakeholders

Although airports are governed by FAA regulations and adhere to the terms of use-and-lease agreements with airlines, other stakeholders (shown in Figure 3.2) can affect an airport's ability to embark on major capital projects or change its operations. Such influence can be either formal or informal. Here, we describe the particular interests of some of these stakeholder groups.

Passengers: Airports rely on passenger-generated revenues and thus have reason to create a positive experience for passengers. The industry tends to divide passengers into two broad categories: business and leisure. Broadly speaking, business travelers tend to be more focused on convenience and efficiency over price, while leisure travelers have the opposite priorities. There are several national passenger advocacy organizations, such as Travelers United, the Aviation Consumer Action Project, FlyersRights.org, and the Global Business Travel Association.

Neighbors: These stakeholders include residents of the communities surrounding the airport as well as the elected officials who represent them. They might support the airport's direct and indirect effect on generating jobs and economic activity through attracting and retaining businesses. They might have concerns about airport-generated issues that affect the quality of life in those neighborhoods, such as traffic and noise. They might participate in comment periods for public outreach on various projects, and in some cases, they form formal organizations. For example, more than 20 years ago, Chicago and local elected officials formed an O'Hare Noise Compatibility Commission of the communities surrounding ORD. The organization conducts regular noise monitoring and plays an oversight and advisory role on sound insulation programs.

Travel industry: The travel industry—outside of the airlines—broadly includes hotels, tourism and convention promotion (e.g., local attractions), and other businesses that depend on tourism and business travel revenues. The industry's interests in airports generally include ease of access and cost of travel to specific locations.

Airport-related businesses and employees: This group includes fixed-base operators, concession holders (retail and restaurants in the airport), ground transportation providers and rental car operators, janitorial and other service providers, and other businesses whose employees work at airports. These groups might have interests ranging from airport fees and how

---

[52] For example, with regard to noise, FAA regulations preempt those of state and local entities, generally speaking, but the airport operator can implement its own rules. See Beckman, 2012.

Figure 3.2
Key Commercial Service Airport Stakeholders

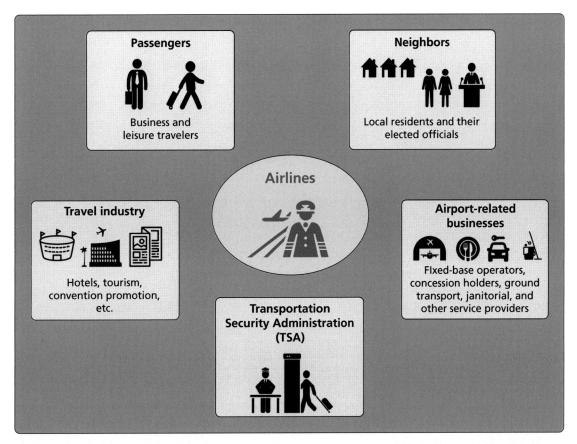

SOURCES: RAND design with Noun Project icons by Luis Prado, Gan Khoon Lay, Juan Prado Bravo, Adrien Coquet, Atif Arshad, Mike Wirth, monkik, Krisada, Bankunetsu Kaito, Lnhi, and lambe Ndomble.

they are set; commuting, working conditions, and security for their employees; and access to potential customers.

TSA: Formed after the September 11, 2001, terrorist attacks, the TSA is responsible for screening passengers and cargo. This role requires physical space for screening lines and equipment, as well as coordination with airport security staff.

Summary of Findings

Airports are complex and highly regulated businesses whose particular financial profile depends critically on the nature of their relationships with airlines and their geographic location. Airports and airlines generally formalize their relationships via use-and-lease agreements, which govern the rates paid by airlines for use of an airport's facilities, the rate-setting mechanism (generally residual or compensatory, with hybrid models possible), and the ability of signatory airlines to access such privileges as preferential gate use and MII provisions. The terms of these agreements help determine whether airlines or airports have the upper hand when they disagree. Other factors that influence this balance of power include whether airlines can block competitors from entering an airport, whether an airline uses an airport as a hub, the proportion of flights an airline controls from an airport, and the size of the market served by the airport.

Another source of complexity is airports' wide array of expenses and funding sources. Although expense categories tend to be fairly straightforward—capital, operating, and debt service—funding sources include aeronautical (derived from airside operations), non-aeronautical (derived from landside operations), PFCs (user fees paid by passengers), grants (including AIP), and non-operating revenues (including bond proceeds).

Airports' use of funding sources is governed by a wide variety of congressional mandates through the reauthorization bills, FAA regulations, and use-and-lease agreements. Some of these vary by funding source. The AIP and PFC are the two sources with the largest degree of federal involvement, because AIP funds come from the AATF and the PFC is subject to FAA approval of projects. AIP funds are designed to provide a stable funding source for smaller airports, while PFCs tend to track enplanements, which are far higher at large- and medium-hub airports. Airports can also access the municipal bond market, although the impact of bond funding tends to decrease with airport size. Although the FAA has allowed a limited number of airports to pursue privatization, this option has not proven as popular in the United States as it has in other countries.

The FAA imposes some specific restrictions on airports and their revenues (which encompass almost every type of revenue generated on airport property), including requirements for financial self-sufficiency, that rates paid by airlines be nondiscriminatory and reasonable, and that revenues be used exclusively for airport purposes on airport property. In addition, a small number of airports are subject to further constraints (specifically, slot restrictions and perimeter rules). Capital projects are subject to environmental review. Airports are subject to other forces, as well, in terms of state and local regulations and numerous other stakeholders, ranging from passengers to local elected officials. Airports must also follow FAA guidance in developing master plans, which guide capital planning.

CHAPTER FOUR

Status of and Trends in Airport Funding and Expenses

In this chapter, we seek to draw a picture of how airports raise and spend money to provide services to travelers and airlines and meet all required safety, security, environmental, and other regulatory requirements. Expenses and funding streams differ across airport size classes, but even within a hub category, for example, variations among airports can be significant. Understanding similarities and differences in expenses and funding helps to explain how current utilization and future changes in AIP, PFCs, bonds, and other funding sources might affect airport finances, competition and fares at individual airports, and competition and capacity constraints more generally throughout the NAS.

Data Sources and Analysis

The FAA's CATS database, through which NPIAS commercial service airports file annual financial reports, itemizes the various categories of expenses and revenues. As of January 2019, all 30 large-hub primary airports, 31 medium-hub primary airports, and 72 small-hub primary airports had reported revenue and expenses. For other categories, 194 non-hub primary airports out of 213 and 76 nonprimary commercial service airports out of 104 had reported (FAA, undated c). In total, 403 airports out of 450 commercial service airports had submitted their financial reports to CATS.

The most-recent and most-complete data available in CATS are for fiscal year (FY) 2017.[1] In the database, PFCs and government grants, including AIP grants, are included together in the non-operating revenue category. However, for the purposes of this report, these two items have been separated into individual categories.

Overview of Funding and Expenses in 2017

According to the CATS data, the 403 airports that reported to the FAA collectively generated $28.8 billion in revenue in 2017.[2] Of this total, $11.8 billion (41.0 percent) was from aeronautical operating revenue, $10.1 billion (35.1 percent) was from non-aeronautical operating revenue, and $1.4 billion (4.9 percent) was from non-operating revenue, as shown in Figure 4.1.

---

[1]   Airports report data to CATS aggregated by their fiscal year, which varies from airport to airport. We describe data from fiscal years ending in 2017 as 2017 data.

[2]   Appendix D provides the data cited in this section in tabular form.

Figure 4.1
Inflow and Outflow of Funds for the 403 Commercial Service Airports Reporting to CATS, 2017

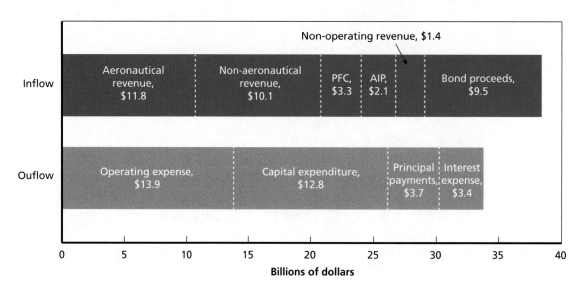

All of those revenues are generated from economic activity at the airports. The revenues associated with either direct federal funding, largely through AIP grants (7.3 percent),[3] or federal oversight through the PFC program (11.5 percent), made up less than 19 percent of the total revenue generated in 2017. However, these sources are the most significant sources of funds for airport capital projects.

On the other side of the ledger, the 403 reporting airports incurred $30.1 billion in expenses. Of this total, $13.9 billion (46.2 percent) came from operating expenses, such as worker salaries, utilities, and contractual services; $3.4 billion (11.3 percent) came from non-operating expenses, which are composed primarily of payments of interest on borrowed funds; and $12.8 billion (42.5 percent) came from capital expenditures. In the same year, commercial service airports raised $9.5 billion in bonds and repaid $3.7 billion of existing long-term bonds.[4]

U.S. commercial service airports are operated essentially as nonprofits. However, differences in total inflow and outflow of funds exist within a given year. The difference becomes a carryover of either positive or negative funds into the next year. These funds are not considered profits; instead, they are categorized either as restricted cash for specific bond payments and capital expenditure or unrestricted cash reserves to account for solvency in times of economic difficulties, such as when the carryover might be negative. Such practice is also encouraged by credit rating agencies and becomes important when new bonds are being issued.

---

[3]   A small percentage of grants come from non-AIP federal programs for security and some limited state programs.

[4]   The CATS database defines *debt service* as both principal and interest paid in relation to long term bonds; the database does not provide the amount of the principal and interest separately. However, non-operating expenses also include payments of interest on long-term bonds, as well as interest payments from all other types of debt. To avoid double-counting the interest, we have subtracted non-operating expenses from debt service. Because we cannot subtract only the long-term bond debt, the value we report as debt service might undercount the principal payments on long-term bond debt. Long-term bonds constitute an average of 94 percent of all types of debt reported by the airports in CATS for the period of 2009 to 2017. We therefore expect the difference between the value we report for debt services and the actual long-term principal paid to be minor.

Revenue, by Airport Size

When compared with the overall trend, the proportions within revenue, expense, and debt activities vary by the size category of the airport. As shown in Figure 4.2 and Table 4.1, the top three sources of revenue (funding sources other than bond proceeds) were aeronautical operating revenue, non-aeronautical operating revenue, and PFCs for large-hub and medium-hub primary airports in 2017. For large-hub airports, aeronautical operating revenue was the largest source, accounting for 45.6 percent of the total revenue. For medium-hub airports, the largest source of revenue was non-aeronautical operating revenue, with 39.6 percent. Also, long-term bonds are used more by larger airports than smaller airports.[5]

The top three sources of revenue for small-hub airports were non-aeronautical revenue at 40.0 percent, aeronautical operating revenue at 30.5 percent, and AIP and other grants at 15.1 percent. Non-hub primary airports were similar to small-hub airports but relied more heavily on AIP and other grants, accounting for 36.0 percent of the revenue in 2017. Nonprimary commercial service airports also were more dependent on AIP and other grants, with about half of their revenue coming from those sources. As the size of airports gets smaller, they tend to rely more on non-aeronautical sources of revenue and external assistance.

Expenses, by Airport Size

Unlike the differences in primary sources of revenue between airports of different sizes, the proportions of expense categories for the commercial service airports are similar across the airport size categories. Excluding principal payments, all sizes of airports spent more than 40 per-

Figure 4.2
Proportion of Funding Sources, by Airport Size, 2017

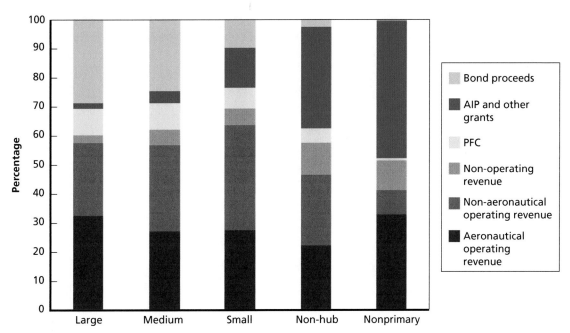

SOURCE: CATS (FAA, undated c).

---

5   For an in-depth analysis of long-term bonds, see Chapter Seven.

Table 4.1
Funding, by Airport Size, 2017 (millions of dollars)

Funding Category	Source	Large-Hub Primary (30 Airports)	Medium-Hub Primary (31 Airports)	Small-Hub Primary (72 Airports)	Non-Hub Primary (194 Airports)	Nonprimary (76 Airports)	Total (403 Airports)
Aeronautical operating	Revenue	8,787	1,585	865	412	151	11,799
Non-aeronautical operating	Revenue	6,766	1,752	1,134	452	38	10,141
Non-operating	Revenue	698	316	180	205	48	1,447
PFC	Revenue	2,429	525	228	88	2	3,271
AIP and other grants	Revenue	601	245	428	650	220	2,144
Bond proceeds	Debt	7,734	1,447	306	46	0.1	9,533
Total		27,015	5,870	3,141	1,853	459	38,335

SOURCE: CATS (FAA, undated c).

cent on operating expenses and another 40 percent or more on capital expenditures, as shown in Figure 4.3 and Table 4.2.

Commercial service airports spend money differently for non-operating expenses, which include interest expenses. As shown in Figure 4.2, larger airports rely on bond issues as a significant source of their capital funding. The size of bond proceeds is comparable to aeronautical and non-aeronautical operating revenue for large-hub and medium-hub airports. These airports can leverage the bond market because of their ability to generate revenue, and as a consequence, they can afford to rely less on assistance from AIP. Details about the bond market and bond activities are further explained in Chapter Seven. Because larger airports issue bonds to raise a significant portion of their capital funds, they also incur interest expenses that are about one-quarter of their operating expenses.

Funding and Expenses, by Urban and Rural Airports

Several definitions of *rural* have been developed by different agencies over the years. Our study uses the definition of a rural airport prescribed by the Internal Revenue Service (IRS) (IRS, 2018). The IRS designates an airport as rural if it

> has fewer than 100,000 commercial passengers departing from the airport by air during the second preceding calendar year and *one of the following is true*:
> • The airport is not located within 75 miles of another airport from which 100,000 or more commercial passengers departed during the second preceding calendar year,
> • The airport was receiving essential air service subsidies as of August 5, 1997, or
> • The airport is not connected by paved roads to another airport (BTS, 2018).

According to these criteria, of the 403 commercial service airports that had submitted financial reports to CATS as of January 2019, 78 airports are considered rural and 325 are considered urban.

Figure 4.3
Proportion of Expenses, by Airport Size, 2017

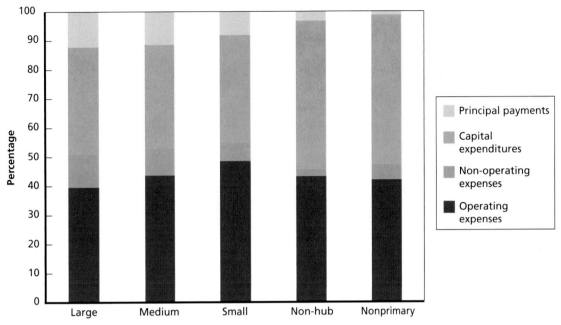

SOURCE: CATS (FAA, undated c).

Table 4.2
Expenses, by Airport Size, 2017 (millions of dollars)

Expense Category	Source	Large-Hub Primary (30 Airports)	Medium-Hub Primary (31 Airports)	Small-Hub Primary (72 Airports)	Non-Hub Primary (194 Airports)	Nonprimary (76 Airports)	Total (403 Airports)
Operating	Expense	9,377	2,119	1,370	841	201	13,907
Non-operating	Expense	2,725	466	172	44	26	3,433
Capital expenditures	Expense	8,749	1,726	1,040	995	247	12,757
Principal payments	Debt	2,807	554	226	60	4	3,651
Total		23,658	4,864	2,809	1,940	478	33,748

SOURCE: CATS (FAA, undated c).

As shown in Figure 4.4 and Table 4.3, the funding activities for an average rural airport are minimal when compared with an average urban airport. Because rural airports are essentially smaller airports by definition, with low passenger traffic, the comparison of funding and expenditures of urban and rural airports is analogous to the comparison between large and small airports. Rural airports tend to rely less on revenue generated from passenger demand, such as aeronautical operating revenue and non-aeronautical operating revenue, and rely more on AIP and other grants. Also, for the same reasons, rural airports have less leverage in the debt market.

Figure 4.4
Proportion of Funding Sources for Rural and Urban Commercial Service Airports, 2017

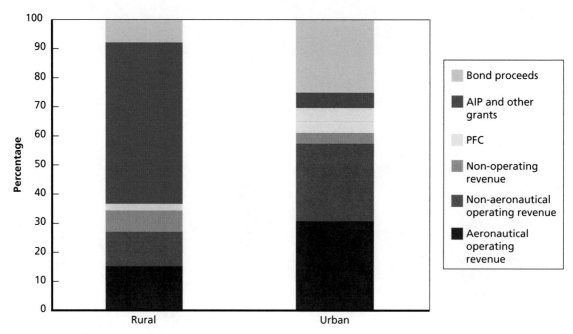

SOURCE: CATS (FAA, undated c).

Table 4.3
Funding Sources for Average Rural and Urban Commercial Service Airports, 2017 (millions of dollars)

Funding Source	Average Rural Airport	Average Urban Airport
Aeronautical operating revenue	0.7	36.1
Non-aeronautical operating revenue	0.5	31.1
Non-operating revenue	0.3	4.4
PFC	0.1	10.0
AIP and state grants	2.5	6.0
Bond proceeds	0.3	29.3

SOURCE: CATS (FAA, undated c).

On the expense side, because rural airports are much smaller in size than urban airports, the overall level of expenses and debt service is much lower than an average urban airport. Table 4.4 shows that the average rural airport's spending was $4.52 million in 2017, whereas the spending was $102.7 million for the average urban airport. Furthermore, debt service and non-operating expenses as proportions of overall spending are significantly lower for rural airports because of their reduced participation in the debt market. Instead, capital expenditures and operating expenses account for nearly all of their spending, as shown in Figure 4.5.

Table 4.4
Expenses for Average Rural and Urban Commercial Service Airports, 2017 (millions of dollars)

Expense Source	Average Rural Airport	Average Urban Airport
Operating expenses	1.5	42.4
Non-operating expenses	0.02	10.6
Capital expenditures	2.9	38.5
Principal payments	0.1	11.2
Total	4.52	102.7

SOURCE: CATS (FAA, undated c).

Figure 4.5
Proportion of Expenses for Rural and Urban Commercial Service Airports, 2017

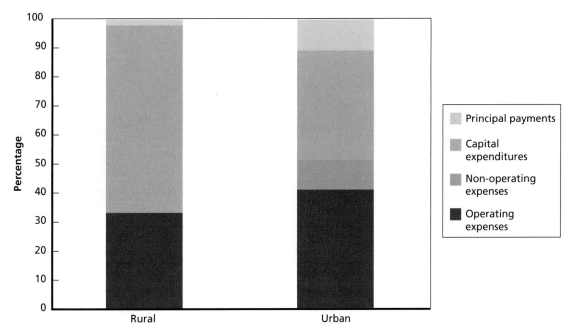

SOURCE: CATS (FAA, undated c).

Trends in Funding and Expenses from 2009 to 2017

Ideally, changes in funding and expenses could be shown for several decades. However, because reporting to CATS changed in 2009 in substantial ways, it is difficult to draw comparisons between data since 2009 and data from before 2009. We therefore focus on relatively recent trends since 2009. Appendix I provides the data in tabular form.

Trends in Funding, by Airport Size

For the period from 2009 to 2017, total annual funding for all commercial service airports consistently increased. Of the five categories previously defined, aeronautical operating revenue was the largest source of revenue, followed by non-aeronautical operating revenue, as shown in Figure 4.6 and Table 4.5. These two sources grew consistently in size and proportion. PFC collections increased by 28.9 percent, from $2.5 billion in 2009 to $3.3 billion in 2017. However, the proportion of PFCs to overall revenue remained between 11 percent and 12 percent throughout the period. In contrast, non-operating revenues and AIP and other grants decreased in size and proportion from 2009 to 2017. Bond proceeds also are a significant source of funding. Bonds will be discussed in detail in Chapter Seven.

Trends examined by airport group size are quite different than trends for airports generally, as shown in Figure 4.7. For large-hub primary airports, the growth in aeronautical operating and non-aeronautical operating revenue mirrors the overall trend. Large-hub primary airports have been receiving fewer AIP and other grants over time, declining from $814 million in 2009 to $601 million in 2017. At the same time, non-operating revenues decreased from

Figure 4.6
Commercial Service Airport Revenue, 2009–2017

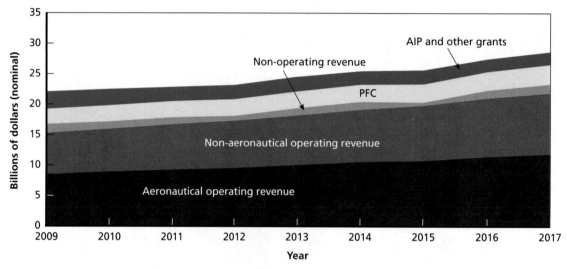

SOURCE: CATS (FAA, undated c).

Table 4.5
Commercial Service Airport Revenue, 2009–2017

Revenue Source	2009	2010	2011	2012	2013	2014	2015	2016	2017
Total revenue (billions of dollars)	22.067	22.579	22.897	23.224	24.603	25.526	25.713	27.519	28.802
Aeronautical operating revenue	38.1%	39.4%	40.2%	40.8%	40.7%	41.3%	41.7%	41.2%	41.0%
Non-aeronautical operating revenue	31.1%	31.2%	33.0%	33.9%	33.5%	33.9%	35.4%	35.2%	35.2%
Non-operating revenue	6.5%	5.6%	4.7%	3.4%	4.7%	4.8%	2.1%	4.7%	5.0%
PFC	11.5%	11.7%	11.7%	11.9%	11.4%	11.2%	11.8%	11.5%	11.4%
AIP and other grants	12.8%	12.1%	10.4%	10.0%	9.8%	8.8%	8.9%	7.4%	7.4%

SOURCE: CATS (FAA, undated c).

2009 to 2015 and then increased back to 2009 levels in 2016. PFC collections increased from $1.9 billion in 2009 to $2.4 billion in 2017, but their proportion to overall revenue generated was consistent throughout this period. This indicates that the rate of growth in revenue from PFC collections is lower than the rate of growth in total revenue.

For medium-hub primary airports, levels of aeronautical operating revenue and PFCs were consistent during the period; non-operating revenues were decreasing but then rebounded in 2017. Similar to large-hub primary airports, AIP and other grants for medium-hub primary airports decreased, from 10.1 percent of total revenue in 2009 to 5.5 percent in 2017. Non-aeronautical operating revenue's share of total revenue increased from 35.1 percent to 39.6 percent. For medium-hub airports, the lack of growth in AIP and other grants appears to have been offset by increases in non-aeronautical operating activities, such as parking, hotel, and terminal services.

The trends for small-hub primary and non-hub primary airports in terms of revenue are similar. Both groups experienced increases in aeronautical and non-aeronautical operating revenues. Also, PFCs have increased both in size and proportion, albeit less than the rate for operating revenues. However, AIP and other grants, which are a significant revenue item for small- and non-hub primary airports, have decreased both in size and in proportion to total

Figure 4.7
Commercial Service Airport Revenue, by Airport Size, 2009–2017

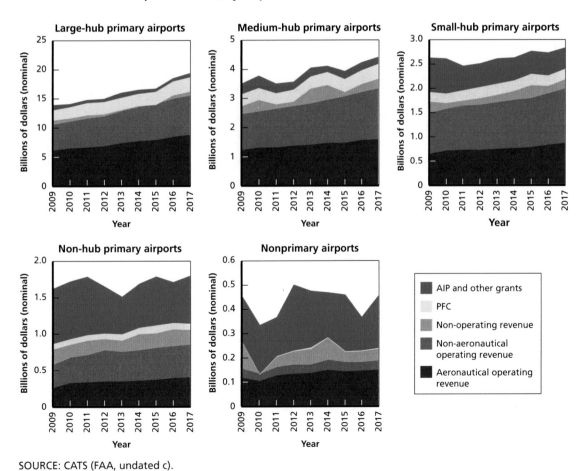

SOURCE: CATS (FAA, undated c).

revenue. Non-operating revenues have also decreased for the two groups, similar to the larger airports.

Nonprimary airports experienced periods of ups and downs in revenues from 2009 to 2017 and, unlike primary airports, did not see overall growth in total revenue. However, the proportions of aeronautical operating revenue and AIP and other grants to total revenue increased, whereas the proportions of other sources decreased.

Trends in Expenses, by Airport Size

As shown in Figure 4.8 and Table 4.6, operating expenses were the largest category of expenses from 2009 to 2017 and have shown consistent growth. Changes in the other categories are relatively small, although the data in Table 4.6 show that non-operating expenses as a proportion of total expenses grew steadily, albeit modestly, until 2014, and then began to contract, whereas the trend for capital expenditures was the opposite. Figure 4.9 disaggregates the data by airport size and shows that all airport sizes experienced trends similar to the overall trend.

The decrease in the proportion of capital expenditures and the increase in the proportion of operating expenses are more significant for the smaller airports than for the larger

Figure 4.8
Trends in Commercial Service Airport Expenses, 2009–2017

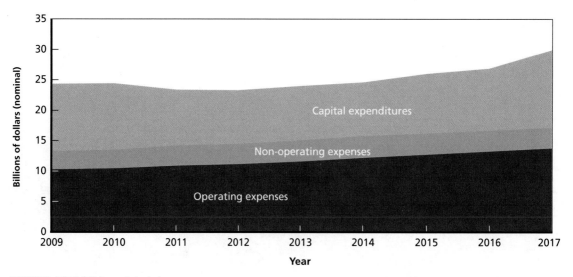

SOURCE: CATS (FAA, undated c).

Table 4.6
Trends in Commercial Service Airport Expenses, 2009–2017

Expense Source	2009	2010	2011	2012	2013	2014	2015	2016	2017
Total expenses (nominal billions of dollars)	24.462	24.547	23.508	23.407	24.087	24.750	26.115	27.055	30.097
Operating expenses	42.5%	43.0%	46.7%	48.1%	48.6%	49.8%	49.1%	49.4%	46.2%
Non-operating expenses	12.3%	12.6%	14.3%	14.2%	14.5%	14.4%	13.5%	12.7%	11.4%
Capital expenditures	45.2%	44.4%	39.1%	37.8%	36.9%	35.8%	37.4%	37.9%	42.4%

SOURCE: CATS (FAA, undated c).

airports. Furthermore, the total spending volume increased for the larger airports. For the smaller airports, total spending decreased initially and then increased back to a level similar to total spending in 2009. Although the total expenses have not increased for smaller airports, more of their revenue appears to be going toward operating expenses and less toward capital expenditures.

Trends in Funding and Expenses, by Urban and Rural Airports

The trends for urban airports and rural airports have developed differently over time. As shown in Figure 4.10, the two largest sources of revenue, aeronautical and non-aeronautical operating revenues, have been steadily increasing for urban airports. Rural airports did not experience much growth in operating revenues but did experience some volatility in non-operating revenue (keeping in mind the very different vertical scales for the two graphs in Figure 4.10). Also, rural airports heavily relied on AIP and other grants as their major source of revenue (similar to smaller airports), accounting for more than 50 percent of revenue on average.

As shown in Figure 4.11, operating expenses for urban airports steadily increased over time, and there was a period of contraction and expansion in capital expenditures for urban airports. In contrast, operating expenses for rural airports marginally increased from 2011 to 2014, but have declined since then. Unlike the trend for smaller airports of devoting propor-

Figure 4.9
Commercial Service Airport Expenses, by Airport Size, 2009–2017

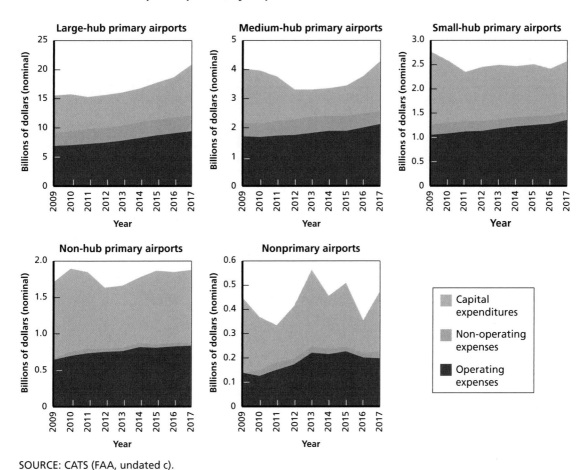

SOURCE: CATS (FAA, undated c).

Figure 4.10
Urban and Rural Airport Revenue, 2009–2017

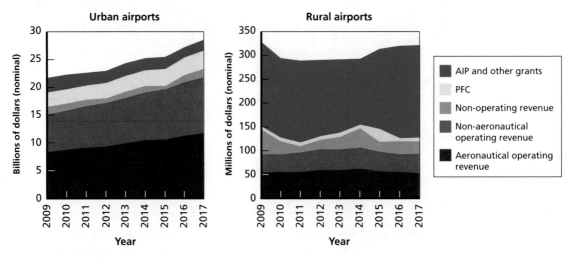

SOURCE: CATS (FAA, undated c).
NOTE: The high rural PFC revenue in 2015 is due to an unusual value at a single airport that is likely a reporting error. We have presented the data as is.

Figure 4.11
Urban and Rural Airport Expenses, 2009–2017

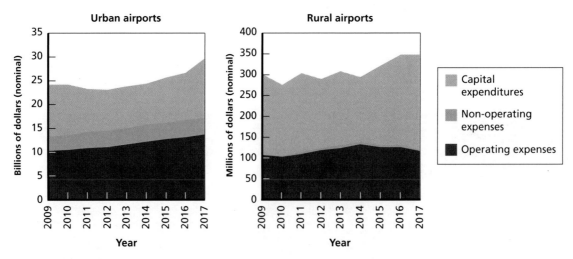

SOURCE: CATS (FAA, undated c).

tionally more of their revenue toward operating expenses and less toward capital expenditures, rural airports have increased their proportion of capital expenditures in recent years. Lastly, because rural airports are less likely to directly participate in the bond market, the share of non-operating expenses is minimal for this group.

Trends in Passenger Facility Charges and Grants Compared with Capital Expenditures

AIP and other grants, together with PFCs, represent a significant portion of the overall funding for airport infrastructure projects, as explained in Chapter Three. Figure 4.12 shows how the non-operating revenues generated from PFCs and AIP and other grants compare with

Figure 4.12
Passenger Facility Charges and Grants Compared with Capital Expenditures for Commercial Service Airports, 2009–2017

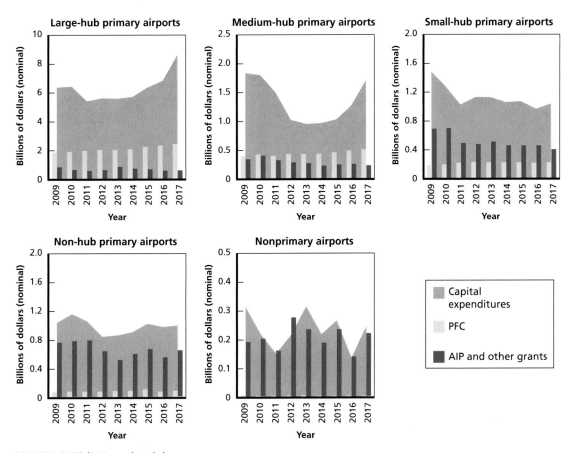

SOURCE: CATS (FAA, undated c).

capital expenditures by airport size. The ratio of the two non-operating revenues to capital expenditures increases as airport size decreases. Furthermore, between PFCs and AIP and other grants, the share of PFCs decreases as airport size decreases. These trends indicate that although AIP and other grants contribute to overall capital expenditures for larger airports, these airports rely more on PFCs and other revenue sources. In contrast, smaller airports rely significantly on AIP and other grants to fund their capital expenditures.

Summary of Findings

In 2017, the 403 airports that submitted their financial reports to the CATS database collectively generated $28.8 billion in revenue. This total amount was made up of $11.8 billion in aeronautical operating revenue, $10.1 billion in non-aeronautical operating revenue, $3.3 billion in PFC collections, $2.1 billion in AIP and other grants, and $1.4 billion in non-operating revenue. In addition to these sources, the airports generated $9.5 billion of funding from bond proceeds. In the same year, the airports incurred a total of $17.3 billion in operating and non-operating expenses and $12.8 billion in capital expenditures, along with $3.7 billion in principal payments on long-term bonds.

The proportions of funding sources and expenses varies by airport size. Larger airports tend to generate the majority of their revenues from operations. Their ability to generate significant revenue also allows them to raise the capital required for infrastructure projects through bond issuance. In contrast, smaller airports rely on AIP and other grants to generate funding and have limited access to the bond market. Despite these difference in the funding mix, the proportions of expenses are similar across airport sizes. One difference, however, is that larger airports incur more interest expenses because of their active participation in the bond market.

From 2009 to 2017, aeronautical and non-aeronautical operating revenues across airports of all sizes steadily increased. However, the rate of increase declines with the size of the airport. Also, the proportion of AIP and other grants compared with other sources of revenue decreased during this period for all airports except nonprimary ones. Similarly, the proportion of PFC collections to overall revenue has remained consistent for all airport sizes with the exception of nonprimary airports, for which the proportion has decreased.

Growth in revenue was more significant for larger airports, and so was the growth in their expenses. Overall expenses for smaller airports declined and then increased, whereas expenses increased consistently from 2009 to 2017 for the larger airports. Among the individual expense items, the proportion of capital expenditures to overall expenses declined, but the proportion of operating expenses to overall expenses increased.

CHAPTER FIVE

Federal Role in Airport Infrastructure Funding: Airport Improvement Program

The federal government is involved most directly in airport planning and development through the AIP, a grants-in-aid program dating back to 1970 that distributes funds to airports primarily for airside projects. The AIP is the focus of this chapter. Beginning in 1990, Congress authorized a complementary program to the AIP: an option allowing airports, subject to FAA approval, to receive revenues from PFCs to fund capital improvement projects. Large and medium hubs give up a portion of their AIP grants in exchange for collecting a PFC. PFCs are collected by the FAA through airline ticket purchases and then remitted to the airports where the charges were collected. PFCs are discussed in detail in Chapter Six.

Airports of all sizes receive AIP grants, but the program is redistributive by design: Grants account for a higher share of capital funding at smaller airports than at larger ones, and these smaller airports also have a lower nonfederal funding match. Funding for AIP grants flows from the AATF, which receives revenues from various excise taxes imposed on users of the airport system and funds the AIP and other FAA programs. Congress must periodically reauthorize revenue collection and funding authorities and can appropriate additional amounts from the General Fund for AIP grants or other purposes.

In this chapter, we begin by describing the AATF, including past trends and future projections for revenues and expenditures from the trust fund as well as the effects of ancillary fees on trust fund receipts. The discussion then moves to a description of the AIP: its history, categories of eligible projects, the complex array of formulas and set-asides that govern how grants are made, and variations in the use of the AIP among airports of different sizes to meet their capital investment needs.

Airport and Airway Trust Fund

The AATF is the principal source of funding for the AIP and for FAA programs more generally. It was established by the Airport and Airway Development Act of 1970 (P.L. 91-258) and subsequently reactivated by the Airport and Airway Improvement Act of 1982 (Pub. L. 97-248).[1] Appendix E includes summaries of key statutes relevant to the AATF and the various FAA-administered infrastructure funding programs. Prior to the creation of the AATF, federal aviation programs were funded entirely from the General Fund (Joint Committee on Taxation [JCT], 2019, p. 10). Revenues flow into the AATF from a variety of excise taxes collected from

---

[1] The AATF authorization lapsed in FYs 1981 and 1982. See Tang, 2019, p. 1.

users of the aviation system. These taxes, along with their current rates as of calendar year 2019, are listed in Table 5.1.

About two-thirds of the $15.8 billion in FY 2018 AATF revenue came from the transportation of persons—i.e., the ticket tax (including on frequent flyers) and the segment fee (see Figure 5.1). About one-quarter came from the use of international air facilities, which includes receipts from the charge imposed on flights to and from Alaska and Hawaii. By contrast, less than 10 percent of revenues came either from fuel taxes or from charges for transporting cargo. As for outlays from the AATF, about 60 percent in FY 2018 were for FAA Operations, including air traffic control and aviation safety activities. These amounts from the AATF accounted for nearly 90 percent of the FAA Operations budget, with the remainder of funding coming from the General Fund. About 20 percent of AATF outlays in FY 2018 were for the AIP, just less than 20 percent of AATF outlays were for Facilities and Equipment, and a small amount was for Research, Engineering, and Development.

The heavy reliance of the AATF on revenues derived from passengers means that airports with large numbers of enplanements are major drivers of AATF revenue generation, though it should be noted that smaller airports often are the origin or final destination of passengers who connect through larger airports. The AIP, then, uses a portion of AATF revenues to support the needs of the air system more broadly, with a deliberate focus on smaller airports that have less ability to generate revenue but that are critical to the functioning of the air system.[2] This intentionally redistributive element of the AIP means that large airports with more enplane-

Table 5.1
Excise Taxes Contributing to the Airport and Airway Trust Fund

Excise Tax	Rate for Calendar Year 2019
Domestic passenger ticket tax	7.5% of fare
Domestic passenger flight segment[a]	$4.20 (indexed annually to CPI)
International departure and arrival taxes	$18.60 (indexed annually to CPI)
Flights between continental United States and Alaska or Hawaii	$9.30 (indexed annually to CPI)
Frequent flyer tax	7.5% of fare
Domestic freight and mail	6.25% of amount paid for the transportation of property by air
Domestic commercial fuel tax	4.3¢ per gallon
Domestic general aviation gasoline tax	19.3¢ per gallon
Domestic general aviation jet fuel tax	21.8¢ per gallon
Domestic general aviation jet fuel surtax on fractional ownership	14.1¢ per gallon

SOURCES: FAA Order 5100.38D, 2019, Table V-1; Tang, 2019; JCT, 2019.
NOTE: CPI = Consumer Price Index.
[a] Flight segment fee not charged on flights that begin or end at a rural airport, defined by the IRS as described in Chapter Four.

---

[2]   See, for example, the discussion of the role of GA airports in FAA, 2012a. This report, commonly known as the ASSET report, lists the following as types of aeronautical functions that serve the public interest and that are carried out by GA airports: emergency preparedness and response; critical community access; other aviation-specific functions; commercial, industrial, and economic activities; and destination and special events.

ments receive a smaller share of AIP grants than their enplanements suggest that they generate in AATF revenues.[3]

Effect of Ancillary Fees on Collections

Many ancillary fees charged by airlines (e.g., on checked baggage or for preferred seat selection) are excluded from taxation and do not face the 7.5 percent excise tax. These fees vary by airline; currently, most U.S. carriers charge a fee for checked baggage, with Southwest being the most prominent exception. Figure 5.2 compares two ticket prices, one in which baggage is included in the ticket price and one in which baggage is not included (but that has the same price when summing the base fare and the baggage fee). The federal percentage-based excise tax treats these two tickets differently for otherwise identical flights; specifically, more tax is collected on the ticket that does not charge a separate baggage fee.

Had the $4.9 billion in baggage fees collected by airlines in 2018 been subject to the tax, excise tax revenues would have been about $367 million higher that year.[4] The GAO has made similar estimates in the past and has noted that it makes "a simplifying assumption that the additional tax due would not have caused any passengers to choose not to purchase tickets"

Figure 5.1
Airport and Airway Trust Fund Revenues and Outlays, FY 2018

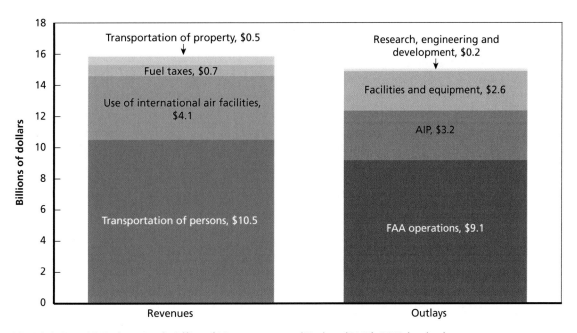

SOURCES: FAA, 2019c (revenues); Office of Management and Budget (OMB), 2019 (outlays).

---

[3]   According to an analysis prepared by the Director of Aviation at Raleigh-Durham International Airport that was shared with us, the median large-hub airport was responsible for about $14 of AATF excise tax contributions for each $1 in AIP grants received over the period from FY 2009 to FY 2016, the median medium hub was responsible for about $7 in AATF contributions for every $1 in AIP grants, and the median small-hub airport was responsible for about $2 in AATF contributions for each $1 in AIP grants. It is important to keep in mind that, in addition to the AIP, the AATF funds the FAA's Facilities and Equipment program and its Research and Development program, as well as a large portion of FAA Operations (more than 80 percent on average in the past five years). The AATF also has a growing uncommitted balance. Therefore, not all AATF revenues are expended each year, and not all expenditure is on AIP grants.

[4]   This amount is 7.5 percent of the $4.9 billion in baggage fees collected in 2018. See BTS, 2019f.

Figure 5.2
Differences in Ticket Prices as a Consequence of Ancillary Fees

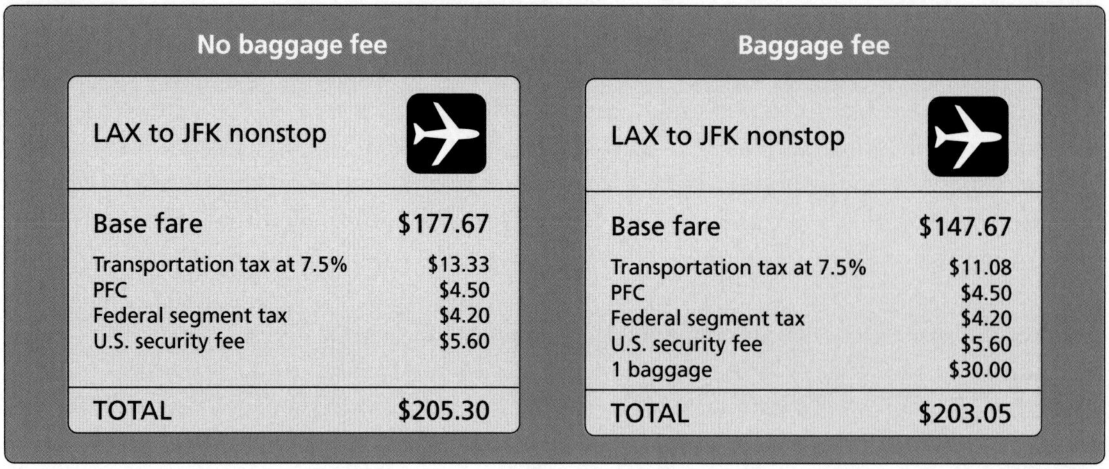

No baggage fee		Baggage fee	
LAX to JFK nonstop ✈		**LAX to JFK nonstop** ✈	
Base fare	$177.67	Base fare	$147.67
Transportation tax at 7.5%	$13.33	Transportation tax at 7.5%	$11.08
PFC	$4.50	PFC	$4.50
Federal segment tax	$4.20	Federal segment tax	$4.20
U.S. security fee	$5.60	U.S. security fee	$5.60
		1 baggage	$30.00
TOTAL	**$205.30**	**TOTAL**	**$203.05**

NOTE: LAX = Los Angeles International Airport.

(we make the same assumption in this report), adding that "[a]ny such reduction in purchases presumably would have been small and would have had the effect of making the increase in potential taxes collected a little smaller than our estimate" (GAO, 2017a, p. 18).

Other ancillary fees not subject to taxation are not separately reported, and potential AATF revenues cannot be estimated for them. GAO, 2010, p. 35, states as a "matter for Congressional consideration" that

> [i]f Congress determines that the benefit of added revenue to the Airport and Airway Trust Fund from taxation of optional airline service fees, such as baggage fees, is of importance, then it should consider amending the Internal Revenue Code to make mandatory the taxation of certain or all airline imposed fees and to require that the revenue be deposited in the Airport and Airway Trust Fund.

Some ancillary fees, however, are taxed already: specifically, those that are "required as a condition of receiving domestic air transportation" (e.g., change fees) (GAO, 2010, p. 21).

Jet Fuel Tax Collection

Another factor that has been studied by the GAO that might reduce revenues to the AATF concerns jet fuel taxes that first flow into the Highway Trust Fund but then are transferred to the AATF when a vendor requests a refund of the few cents' difference in tax rates for diesel fuel and jet fuel (GAO, 2016b). This process originated in the early 2000s because of concerns that jet fuel could substitute for diesel fuel when facing a lower tax rate, depriving the Highway Trust Fund of revenue. The 2005 Safe, Accountable, Flexible, Efficient Transportation Equity Act: A Legacy for Users (Pub. L. 109-59) equalized the tax rate at sale and resulted in the excise tax revenues first going to the Highway Trust Fund. However, it allowed vendors of jet fuel to request a refund of the $0.025-per-gallon difference in the tax rates, with this request triggering a transfer of the balance of the tax revenue to the AATF. GAO, 2016b, finds that, over the previous decade, the failure to request these refunds resulted in $1 billion to $2 billion not being transferred to the AATF that should have been. To be clear, the GAO did not find evidence that the revenues were not being transferred when the refunds were claimed, but rather that vendors were failing to request these refunds of the difference between the diesel and jet fuel taxes—costing themselves money in addition to depriving the AATF of revenue.

Trends and Projections in Airport and Airway Trust Fund Balances

As noted earlier, the AATF, in addition to funding AIP grants, wholly funds the FAA's Facilities and Equipment program and its Research, Engineering, and Development program. The AATF also funds much of the FAA Operations budget, with the AATF share of this funding varying over time, often in tandem with the AATF balance. This funding is not without controversy. For much of the AATF's early history, there was a debate over Congress' intent in establishing the fund and whether it could be used for purposes other than financing airport or other aviation infrastructure. In 1999, the GAO reviewed the AATF's legislative history and concluded that it "was not created solely to finance aviation infrastructure" (GAO, Office of the General Counsel, 1999). Nonetheless, some observers continue to consider the funding of FAA Operations from the AATF as an effort to "raid" the AATF (Wu, 2016).

Over the past five years (FYs 2014 to 2018), the AATF share of the FAA Operations budget averaged 83 percent, up considerably from the previous five-year period in the aftermath of the Great Recession, when the AATF share of the Operations budget was about half (OMB, 2019, Outlays). Therefore, the balance of the AATF depends not only on excise tax revenues and AIP expenditures but also on the level at which these other programs are funded and, perhaps most importantly, how much of the Operations budget is funded by the AATF. In each of the past five years, a majority of AATF outlays have been for FAA Operations.

Figure 5.3 shows the trend for AATF revenues and outlays over the past 20 years. The chart does not include interest earnings, which depend on interest rates and the balance held

Figure 5.3
Airport and Airway Trust Fund Revenues and Outlays, FYs 1999–2018

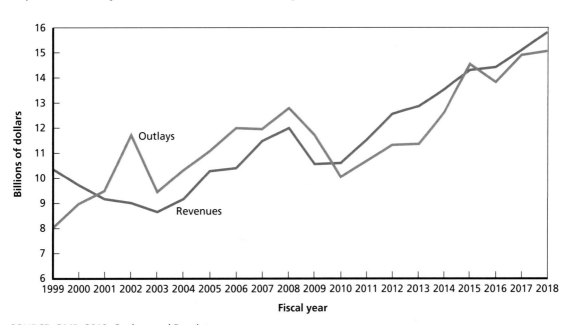

SOURCE: OMB, 2019, Outlays and Receipts.
NOTE: Revenues exclude interest earnings on AATF balances.

in the AATF. Revenues fell in the early 2000s (around the time of the 2001 recession and September 11, 2001, attacks), grew during the mid-2000s, dropped during the Great Recession, and have increased every year since 2009. Outlays typically exceeded revenues during the 2000s, with this trend reversing in the 2010s.

Revenues are determined largely by economic trends—in passenger and cargo volumes and the amount of fuel purchased—though policymakers establish the levels of the excise taxes. Policy decisions more directly drive the trends in outlays. For example, beginning with passage of AIR-21 (Pub. L. 106-181, 2000) until the passage of the FAA Modernization and Reform Act of 2012 (Pub. L. 112-95), it was "out of order" for Congress to consider appropriations legislation that did not use all AATF revenues forecast in the President's Budget for the relevant fiscal year or that did not fund the AIP or the Facilities and Equipment accounts at their authorized levels (GAO, 2012a). Although a point of order must be raised in order to enforce these "spending guarantee" mechanisms and, even if raised, the point of order can be waived by Congress on a case-by-case basis, AATF expenditures in practice roughly equaled *projected* revenues during the 2000s (GAO, 2012a). This result could be more attributable to the widespread support for the AIP, in particular, than to the point of order provisions, because the Facilities and Equipment account was often not funded at authorized levels during the 2000s (Kirk, 2008).

A core motivation behind the spending guarantee mechanisms was to make it more likely that revenues to the AATF would be spent on aviation programs, rather than allowing a large unexpended balance to accumulate that could be used to offset other budgetary priorities. To be clear, this money typically is not actually appropriated for nonaviation priorities. Rather, the federal government lends the balance to itself for spending on other programs; unspent funds are invested in Treasury securities that are ultimately intermixed with all other sources of revenues to the General Fund. As a Congressional Research Service report from 2008 put it,

> Although the inclusion of the aviation trust fund within the unified budget was not a major issue during debate over the trust fund's creation, the unified budget has, historically, had an impact on trust fund spending levels. Within the context of the unified budget, an excess of aviation trust fund revenues over expenditures can be seen as an offset in federal deficit computations. In some cases, however, the balance may be seen as having been spent on non-aviation programs or purposes. Because the balance is invested in short-term Treasury notes (the interest is payed [sic] to the aviation trust fund), the federal government is lending itself an amount roughly equal to the balance. This, in effect, frees up the money for spending elsewhere in the budget without pushing up the overall budget deficit or putting pressure on budgetary ceilings established by the congressional budget process (Kirk, 2008, p. 3).

However, to the extent that *actual* revenues to the AATF for a given fiscal year fall short of *projected* revenues, appropriating at the level of projected revenues results in drawing down the balance in the AATF. This drawdown occurred often during the 2000s, as Figure 5.4 depicts. As GAO, 2012a, p. 24, notes, three key factors can contribute to gaps between projected and actual revenues: "exogenous shocks, the timing of forecasts, and lags in recognizing structural changes to the airline industry." Notably, because revenue projections are put together well in advance of a fiscal year, they cannot capture unexpected developments in the economy.

The mismatch between AATF projected and actual revenues in the 2000s resulted in a dwindling uncommitted balance in the AATF, from more than $7 billion in FY 2000 to just

Figure 5.4
Difference Between Actual and Projected Airport and Airway Trust Fund Revenues, FYs 1999–2018

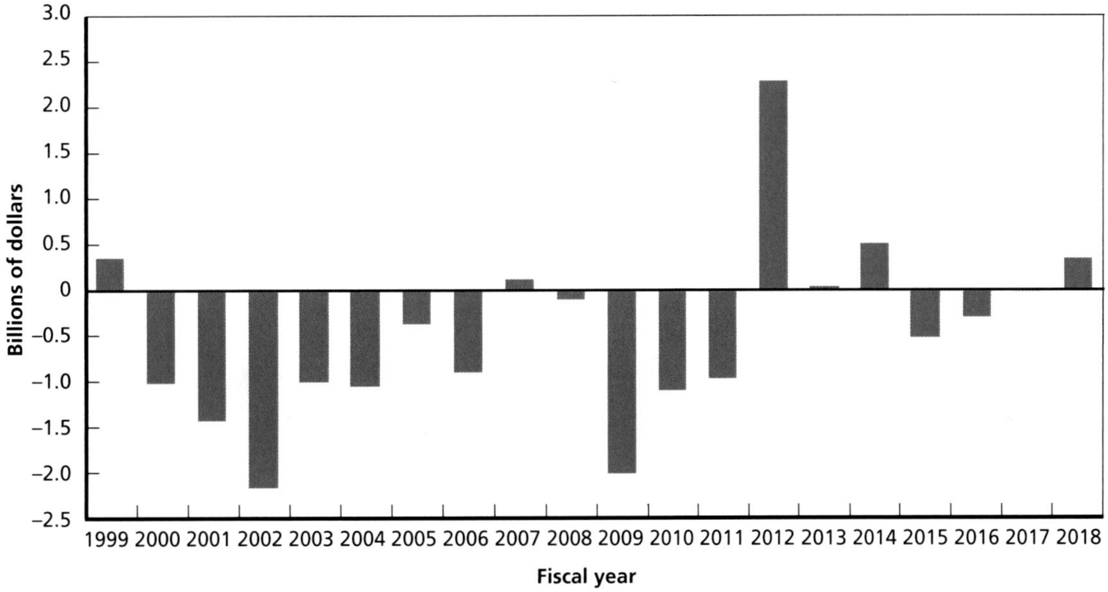

SOURCE: OMB, undated.
NOTES: Projections are those included in the President's Budget for each fiscal year (e.g., the FY 1999 budget released in early 1998); actuals reflect historical data in the FY 2020 budget tables. Interest earnings are excluded.

$300 million at the end of FY 2009 (see Figure 5.5). In part because of concerns that those trends would have fully depleted the AATF balance,[5] the FAA Modernization and Reform Act of 2012 (Pub. L. 112-95) adjusted the spending guarantee mechanism to require spending from the AATF to be 90 percent of the estimated revenues plus an adjustment to reflect any difference between actual receipts in the second preceding fiscal year (i.e., those that are known when appropriations are being made for the upcoming fiscal year) and the amount appropriated for that year.[6] However, the enforcement mechanism for this spending guarantee remained weak: a point of order that is not raised in practice. The 2010s saw the uncommitted balance in the AATF rebound to $6.1 billion at the end of FY 2018 (JCT, 2019, Table 2).

The Congressional Budget Office projects that the uncommitted balance in the AATF will grow rapidly over the coming decade, to $22.5 billion at the end of FY 2024 and $47.7 billion at the end of FY 2029 (JCT, 2019, Table 2). Figure 5.6 plots the projections for the uncommitted balance along with the projections for AATF revenues (*including interest*, because interest earnings contribute to the accumulation of an uncommitted balance) and outlays over the FY 2019 to FY 2029 period. If these amounts were to materialize, they would represent a

---

[5]   The uncommitted balance in the AATF refers to funds not yet appropriated for a specific purpose. Per the GAO,

The uncommitted balance is the revenue that would remain in the trust fund after subtracting the committed balance. The financial condition of the trust fund generally can be evaluated by looking at the uncommitted balance and the cash balance. The uncommitted balance is used to evaluate FAA's ability to enter into future commitments as provided in authorization and appropriations acts. The cash balance reflects all cash on hand in the trust fund—both that which may be required to satisfy outstanding obligations and funds for which no commitments may have been made (GAO, 2012a, p. 2).

[6]   GAO testimony before the U.S. Senate Committee on Finance in 2011 discussed the AATF's declining balance and policy options to stabilize the trust fund. See Dillingham, 2011. The options mentioned in the GAO testimony included the option later adopted in the FAA Modernization and Reform Act of 2012 (Pub. L. 112-95).

Figure 5.5
End-of-Year Airport and Airway Trust Fund Uncommitted Balance, FYs 2000–2018

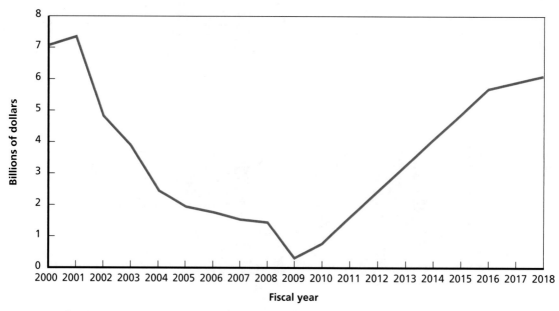

SOURCES: Dillingham, 2011 (FYs 2000–2010); CBO, as cited in Tang and Elias, 2017 (FY 2016); CBO, as cited in JCT, 2019 (FY 2018).
NOTE: Values for 2011–2015 and 2017 are interpolated.

Figure 5.6
Airport and Airway Trust Fund Projections: Revenues, Outlays, and Uncommitted Balance, FYs 2019–2029

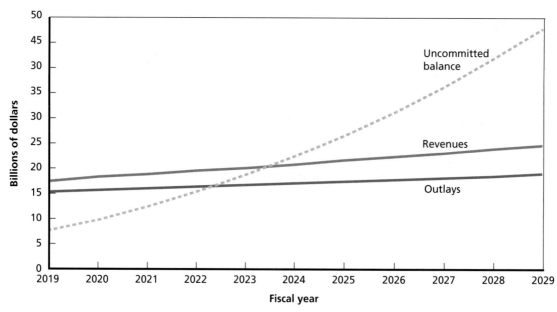

SOURCE: CBO Projections in JCT, 2019, Table 2.
NOTE: Revenue projections include interest earned.

significant pot of funding that could be tapped for infrastructure or other needs of the FAA and the aviation system.

Past history gives reason to question whether these large uncommitted balances will indeed materialize. For example, in 2006, the CBO projected that the uncommitted balance would reach $18.6 billion by FY 2016 (Marron, 2006, Table 1), but the Great Recession and other factors intervened; the uncommitted balance ended up being about $5.7 billion at the end of FY 2016 (Tang and Elias, 2017, p. 8). Five years later, in 2011, the CBO projected that the cash balance (which includes amounts that have been obligated but not yet spent) would rise, from $9.4 billion at the end of FY 2010 to $32.1 billion in FY 2018 (JCT, 2011, Table 2); this balance was $15.3 billion at the end of FY 2018, less than half the projected amount (JCT, 2019, Table 2).

In addition to policy changes in the amounts appropriated for various FAA programs and fluctuations in revenues driven by economic and industry developments (e.g., ancillary fees, which are not taxed), budgetary assumptions (which might not hold in practice) contribute to the projections. For example, revenues are assumed to grow roughly with nominal gross domestic product, while most non-AIP categories of spending are assumed to grow with inflation only. AIP grants are assumed to hold steady (at $3.35 billion), as is the approximate share of FAA Operations funded by the AATF versus that funded by the General Fund. If these assumptions do not hold—for example, if policymakers increase spending for FAA Operations faster than the rate of inflation or fund an even higher share of FAA Operations from the AATF rather than from the General Fund than assumed in the projections—the actual uncommitted balance will fall short of the projection.

Uncertainty with respect to future developments—in the macroeconomy, in the aviation industry, and in the world generally—weighs on the side of managing the AATF with an abundance of caution and being prepared to adjust both revenue and spending levers as conditions evolve. For example, although fuel excise taxes represent a small share of AATF revenues, improved fuel efficiency or a shift to electric-powered aviation could depress AATF revenue collections. Greater reliance on untaxed categories of ancillary fees rather than base fares, which face the 7.5 percent excise tax, also would lower AATF revenues, as would any developments in the airline industry that result in lower airfares. Economic downturns or international or national security developments that result in less air travel could intervene, as they have periodically in the past. On the other side of the ledger, unexpected developments also could affect the need for building or rebuilding aviation infrastructure (for example, if an attack or natural disaster resulted in damage to U.S. airports).

These cautionary notes should not keep policymakers from considering devoting more AATF resources to aviation infrastructure, particularly if annual revenues continue to outstrip outlays, as the CBO projects. But these notes underscore that any policy changes that tap the uncommitted balance to fund additional airport infrastructure would not only need to be mindful of the other moving pieces of the FAA budget but also be designed to guard against the possibility of draining down the balance, should revenues fail to materialize. As GAO, 2012a, p. 22, notes,

> According to an industry expert, the effects of certain exogenous events—events caused by factors outside the aviation industry—on demand for air travel are such that it is common for demand to drop much more quickly in response to a negative shock than it will build in response to overall good economic conditions. Thus, the likelihood that there will be years

when revenues are considerably overforecast may be higher than the likelihood that there will be years when revenues are considerably underforecast.

Airport Improvement Program

The AIP provides grants to airport sponsors (typically, public agencies that own public-use airports) for projects that align with prescribed federal policy priorities. Most AIP funds are apportioned to airports by formulas—for example, according to their enplanements or amount of cargo processed. We refer to these amounts as AIP *entitlements* or *apportionments*, using the terms synonymously, because both terms appear in statute and FAA policy guidance. Other AIP funds are awarded competitively. The federal share for projects at large- and medium-hub airports is 75 percent, and the federal share at smaller airports is typically 90 percent. Four broad categories of projects for which grants are available are airport master planning, airport development, noise compatibility planning, and noise compatibility projects. Airports must be listed in the NPIAS to receive grants. Precise formulas and regulations governing how funds are distributed and projects for which funding is available have evolved over time and are detailed in the FAA's *Airport Improvement Program Handbook*, most recently updated in 2019 (FAA Order 5100.38D, 2019).

The FAA's funding priorities are reflected quantitatively in an equation, known as the National Priority System (NPS) equation, used to assess how well potential projects align with FAA goals and objectives (FAA Order 5090.5, 2019). The NPS equation takes as its inputs the size of the airport, the purpose of the project (e.g., capacity), the component involved (e.g., a runway), and the type of work being done (e.g., extension/expansion). The equation yields a rating, known as the National Priority Rating (NPR), that ranges from 0 to 100, where a rating of 100 indicates projects that most closely align with FAA objectives. The NPS equation weights airside projects more heavily than landside projects, safety and security projects more than projects for other purposes, and projects at larger airports more than those at smaller airports. Additional details on the NPR and the NPS equation can be found in Appendix G.

Origins and Objectives

The federal role in airport development has its origins in the years after World War II, when policymakers established the Federal-Aid Airport Program in the Federal Airport Act of 1946 (Pub. L. 79-377) to support building airfields, terminals, and access roads. This funding came from the General Fund, was often used to support converting military airports for civilian use, and by the late 1960s, proved to be insufficient to address growing capacity needs at U.S. airports (Tang, 2019). The Airport and Airway Development Act of 1970 (Pub. L. 91-258) established the AATF and levied taxes on aviation users that flowed into the trust fund. The law also created the Airport Development Aid Program and the Planning Grant Program, precursors to the AIP that made grants using AATF funds to support airport infrastructure development. Although the "demands of interstate commerce" were cited in the 1970 legislation as a rationale for the establishment of the Airport Development Aid Program and the Planning Grant Program, neither these programs nor the subsequent AIP explicitly consider the economic impact of projects seeking funding.

After revenue collection authority lapsed in FYs 1981 and 1982, the AAIA (Pub. L. 97-248) reestablished this authority and created the AIP in its current iteration. The mechanics of the program, its level of funding, and the distribution of AIP grants across categories of airports and types of projects has evolved over time through a series of reauthorization acts, but the basic structure established in 1982 remains: Users pay excise taxes into the AATF, and a portion of this money is allocated to AIP grants each year. Most recently, the AIP was reauthorized through FY 2023 in the FAA Reauthorization Act of 2018 (Pub. L. 115-254).

The policy objectives of the AIP, which undergird a federal role in aviation more broadly, are codified at 49 USC § 47101. The FAA summarizes these objectives as follows:

    a. Providing a safe and secure airport and airway system.
    b. Minimizing airport noise impacts on nearby communities.
    c. Developing reliever airports, cargo hub airports, and intermodalism.
    d. Protecting natural resources.
    e. Reducing aircraft delays.
    f. Converting former military air bases to civil use or improving joint-use airports.
    g. Carrying out various other projects to ensure a safe and efficient airport system (FAA Order 5100.38D, 2019, p. 1-5).

We now turn to a discussion of AIP-eligible projects that align with these broad policy goals.

Eligible Projects

AIP grants can go toward airport planning, airport development, airport noise compatibility planning, and airport noise compatibility programs (49 U.S.C. § 48103). Each of these terms is defined in statute, and selections from the relevant provisions in statute are listed below.

- **Airport planning:** includes integrated airport system planning, developing an environmental management system, and developing a plan for recycling and minimizing the generation of airport solid waste (49 U.S.C. § 47102).
- **Airport development:** a wide-ranging term that includes (but is not limited to) constructing, repairing, or improving a public-use airport (including building or rehabilitating runways, taxiways, aprons, and drainage systems); acquiring or installing navigation aids and safety or security equipment; acquiring land or airspace for future development, to mitigate airport hazards, or to build a deicing pad; taking steps to comply with the Americans with Disabilities Act of 1990; implementing certain projects to reduce emissions and retrofit vehicles and ground support equipment; constructing or improving on-airport systems to transport passengers, cargo, or baggage; and implementing select projects in nonrevenue-producing areas of terminals (49 U.S.C. § 47102).
- **Airport noise compatibility planning:** developing information necessary to prepare and submit a noise exposure map or a noise compatibility program (49 U.S.C. § 47505).
- **Airport noise compatibility program:** includes constructing barriers, acoustic shielding, and sound-insulating buildings and acquiring land, air rights, easements, development rights, and other interests (49 U.S.C. § 47504).

Boxes 5.1 and 5.2 replicate information from the FAA website overview of the AIP that summarizes projects that are generally eligible and ineligible.

Box 5.1
Airport Improvement Program–Eligible Projects
- Runway construction and rehabilitation
- Taxiway construction and rehabilitation
- Apron construction and rehabilitation
- Airfield lighting
- Airfield signage
- Airfield drainage
- Land acquisition
- Weather observation stations
- Navigational aids, such as runway end identifier lights and precision approach path indicators
- Planning studies
- Environmental studies
- Safety area improvements
- Airport layout plans
- Access roads only located on airport property
- Removing, lowering, moving, marking, and lighting hazards
- Glycol recovery trucks and glycol vacuum trucks[a]

SOURCE: FAA, 2017c.

[a] To be eligible, the vehicles must be owned and operated by the airport and meet the Buy American Preference specified in the AIP grant.

Box 5.2
Airport Improvement Program–Ineligible Projects
- Maintenance equipment and vehicles
- Office and office equipment
- Fuel farms[a]
- Landscaping
- Artworks
- Aircraft hangars[a]
- Industrial park development
- Marketing plans
- Training
- Improvements for commercial enterprises
- Maintenance or repairs of buildings

SOURCE: FAA, 2017c.

[a] May be conditionally eligible at nonprimary airports.

Funding Levels

Congress grants the FAA the authority to incur obligations to spend money from the AATF on AIP grants in periodic FAA reauthorization acts;[7] most recently, the FAA Reauthorization Act of 2018 (Pub. L. 115-254) authorized annual AIP spending of $3.35 billion from FY 2019 to FY 2023. However, Congress also imposes a separate, sometimes lower limitation on obligations that can be made in a particular fiscal year. Effectively, the annual obligation limitation is equivalent to an appropriation, and as is the case with other government programs that both are authorized and receive appropriations, this limit might differ from the authorized amount because of diverging priorities of authorizers and appropriators in Congress. Congress may further direct that a portion of the funding that would otherwise be available for AIP grants be spent on other FAA programs, such as the Airport Cooperative Research Program (ACRP), Airport Technology Research, and administrative expenses.[8] Figure 5.7 plots the authorization and the obligation limitation for the AIP over time. The obligation limitation line on the chart

---

[7] This is known as *contract authority*, which "permits you to incur obligations in advance of an appropriation, offsetting collections, or receipts that enable you to make outlays to liquidate the obligations." See OMB, 2016, p. 4.

[8] For example, see language in the Consolidated Appropriations Act, 2019 (Pub. L. 116-6).

is shown after subtracting amounts directed to be spent for non-AIP purposes in appropriations legislation (e.g., for the ACRP or Airport Technology Research). The line shows that the annual AIP grant obligation limitation typically has fallen short of the authorized level, most notably in the 1990s, when there was a significant push for deficit reduction (Tang, 2019, p. 4).

Congress also may authorize and appropriate amounts for AIP grants from the General Fund in addition to the amounts from the AATF. In the Consolidated Appropriations Act, 2018 (Pub. L. 115-141), Congress provided a $1.0 billion supplemental appropriation to AIP discretionary programs, to be made available through the end of FY 2020 and with priority given to small- and non-hub primary airports and nonprimary airports that are regional, local, or basic airports located away from metropolitan or micropolitan areas (FAA, 2019h). The FAA Reauthorization Act of 2018 (Pub. L. 115-254) authorized supplemental funding of more than $1 billion from the General Fund in each of the five fiscal years from FY 2019 to FY 2023, with at least half to go to airports other than large and medium hubs; the Consolidated Appropriations Act, 2019 (Pub. L. 116-6) appropriated $500 million (less than half the authorized amount), to be made available through the end of FY 2021 as discretionary AIP grants. These supplemental amounts are not included in Figure 5.7.

The Obama administration's FY 2014 through FY 2017 budgets proposed decreasing the AIP obligation limitation to less than $3 billion in tandem with other changes to both the AIP and the PFC program.[9] This proposal, which was not adopted by Congress, would have raised

Figure 5.7
Airport Improvement Program Funding Authorized and Airport Improvement Program Obligation Limitation, FYs 1982–2018

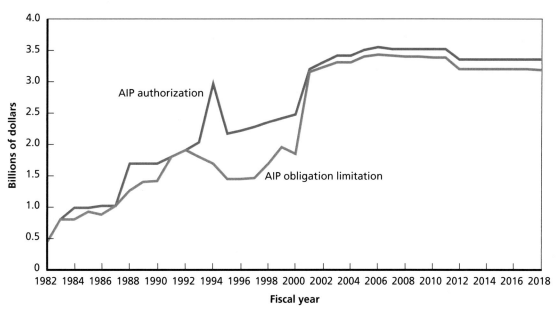

SOURCES: FAA, 2017b (through FY 2016); Tang, 2019, Table 1 (FYs 2017 and 2018).
NOTE: The 1994 authorized funding amount is an anomaly that resulted from the timing of when the existing authorization lapsed and extensions passed during that year. In FY 2013, the FAA later was permitted to transfer $253 million from the AIP (or other accounts) to FAA Operations to mitigate the effects of sequestration on the agency and the air system (Pub. L. 113-9, 2013); this transfer is not reflected in the figure.

---

[9]   See, for example, USDOT, 2016.

the maximum allowable PFC cap while eliminating AIP entitlement funding for large-hub airports. Importantly, it would have pushed AIP funding below the $3.2 billion per year level that triggers several changes to the way entitlement funding is distributed, freeing up more money for discretionary grants.[10] Legislation introduced in 2019 (H.R. 3791) and previously introduced in 2017 (H.R. 1265) also would reduce the AIP obligation limitation but would simultaneously reduce the trigger level, resulting in an even higher share of AIP grants being made as entitlements and leaving very little for discretionary grants. The following sections provide details on how grants are currently distributed.

Distribution of Airport Improvement Program Grants by Funding Program

A complex set of apportionment formulas and set-aside requirements govern how AIP funding is distributed across airports and individual projects. On balance, a majority of funding is allocated as entitlement funding to airports according to their number of enplanements or other formulas, while a substantially smaller share is available for discretionary grants. Smaller airports, which have less ability to generate revenues on their own (e.g., through enplanement-based PFCs), receive about three-quarters of AIP grant dollars, while large- and medium-hub airports receive about 25 percent of AIP dollars. The comparatively small share of AIP that goes to large- and medium-hub airports is by design and, in part, is a choice by the large- and medium-hub airports themselves, with these airports willingly forgoing a sizable share of their AIP entitlements (50 percent to 75 percent) in exchange for the ability to impose a PFC. As described in Chapter Six, large- and medium-hub airports are able to collect significantly more money through the PFC program than they forgo in AIP grants.

The overwhelming majority of AIP dollars support airside infrastructure, consistent with the NPR system, which prioritizes these projects as part and parcel of prioritizing safety. In the remainder of this chapter, we discuss each of these aspects of the distribution of AIP grants in turn: the allocation across funding programs, across types of airports, and across categories of projects.

Annual entitlement and discretionary funding amounts, and the distribution between these two broad categories, depend on the amount of funding made available for AIP grants each year. Figure 5.8 displays the breakdown for FY 2018, for entitlement and discretionary funding and by individual funding program. As the figure shows, about two-thirds of funding was distributed through entitlement programs. More than 20 percent was reserved as protected entitlements for airports that did not spend the entirety of their apportioned funds during the prior years.[11] These allocations left less than 10 percent of funding to be distributed as discretionary funds, which are subject to percentage set-asides; however, any entitlements unused in FY 2018 were converted to additional discretionary funding in that year. In the following subsections, we describe each of the programs receiving AIP funding.

---

[10]   Note that this $3.2 billion threshold refers to the AIP line item in appropriations legislation, which (as noted earlier) directs a portion of the funding to the ACRP and other non-AIP programs.

[11]   For large-, medium-, and small-hub primary airports, entitlement funds can be carried forward for two additional fiscal years beyond the year in which they were apportioned; non-hub primary and nonprimary airports have three additional years.

Figure 5.8
Distribution of Airport Improvement Program Funding, by Funding Program, FY 2018

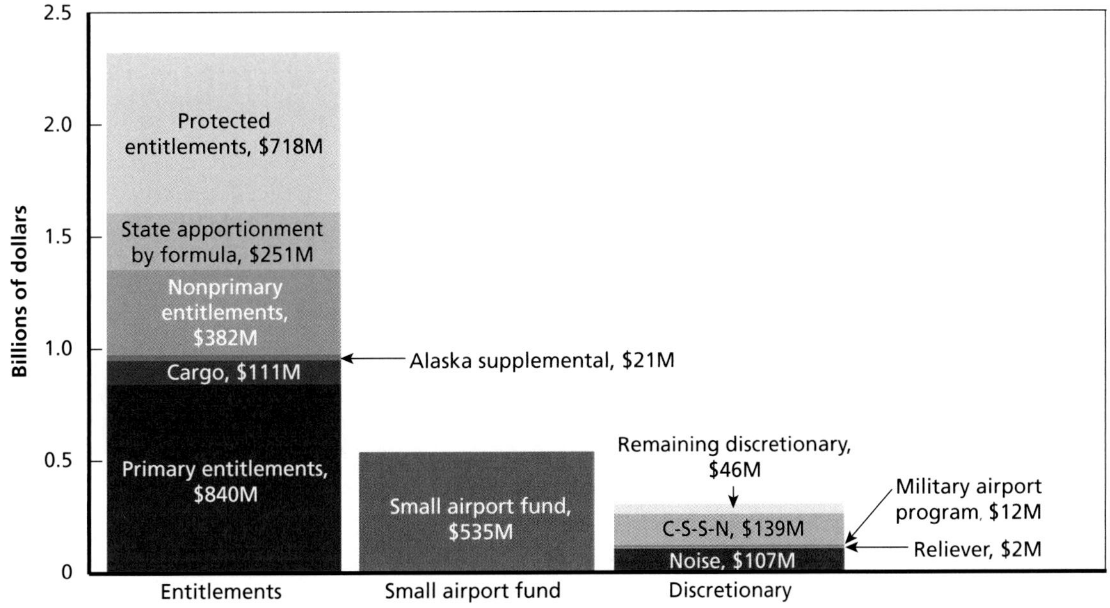

SOURCE: Personal communication with FAA staff, October 12, 2019.
NOTE: C-S-S-N = capacity, safety, security, noise.

Primary Entitlements

About one-quarter of all AIP funding, the largest single pot of money, is apportioned to primary airports at the beginning of each fiscal year via formulas that distribute amounts according to the number of enplanements at the airport in the previous full calendar year. For example, to determine each primary airport's apportioned amount for FY 2019, the number of passengers who boarded at the airport in calendar year 2017 is used. Table 5.2 lists the funding amounts per passenger, depending on the number of enplanements. The table lists the amounts specified in statute that are apportioned when the AIP obligation limitation is below $3.2 billion and the levels when the obligation limitation is $3.2 billion or higher, as it has been each year since the early 2000s. When the $3.2 billion threshold is hit, the minimum entitlement for primary airports is $1 million and the maximum entitlement is $26 million. If the threshold is not hit, the minimum entitlement would be $650,000 and the maximum would be $22 million.

Importantly, large- and medium-hub airports forgo a portion of their primary entitlements if they impose a PFC, as virtually all of them do. Large and medium hubs that charge a PFC of $3 or less forgo AIP apportionments equal to 50 percent of their projected PFC revenues for the year, up to 50 percent of their primary apportionment, while those that charge a PFC of more than $3 forgo an amount equal to 75 percent of projected PFC revenues, up to 75 percent of their primary apportionment (49 U.S.C. § 47114). In FY 2018, all but one of the 30 large-hub airports and all but three of the medium-hub airports forfeited 75 percent of their primary entitlements; the largest entitlement was about $12.3 million for CLT, the only large hub that turned back 50 percent of its entitlement rather than 75 percent (FAA, undated d). By statute, 87.5 percent of these forgone AIP entitlements go to the Small Airport Fund, while the remaining 12.5 percent are available as discretionary funds (49 U.S.C. § 47116).

Table 5.2
Airport Improvement Program Primary Airport Entitlement Amounts, by Number of Enplanements

Number of Enplanements	Apportionment Amount per Enplanement (Below $3.2 Billion Appropriation Threshold)	Apportionment Amount per Enplanement (Above $3.2 Billion Appropriation Threshold)
First 50,000	$7.80	$15.60
Next 50,000	$5.20	$10.40
Next 400,000	$2.60	$5.20
Next 500,000	$0.65	$1.30
1 million and above	$0.50	$1.00

SOURCE: FAA Order 5100.38D, 2019, Table 4-1.

Cargo Entitlements

Although this report is focused solely on passenger air transportation, we address the cargo entitlements program in the interest of completeness. Airports with more than 100 million pounds of cargo-only aircraft landed weight per year receive cargo entitlement funding. The total amount of money subject to cargo apportionment is equal to 3.5 percent of all AIP funding available in the fiscal year, and it is distributed to airports according to their share of total landed weight at airports eligible to receive this funding (49 U.S.C. § 47114).[12] The relevant year for determining apportionments is also the last full calendar year (FAA Order 5100.38D, 2019, p. 4-1). In FY 2018, 119 airports received funding through the cargo entitlement program, with Memphis International receiving the most funding ($16.9 million) because it accounted for about 15 percent of total landed weight among eligible airports (FAA, undated a). In general, the set of airports receiving cargo entitlements overlaps with airports receiving primary entitlements by boarding passengers.

Nonprimary Entitlements, State Apportionments, and Alaska Supplemental Funds

General aviation, reliever, and nonprimary commercial service airports are apportioned 20 percent of all AIP funding available. In years in which total funding available is $3.2 billion or greater, each of these airports receives an apportionment equal to the lesser of $150,000 or one-fifth of the airport's five-year capital needs as included in the NPIAS (49 U.S.C. § 47114).[13] These amounts are the nonprimary entitlements in Figure 5.8. After this funding is allocated, the balance is distributed according to a formula that equally weights state population and state land area, with these apportionments made available for projects at nonprimary airports in the states (state apportionment by formula in Figure 5.8) (FAA, 2017a, p. 13). The FAA ultimately makes funding decisions, though there is collaboration with the states and these funds may go toward addressing state priorities (Tang, 2019).

In addition, there is a separate apportionment for Alaskan airports, known as the Alaska Supplemental Fund, that stems from a requirement that these airports receive at least as much funding as they received in FY 1980 under a previous version of the AIP (FAA, 2017a, p. 13).

---

[12] Note that in years in which AIP funding is less than $3.2 billion, no single cargo service airport may receive more than 8 percent of all cargo entitlement funding.

[13] When AIP funding is below $3.2 billion, this 20-percent-of-funding pot is all distributed via the state apportionment formula, without the separate nonprimary entitlement amount for each nonprimary airport.

When total AIP funding is more than $3.2 billion, this amount doubles to twice the FY 1980 level, or $21.3 million.

Protected Entitlements

Apportioned amounts that are not used in the fiscal year for which they are initially apportioned may be carried over to subsequent years, subject to the limitations listed in Table 5.3. In the year in which these amounts are deferred, they convert to additional discretionary funding, neither subject to the set-aside percentages described below nor included within the "discretionary" categories in Figure 5.8. In subsequent years, these deferred amounts become protected entitlements available to the original recipients, subtracting from the pool of funding that otherwise would be subject to discretionary awards (and the associated set-asides) and appearing as the "protected entitlements" category in Figure 5.8.

Small Airport Fund

The Small Airport Fund receives 87.5 percent of forgone primary entitlements at large- and medium-hub airports that impose a PFC, as described above. The amounts are reapportioned as follows, with the proportions established in statute and constant from year to year (FAA Order 5100.38D, 2019, Table 4-1):

- One-seventh to small-hub airports
- Four-sevenths to non-hub primary and nonprimary commercial service airports
- Two-sevenths to general aviation and reliever airports and certain privately owned, public-use airports with at least 2,500 passenger enplanements.

Funds are awarded competitively within these categories.

Discretionary Funding

AIP funding available after subtracting current-year entitlements and protected entitlements is used for competitively awarded discretionary grants. However, there are statutorily required set-asides and other criteria that govern how these funds can be distributed (see FAA Order 5100.38D, 2019, Table 4-1, for specific references to statute). These criteria are as follows:

Table 5.3
Expiration of Airport Improvement Program Apportionment Funds, by Program and Airport Type

Airport Type	Funding Program	Expiration
Small, medium, or large hub	Primary or cargo entitlement	Two years after year of original apportionment
Non-hub primary	Primary or cargo entitlement	Three years after year of original apportionment
Nonprimary	Nonprimary or cargo entitlement	Three years after year of original apportionment
N/A	State apportionment or Alaska supplemental	Two years after year of original apportionment

SOURCE: FAA Order 5100.38D, 2019.
NOTE: N/A = not applicable.

- At least 35 percent of discretionary funds are set aside for noise and environmental projects, including the Voluntary Airport Low Emissions program.[14]
- At least 4 percent of discretionary funds must be devoted to the Military Airport Program for converting current or former military airports to full or partial civilian use.
- Two-thirds of 1 percent of discretionary funds is set aside for certain reliever airports that meet specific criteria in years in which total AIP funding is at least $3.2 billion.
- Seventy-five percent of remaining discretionary funds after the above amounts are set aside are to be used for capacity, safety, security, and noise projects at primary and reliever airports, along with 75 percent of the 12.5 percent of forgone entitlements (from imposing PFCs) that are not allocated to the Small Airport Fund.

Within these constraints, the FAA has discretion to award grants to airports using the prioritization formula described earlier and other qualitative criteria. Any supplemental appropriations made that are subject to the authorizing language in the FAA Reauthorization Act of 2018 (Pub. L. 115-254) are added to the discretionary pot and are not subject to set-asides, with the exception that at least half of these funds are to go to airports other than large and medium hubs.

State Block Grant Program

The State Block Grant Program provides states (rather than the FAA Airport District Office) with administrative responsibility over AIP grants to nonprimary airports. The State Block Grant Program is not identified separately in Figure 5.8; rather, it is the administrative mechanism through which grants to nonprimary airports (across displayed categories) are distributed. The program was initially established in 1987 and recently expanded from ten to 20 states in the FAA Reauthorization Act of 2018. Under the block grant program, states are granted flexibility to select projects to fund from state apportionment funds, although the FAA retains the authority to decide on discretionary awards, taking state priority lists into account. The FAA distributes both entitlement and discretionary funds for the states in the block grant program to administer (FAA Advisory Circular 150/5100-21, 2016). As of FY 2018, the ten states in the program were Georgia, Illinois, Michigan, Missouri, New Hampshire, North Carolina, Pennsylvania, Tennessee, Texas, and Wisconsin.

Letter of Intent Program

The Letter of Intent (LOI) program allows primary and reliever airports to receive a formal document stating the FAA's intention to fund large-scale capacity projects in subsequent fiscal years, assuming funds are made available by Congress. The LOI program also is not separately identified in Figure 5.8; the program involves the FAA stating an intention to fund projects through one or a combination of the displayed programs (e.g., primary entitlements). The benefit of the program is that airports can begin projects without waiting for the actual AIP grants, which come in future years, and they are then able to have their AIP-eligible project costs reimbursed with those future-year AIP grants. The LOI program is limited to projects that enhance or preserve capacity. Large and medium hubs using the program must demon-

---

[14] The Voluntary Airport Low Emissions program was established in 2004 to help airports meet their requirements under the Clean Air Act, including by financing low-emission vehicles, refueling and recharging stations, gate electrification, and other airport air quality improvements. See FAA, 2018f.

strate that the project covered by the LOI would "significantly enhance system-wide airport capacity" (FAA Order 5100.38D, 2019, p. 5-6). In FY 2016, 12 payments were made system-wide under the LOI program, with those payments totaling about $120 million (FAA, 2017a, Table 8).

Grant Assurances

When airports receive AIP funding, they bind themselves to a detailed list of grant assurances that reflect federal priorities incorporated into statute over time.[15] Details are provided in Appendix G.

Distribution of Airport Improvement Program Grants by Airport Size

Figure 5.9 shows the distribution of the dollars of AIP grants over the past ten fiscal years (FYs 2009–2018), by airport size. Nearly three-quarters of AIP dollars went to airports other than large and medium hubs over the FY 2009–2018 period. Note that state block grants, by the nature of the program, go to nonprimary (i.e., smaller) airports but may be distributed across categories of nonprimary airports. Planning grants are a subset of AIP grants that fund aviation system planning in a geographic area and that go to "planning agency sponsors," such as metropolitan or state planning agencies, rather than to airports themselves.[16] In terms of the number of grants, GA airports accounted for more than half, while large and medium hubs

Figure 5.9
Billions of Dollars of AIP Grants Awarded, by Airport Category, FYs 2009–2018

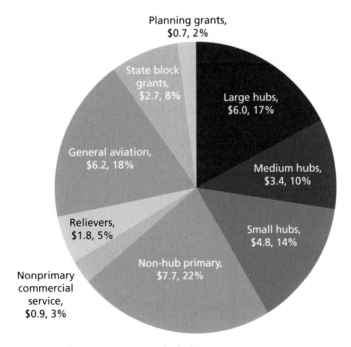

SOURCE: FAA, 2019a; RAND calculations.
NOTE: Total percentage does not sum to 100 because of rounding.

---

[15] See 49 U.S.C. § 47105, 49 U.S.C. § 47106, and 49 U.S.C. § 47107.

[16] See FAA Order 5100.38D, 2019, Table 2-11, for a discussion of criteria for being considered a planning agency sponsor.

received less than 10 percent of all grants. However, the average grant amount at GA airports was less than one-tenth of the average grant to large and medium hubs.

In total, large hubs received about $6 billion in AIP grants over this ten-year period, or a little more than $500 million per year. This amount suggests that large-hub airports would be in line to receive about $3 billion in AIP grants over the next five years, though this projection assumes that the AIP obligation limitation, the AIP grant apportionment processes, and the approximate distribution of discretionary funds by airport size remain the same for the next five years as they were, on average, over the past ten years. These assumptions might not hold in practice. For example, the availability of supplemental discretionary funds (from the General Fund rather than the AATF) could increase this amount, either by large-hub airports receiving such funds directly or by the funds going to meet the needs of smaller airports and, therefore, freeing up a larger share of AATF-funded AIP grants for large-hub airports.[17] The percentage of large hubs' capital expenditures that comes from AIP grants has declined, down to 5 percent in 2018 from approximately 10 percent to 15 percent between 2009 and 2015.

As noted above, smaller airports, and airports outside metropolitan areas in particular, received priority consideration for $1 billion in supplemental AIP funds appropriated in the Consolidated Appropriations Act, 2018 (Pub. L. 115-141). No supplemental discretionary grants from this pot of funding went to large-hub airports, though large hubs continued to receive both entitlement and regular discretionary funds, in tandem totaling about $525 million in FY 2018.[18] Although Congress authorized supplemental funds of more than $1 billion for each year from FY 2019 to FY 2023 in the FAA Reauthorization Act of 2018 (Pub. L. 115-254), it appropriated $500 million in the Consolidated Appropriations Act, 2019 (Pub. L. 116-6). At least half of this funding is to go to airports other than large and medium hubs.

Distribution of Airport Improvement Program Grants by Type of Project

About two-thirds of AIP grant dollars in FY 2018 went to airside projects, consistent with the higher weight given to these projects in the NPS equation that generates the NPR for each potential project, while a much smaller share went to landside projects. Runway, taxiway, and apron projects account for a majority of AIP grant dollars. In contrast, terminal projects received just 5 percent or less of AIP grant dollars in recent years. Details of AIP grants by type of project are provided in Appendix G.

Summary of Findings

The AIP is the principal mechanism through which the federal government funds airport infrastructure in support of its interest in safe, efficient passenger and cargo air transit. A complex array of entitlement formulas and discretionary set-aside requirements established by Congress govern the distribution of AIP grants. It is, by design, a redistributive program, supporting smaller airports with little ability to generate revenues on their own but that are critical

---

[17] The FAA notes this latter possibility in FAA, 2018d. Specifically, FAA, 2018d, p. 2, states, "Moreover, to the extent that the FAA is able to apply these supplemental funds to projects that meet the criteria for 'Priority Consideration,' it may also provide additional AIP funds for other projects elsewhere."

[18] A list of projects funded in the first round of supplemental appropriations is available at FAA, 2018e. FAA, 2019e, notes the hub-level breakdown of projects funded in the second round of these appropriations.

to maintaining the functionality and connectivity of the NAS. The AIP's regulations on what can be funded and the NPS equation that determines the prioritization of projects result in AIP grants flowing mostly to airside projects.

The AATF is the primary funding source for the AIP and several other FAA programs, including FAA Operations. Various excise taxes fund the AATF, with the largest share of AATF dollars coming from passengers. Passengers pay a flight segment fee that is indexed to the CPI, along with a ticket tax of 7.5 percent of the fare. Other excise taxes are based on international travel, cargo, and fuel use.

Under current law, the authorized amount of AIP grants funded by the AATF is $3.35 billion through FY 2023, while supplemental discretionary funding is authorized at a level of more than $1 billion per year. However, both funding sources require annual appropriation decisions by Congress; for example, FY 2019 supplemental discretionary appropriations were $500 million, less than half the authorized amount. The CBO projects that the AATF's uncommitted balance will grow over the coming decade, from $6.1 billion at the end of FY 2018 to nearly $50 billion by the end of FY 2029 (CBO projections cited in JCT, 2019, Table 2).

If this projected amount were to materialize, it would offer a sizable amount of resources that could be put toward federal air system priorities rather than be allowed to grow and essentially serve as an offset for other portions of the federal budget. However, past experience suggests that policymakers should use caution when interpreting these projections or using them as the basis for policy decisions. Unexpected economic or national security developments could cause revenues to fall short of projected levels, as could developments in the airline industry, such as further shifts toward untaxed categories of ancillary fees or substantial gains in fuel efficiency. Meanwhile, Congress could appropriate more for other categories of FAA spending from the AATF than expected under current law. These and other potential changes in the assumptions on which AATF revenues and outlays are based suggest that Congress should consider a longer-term plan for stable funding and consider the relationship between AIP grants and the use of PFCs, discussed in the next chapter.

CHAPTER SIX

Federal Role in Airport Infrastructure Funding: Passenger Facility Charge Program

A PFC is a federally authorized user fee paid by a passenger at the time of ticket purchase and remitted to the airport at which the passenger boards. With the approval of the FAA, an airport has the choice of opting into the PFC program. Currently, 98 of the top 100 airports enplaning passengers impose a PFC, including all 30 large-hub airports; nearly all of these airports collect the maximum allowable fee of $4.50 per flight segment (FAA, 2019f). PFC revenues can be used for a wider range of projects than can AIP grants, and they can also be used to pay for debt service and financing costs. PFC revenues account for a notably higher share of all airport revenues at medium- and large-hub airports than at smaller airports, and they are more likely than AIP grants to go toward landside projects. There is an ongoing debate over whether the maximum allowable PFC should be increased above $4.50, the amount it has been since April 2001, when the cap increase included in the 2000 FAA reauthorization took effect.

In this chapter, we begin by providing background on the PFC program, a description of eligibility criteria, and a discussion of how PFC aggregate collections and airport-level charges have evolved over time. We then consider four issues related to PFCs: (1) the purchasing power of the PFC since its cap was last increased, (2) the extent to which airports have committed their future PFC revenues with the current PFC cap, (3) the effect of PFCs on competition, and (4) the potential effects on passengers, airports, and airlines of indexing the PFC cap to inflation or of other proposed changes to the PFC program.

Background

The Aviation Safety and Capacity Expansion Act of 1990 established the PFC program,[1] permitting the FAA to authorize local commercial airport sponsors to collect a fee from paying passengers for boarding aircraft. The PFC program is an explicitly carved-out exception to the 1973 Anti-Head Tax Act,[2] which otherwise prohibits states, localities, and airport owners or lessees from charging a per-passenger tax on air travelers.[3]

---

[1] This legislation was Section 9110 of the Omnibus Budget Reconciliation Act of 1990 (Pub. L. 101-508).

[2] This legislation was Section 1113 of the Airport Development Acceleration Act of 1973 (Pub. L. 93-44).

[3] The 1973 Anti-Head Tax Act followed in the wake of a 1972 Supreme Court decision that ruled that two state-levied charges on air travelers were constitutional and did not pose an unreasonable burden on interstate commerce because "these charges reflect a fair, if imperfect, approximation of the use of facilities for whose benefit they are imposed" (Evansville Airport v. Delta Airlines, 1972).

The maximum allowable fee was set initially at $3 per flight leg, with a maximum allowable charge per passenger per round trip of $12, and later was increased to a maximum of $4.50 per flight leg and $18 per round trip, effective in 2001.[4] The fee is collected by airlines at the time of ticket sale, with proceeds remitted on a monthly basis to airport sponsors and airlines keeping $0.11 per PFC imposed as compensation for handling the funds (USDOT, 2004b).

The PFC program was established to fund projects to "preserve or enhance safety, security, or capacity," "reduce noise or mitigate noise impacts," or "furnish opportunities for enhanced competition between or among air carriers."[5] It was intended to complement the AIP and to allow an additional source of revenues for airport infrastructure projects at a time of elevated concern about the adequacy of existing airport infrastructure for meeting the nation's needs and about federal budget deficits (Tang and Elias, 2017). GAO reports and testimony issued around the time of the PFC program's creation shine a light on one of the motivating factors for the PFC: promoting competition. GAO, 1990, pp. 2–3, states,

> A PFC gives airports a source of revenue for financing airport expansion projects independent of airline control and reduces airports' need to rely on airlines to pay for or guarantee capital projects. Airports that are less reliant on airline financing and guarantees should be better able to resist pressure to enter into long-term contracts containing restrictive provisions. Fewer restrictive contracts, in turn, should give airports more flexibility both in stimulating competition and in reducing congestion and delay.

> [...] While PFC funds must be used for specific projects approved by the Secretary of Transportation, incumbent airline approval of those projects will not be required, even if the PFC funds are used to support a bond issue or combined with funds from other sources, such as federal grants.

The process through which airport sponsors apply to impose a PFC and gain approval for specific PFC-eligible projects is detailed in FAA Order 5500.1, last updated in 2001.[6] Key elements of the application process include

- developing a project plan and schedule for each proposed project
- providing "adequate justification" for why projects meet PFC objectives
- listing the proposed PFC rate and the duration over which it will be imposed to yield the revenues needed to fund the proposed project
- documenting that air carriers have been provided with written notice and consulted about the airport's plans to impose a PFC
- responding to any formal comments made by air carriers or other members of the public.

In some cases, these processes dissuade small airports from pursuing the authority to impose a PFC at all because they perceive the potential revenue to be too small to justify the administrative costs of applying.

---

[4]   Section 105 of the Wendell H. Ford Aviation Investment and Reform Act for the 21st Century (Pub. L. 106-181).

[5]   These stated goals for PFC projects are included in the initial authorizing legislation. See Section 9110 of the Omnibus Budget Reconciliation Act of 1990 (Pub. L. 101-508). They are also listed at 14 CFR § 158.15.

[6]   The instructions for preparing a PFC application are available on the FAA's website. See FAA, undated e.

Medium- and large-hub airports face additional requirements. For example, they must submit a written "competition plan" in order to impose a PFC if one or two airlines account for half or more of all passenger enplanements. From 2001 to 2018, these airports also had to meet a stricter "significant contribution" standard for a project to be eligible for PFC funding at $4 or $4.50, though this requirement was eliminated in the most recent FAA reauthorization. Also, medium- and large-hub airports forgo 50 percent of their AIP primary entitlements if they impose a PFC of $3 or less, and they forgo 75 percent of these AIP funds if they impose a PFC of more than $3.

After receiving a PFC application from an airport, the FAA first reviews the application for completeness (which must occur within 30 days of application receipt) and then initiates a full review, all aspects of which are to be completed within 120 days of application receipt. This full review includes FAA determination that

- the amount of revenue collected does not exceed the amount necessary to finance the specific projects
- the projects are eligible for PFC funds
- the projects are adequately justified in accordance with federal policy
- the airport sponsor is in compliance with certain federal policies
- the application includes responses to airline and stakeholder comments.

This full review also includes filing a notice in the Federal Register and allowing for a 30-day public comment period after the notice is published. A Record of Decision is then prepared, either by the FAA Airports office (in certain circumstances, including when a significant policy precedent, legal issue, or controversy arising in air carrier consultation or public comment is present) or by regional FAA Airports Division managers. Airports are then notified of the decision, and all approved and disapproved projects are published on a monthly basis in the Federal Register. After formal FAA approval, the airports must notify their air carriers and provide the charge effective date, which must be the first day of a month, no earlier than 60 days from the date of the notification to the air carriers of the approval to impose the PFC.

Eligible Projects and Implementation

The set of projects on which PFC revenues can be expended fully encompasses AIP-eligible projects, including those for airport development, airport planning, noise compatibility programs, and noise compatibility planning, as described in Chapter Five and defined in the relevant portions of the AIP statute.[7] PFCs can also be used as the local match to an AIP grant or to supplement AIP funding for an AIP-eligible project. PFC eligibility extends to other categories of projects;[8] notably, the following:

- A larger array of landside projects can be funded with PFC revenues, particularly at small-, medium-, and large-hub airports. Hub airports are unable to use AIP grants for projects in revenue-producing areas of terminals but can use PFC revenues for these pur-

---

[7]   See Chapter Five for a discussion of AIP project eligibility requirements with references to statute.

[8]   For a full list, see 14 CFR §158.15 and 14 CFR §158.17. For further information, see FAA Order 5500.1, 2001.

poses, with some limitations (e.g., gates, airline ticketing areas, and passenger check-in facilities are eligible at hub airports, but concession areas, such as food courts, are not).

• PFC revenues can be leveraged to incur debt, and airports can use PFCs to pay principal and interest on this debt. In most cases, bonds backed by PFC revenues must be used to fund projects that are PFC-eligible, though there is an exception in the PFC statute that allows the FAA to waive this condition if the airport has a financial need.[9]

Other PFC-eligible projects include those approved under the FAA's "Program to Permit Cost-Sharing of Air Traffic Modernization Projects," projects to convert or obtain ground support equipment that includes low-emission technology or uses cleaner burning fuels, and noise projects that are not included in noise compatibility plans (a requirement for AIP eligibility being their inclusion in such plans) (FAA, 2015b). Ground access transportation project eligibility is determined by the FAA "on a case-by-case basis after a review of the particulars associated with each unique proposal" and requires these projects to be AIP-eligible and to meet one of the PFC program objectives (enhance safety, capacity, and security; mitigate noise; enhance competition) (USDOT, 2004a, p. 6370).

Because the PFC is charged per airport and not per flight,[10] layovers can increase the cost of otherwise identical flights. This could result in passengers traveling to or from smaller airports, which are more likely to have a connecting flight, and paying more in PFC charges than passengers traveling to or from larger airports, which are more likely to have nonstop flight options. Consider two one-way flights from LAX to JFK, one with a layover at Phoenix Sky Harbor International Airport (PHX) and one that is direct. In this example, both flights have identical base fares, and as a result, most taxes and fees are also identical. The exception is the PFC: the PFC cap is $4.50 per segment, not per flight. A PFC is collected according to a traveler's departure airport for each flight segment. As shown in Figure 6.1, a traveler with a direct, one-way flight from LAX to JFK pays a $4.50 PFC; that money is collected by the airline, which sends those funds to the airport sponsor (less a compensation of $0.11 for col-

Figure 6.1
PFC Comparison

Nonstop itinerary		One-stop itinerary	
LAX to JFK nonstop	✈	LAX to JFK one-stop (PHX)	✈
Base fare	$177.67	Base fare	$177.67
Transportation tax at 7.5%	$13.33	Transportation tax at 7.5%	$13.33
PFC	$4.50	PFC	$9.00
Federal segment tax	$4.20	Federal segment tax	$8.40
U.S. security fee	$5.60	U.S. security fee	$5.60
TOTAL	$205.30	TOTAL	$214.00

---

[9]   *Financial need* is defined in the Code of Federal Regulations as "a public agency cannot meet its operational or debt service obligations and does not have at least a 2-month capital reserve fund." See 14 CFR § 158.3.

[10]   A *flight* is defined as the entirety of a one-way trip from origin to destination, including stops or layovers along the way.

lection and handling costs) on a monthly basis to pay for FAA-approved projects.[11] A traveler with a layover in PHX pays a $9.00 PFC, with $4.39 going to LAX, $4.39 going to PHX, and $0.22 going to the airline.

Current Status of PFC Collections and Project Approvals

There are currently 362 airports collecting a PFC, the vast majority of which charge the maximum allowable amount of $4.50 (FAA, 2019f). Table 6.1 breaks this number down by airport category. Just two of the top 100 airports by passenger volume currently do not charge a PFC, though both have plans in process to impose one in the near future.[12] Since the program was established in the early 1990s, a total of 399 airports have imposed a PFC.

Figure 6.2 plots the share of hub airports (large, medium, and small) that have charged a PFC over the duration of the program, as well as the share of these airports that have charged the maximum allowable PFC since it was increased to $4.50 in April 2001. As the figure shows, the share of hub airports charging a PFC at the maximum rate of $4.50 increased dramatically during the 2000s, continued to increase over the past eight years, and currently sits at approximately 95 percent. As Table 6.1 underscores, these shares are even higher when restricted to large- and medium-hub airports, all 61 of which impose a PFC and all but two of which charge $4.50.

Almost all large and medium hubs charge a PFC of $4.50 despite the provision requiring these airports to forgo AIP primary entitlements equaling 75 percent of anticipated PFC

Table 6.1
PFCs by Airport Category

Airport Category	Number of Airports	Airports Currently Collecting PFCs	Airports Collecting PFCs at the Maximum $4.50 Level
Large hub	30	30	29
Medium hub	31	31	30
Small hub	72	68	67
Non-hub primary	247	193	187
Nonprimary commercial service	126	40	37
Total	506	362	350

SOURCE: FAA, 2019f.
NOTE: Data are as of August 31, 2019; the number of airports in each hub size category is from FAA, 2018a.

---

[11]   14 CFR Part 158, Subpart C, provides the authority and regulations surrounding how airports collect and handle PFC revenue and how they remit these funds to the public agency airport sponsor. 14 CFR Part 158, Subpart D, describes the reporting and auditing requirements involving these funds. Because these regulations impose collection and record-keeping expenses on the airlines, "the collecting carrier is entitled to: (1) $0.11 of each PFC collected. (2) Any interest or other investment return earned on PFC revenue between the time of collection and remittance to the public agency" (14 CFR § 158.53). Carriers are required to remit the funds on a monthly basis.

[12]   These airports are Boise Airport and Greenville–Spartanburg International Airport. See FAA, 2019f. Boise charged a PFC from 1994 to 2015, while Greenville has never charged a PFC. See Day, 2019, and Greenville-Spartanburg Airport Commission, 2019.

Figure 6.2
Percentage of All Hub Airports Charging Any PFC and Percentage Charging a $4.50 PFC, 1992–2019

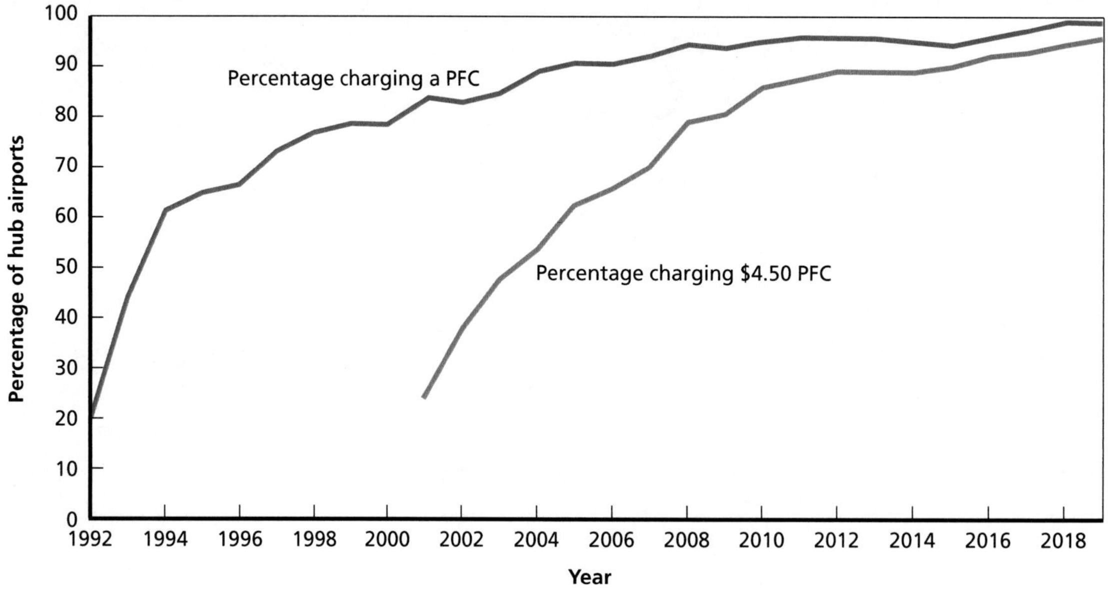

SOURCE: FAA, 2019g.
NOTE: Includes large-, medium-, and small-hub airports, using NPIAS hub definitions. PFC charges are those authorized to be collected as of December 31 of each year through 2018. PFC for 2019 is as of August 2019.

revenues, up to a maximum of 75 percent of the AIP primary entitlements for which they would otherwise be eligible if they impose at that level.[13] Figure 6.3 demonstrates why this is a good deal for these airports. No matter the number of enplanements (the smallest number of enplanements at a medium hub in 2018 was just shy of 2.5 million), the airports gain more in PFC revenues by charging $4.50 per passenger than they forgo in AIP primary entitlements, which are also based on enplanements. That is, there is a sizable gap between the blue line indicating PFC collections and the red line indicating forgone AIP grants.[14] The maximum possible amount of AIP primary entitlements, $26 million, is reached at 22,975,000 enplanements (which ten large hubs hit in 2018),[15] and therefore so is the maximum amount of forgone grants ($19.5 million). For enplanements beyond that number, airports are not forgoing any additional AIP entitlements for charging a PFC, meaning that every $4.50 PFC

[13] A 50 percent turn-back requirement was initially included in the Aviation Safety and Capacity Expansion Act of 1990 (included in Pub. L. 101-508), and the 75 percent turn-back requirement (for charging a PFC above $3) was established in tandem with authorizing higher PFCs in the Wendell H. Ford Aviation Investment and Reform Act for the 21st Century (Pub. L. 106-181, 2000). The rationale for the turn-back requirement is not stated explicitly, though one can infer that it is to enhance the focus of AIP resources on smaller airports, since the vast majority of these forgone AIP entitlements flow into the Small Airport Fund.

[14] The AIP grant apportionment amounts are based on enplanements in the prior calendar year, while the amount forgone is based on estimates of PFC revenues to be collected according to enplanements in the current fiscal year.

[15] Note that $26 million is the maximum AIP primary entitlement when the AIP obligation limitation is at least $3.2 billion (as discussed in Chapter Five). The maximum amount when this threshold is not hit is $22 million. More than 41 million enplanements are needed to reach this maximum, using the AIP primary entitlement formula that does not double apportionment amounts.

Figure 6.3
PFC Collections Versus AIP Grants Forgone, by Enplanements, for Medium and Large Hubs Charging a PFC of $4.50

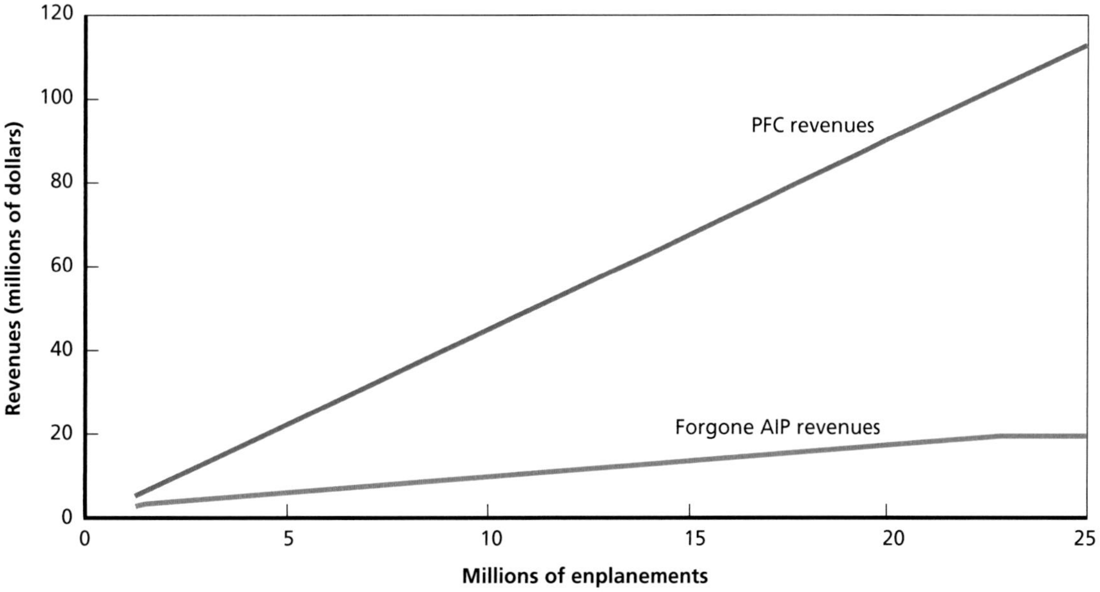

SOURCE: FAA Order 5100.38D, 2019; RAND calculations.

collected past about 23 million enplanements translates dollar for dollar to additional money for infrastructure.

PFC Collections

FAA data show that, from 1992 to 2018, overall PFC collections totaled $56.9 billion (in nominal dollars). Figure 6.4 plots the trend in annual PFC collections in nominal dollars. As the figure shows, collections increased steadily on a year-over-year basis during the 1990s, before leveling off around 2000. Collections picked up again after 2001 (when the maximum allowable PFC was last increased) and peaked in the years prior to the Great Recession, though 2006 revenue is overstated by nearly $500 million dollars as a result of a one-time adjustment to past collections, which led these prior-year collections to be allocated to 2006 (FAA, 2019f). Revenues fell sharply in 2008 and 2009, grew slowly for several years after the recession, and then began to increase more rapidly starting around 2015. Nominal PFC revenues hit all-time highs in each of the past five years, and the FAA expects that collections will continue to increase in 2019 and 2020 (FAA, 2019f).

The increase in nominal PFC collections reflects three factors: (1) an increase in the number of airports that impose a PFC, (2) an increase in the average PFC charged by these airports, and (3) an increase in enplanements. However, as discussed later in this chapter, it is important to keep in mind that inflation has eroded the purchasing power of each dollar of PFC revenues over time, cutting into airports' ability to fund infrastructure projects with these record-high PFC collections.

Figure 6.4
PFC Collections, by Year, 1992–2018

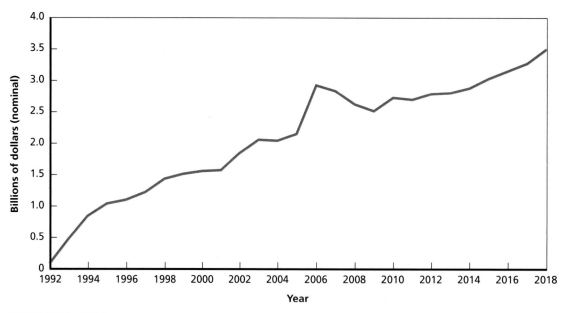

SOURCE: FAA, 2019f.

PFC Project Approvals Across Categories

In addition to the $56.9 billion in actual PFC collections through FY 2018, the FAA has approved future collections totaling about $50 billion to fund PFC-eligible projects, for a total of $107.4 billion in authorized collections over time. In this section, we describe the distribution of the full set of projects that have been approved, whether associated collections occurred in the past or are authorized to occur in the future.

Although more than 50 percent of individual PFC projects are approved at non-hub primary airports, more than 75 percent of the dollars are for projects at large-hub airports. Figure 6.5 displays the distribution of PFC dollars by airport hub size over the duration of the PFC program (through August 2019). Over this period, the average PFC project approval was $6.4 million across all projects at all airports. The average project size increased with hub size. The average large-hub project approval was for $37.8 million, medium-hub projects averaged $8.9 million, and small-hub projects averaged $2.8 million. Non-hub primary projects averaged about $300,000, while nonprimary projects averaged about $50,000 each.

Landside projects account for about 60 percent of the $107.4 billion in approved eligible projects (through August 2019), while airside projects represent about 25 percent of the total. Appendix H shows the distribution of PFC project approvals in detail.

Another way to characterize the distribution of PFC-approved projects is in terms of the stated objective of the project: to preserve or enhance capacity, safety, or security; enhance competition; or mitigate noise. Capacity projects account for about three-quarters of all project dollars, a finding that holds true for all airport categories save for nonprimary commercial service airports. Large- and medium-hub airports devote a higher share of PFC dollars to competition-enhancing projects (9 percent and 13 percent, respectively) than do smaller airports, which dedicate less than 5 percent to these projects.

Figure 6.5
Billions of Dollars of PFC Project Approvals, by Hub Size, 1992 to August 2019

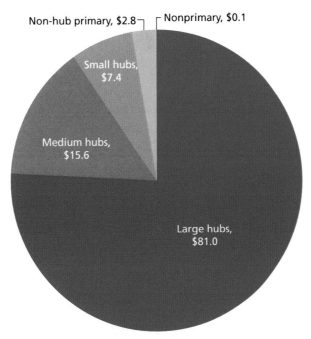

SOURCE: FAA data provided to RAND, current as of
August 28, 2019.

FAA data on PFC project approvals over time also provide a window into how PFC revenue use breaks down between pay-as-you-go expenses, bond principal payments, and interest costs, as well as how this distribution varies by airport category.[16] Across all airports, about 39 percent of PFC revenue is allocated to bond principal, about 33 percent is allocated to interest, and about 29 percent is allocated to pay-as-you-go project expenses. This distribution is despite the fact that the vast majority of individually approved projects (nearly 90 percent) are entirely pay-as-you-go. A key takeaway, therefore, is that big-dollar projects at larger airports tend to be debt financed, with PFC revenues used to service that debt, while smaller projects approved at smaller airports are more likely to have PFC revenues going directly to pay for project costs on a pay-as-you-go basis. Figure 6.6 depicts this relationship, with the share of collections put toward pay-as-you-go expenses decreasing with airport size, from 26 percent at large hubs to 95 percent at nonprimary airports.

Inflation and the Purchasing Power of the PFC over Time

Prices rise over time because of inflation. Therefore, the amount of infrastructure that can be purchased with each dollar declines over time. For this reason, some taxes and fees are indexed

---

[16] The analysis in this paragraph and Figures 6.5 and 6.6 use an Excel workbook that the FAA provided to RAND, which included a table entitled "Projects Summary Report by Objective, Component, Type." This file listed individual PFC project approvals from January 1, 1992, to August 28, 2019, and detailed the approved collection amounts for pay-as-you-go projects, bond capital, and financing and interest.

Figure 6.6
PFC Approvals, by Use of Funding, 1992 to August 2019

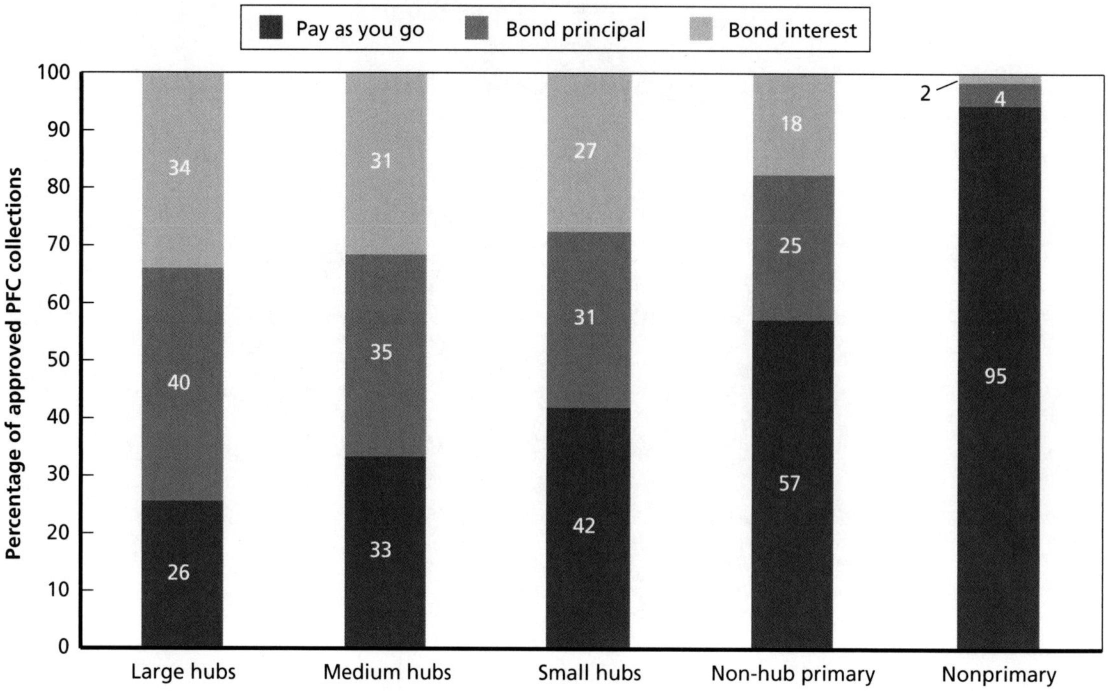

SOURCE: FAA data provided to RAND, current as of August 28, 2019.
NOTE: Percentages might not sum to 100 because of rounding.

to inflation, meaning the amount of the fee or tax changes over time to match changes in prices. For example, both the flight segment tax and the international arrival/departure tax, which fund the AATF, are indexed to the CPI (Tang and Elias, 2017). The PFC is not indexed to inflation, meaning that the amount of infrastructure that can be purchased with the PFC collected from a single passenger has declined over time.

Figure 6.7 shows two ways to measure this decline in purchasing power. The most common measure of inflation is the CPI, which reflects changes in the price of a basket of common consumer goods and services. Because of inflation, $4.50 in 2019 will buy approximately two-thirds of what $4.50 bought in 2000. Specifically, $4.50 in 2019 buys the same amount of CPI goods and services that $3.02 bought in 2000.

Different goods change prices at different rates, so a basket of consumer goods might not be the most accurate reflection of the extent to which inflation has decreased the amount of airport infrastructure that a single passenger's PFC fee can purchase. Some indexes focus more narrowly on a specific type of goods and services.[17] Construction materials have increased in

---

[17] Defining an appropriate inflation index for the PFC is challenging because of the range of materials costs and variations across airport sizes, types, and locations. The choice of the CPI as a reference is based on the assumption that changes of the PFC cap will eventually pass through to passengers, affecting prices of air travel. In contrast, construction cost indexes would represent prices directly faced by airport owners for infrastructure improvements. We examined three construction-related inflation indexes, which used construction materials, average hourly wages, and the price of asphalt, respectively. Using these indexes, a PFC of $4.50 in the year 2000 would purchase $2.72 of construction materials, $2.68 of labor, and $1.74 of asphalt in 2019. These three indexes are from the Bureau of Labor Statistics, and are as follows: (1) Producer Price Index by Commodity for Special Indexes: Construction Materials (construction materials), (2) Average Hourly Earnings of Production and Nonsupervisory Employees: Total Private (average hourly wages), and (3) Producer Price Index by Industry:

Figure 6.7
Reduction of Purchasing Power of PFCs in Constant Year 2000 Dollars

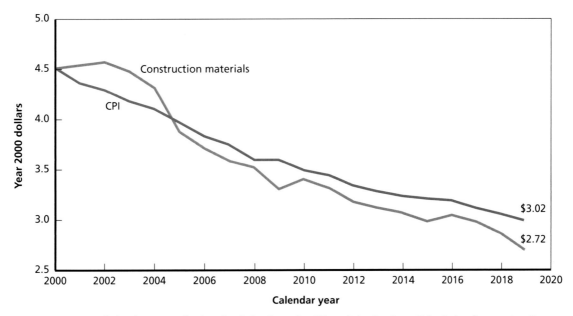

SOURCE: RAND analysis of Bureau of Labor Statistics data, the CPI, and the Producer Price Index for construction materials (Bureau of Labor Statistics, 2019).

price faster than the goods and services in the CPI. Figure 6.7 shows that, as a result of this increase in construction material prices, an airport that collects $4.50 from a passenger in 2019 can only buy as much construction material as $2.72 bought in 2000. This decrease in purchasing power is sometimes referred to as an *erosion* in the value of the PFC.

A thought exercise on this topic is to consider what the $4.50 PFC cap would be in 2018 if it had been indexed to inflation. In other words, what would the dollar value of the PFC cap be in 2018 in order for an individual PFC fee to have the same purchasing power it had in 2000? Because different types of goods have changed at different rates, the answer depends on what type of good is being purchased. As shown in Figure 6.8, the 2018 PFC cap would need to be $6.72 to purchase the same amount of consumer goods and services that $4.50 bought in 2000. Because construction material prices, on average, have risen faster than the CPI, the 2018 PFC cap would need to be $7.44 to purchase the same amount of construction materials that an individual PFC fee bought in 2000. Prices for specific types of construction materials used by airports for specific purposes might have grown at faster or slower rates than this overall average. Construction costs also might have grown at different rates in different parts of the country.[18]

It is important to note that increases in the number of airports that charge a PFC, the number of airports that charge the maximum allowable PFC of $4.50, and the number of pas-

---

Asphalt Paving Mixture and Block Manufacturing: Asphalt Paving Mixtures and Blocks (asphalt). Data were pulled from the Federal Reserve Bank of St. Louis' FRED database.

[18] Turner & Townsend, 2019, p. 15, finds that construction cost inflation varies across several major U.S. cities. This source also finds that airport terminal construction costs vary between certain major U.S. cities and by type of terminal being built (Turner & Townsend, 2019, pp. 98–103). Building costs per square foot are nearly two times higher for "full service" domestic terminals than they are for LCC terminals.

Figure 6.8
Value of PFC Cap If It Had Been Indexed to Inflation

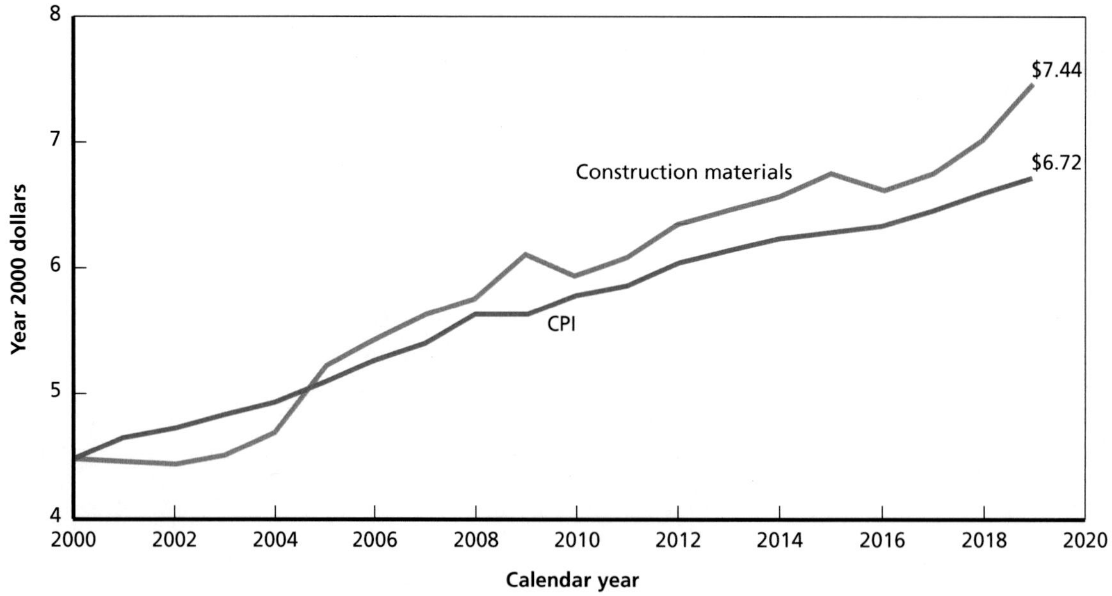

SOURCE: RAND analysis of Bureau of Labor Statistics data, the CPI, and the Producer Price Index for construction materials (Bureau of Labor Statistics, 2019).

sengers at these airports have resulted in the inflation-adjusted value of total PFC collections increasing over time despite declines in the value of a single passenger's PFC. For example, the CPI-adjusted value of total PFC collections increased by about 15 percent from 2013 to 2018 and by more than 50 percent from 2000 to 2018. Therefore, airports collectively could purchase more with their total PFC collections in 2018 than they could in 2000. However, the increasing number of passengers also requires airports to spend more on infrastructure. We are unable to determine whether the value of an individual PFC is eroding faster than airports can benefit from returns to scale. Moreover, to the extent that certain stresses on infrastructure grow in tandem with operations rather than enplanements, and given that larger airplanes have contributed to enplanements growing faster than operations, the erosion of the per-passenger PFC might be less substantial. Put another way, per-plane PFC collections can grow even while the PFC cap stays constant, and if demands on infrastructure are on a per-plane rather than per-passenger basis, the declining purchasing power of the per-passenger PFC would be less consequential.

How Long Are Airports Constrained by Existing PFC Revenues?

One of the questions we are required to consider in this study is how long airports are constrained by current PFC collections—in other words, how far into the future have airports committed their PFC revenues? One way to shed light on this question is to consider how long airports are approved to collect PFCs, which is determined by estimating the amount of time it will take these airports to collect the PFC revenues needed to fund approved projects. For example, if an airport is approved to collect a PFC until 2030, that means it has received

FAA approval for projects that will cost an amount that will take until 2030 to raise in PFC collections according to the approved PFC rate and the expected passenger traffic.[19] The only way to fund additional projects (other than those already approved) using a PFC would be by using revenues received after 2030 or, in the case of the small number of airports collecting a PFC at less than the maximum rate of $4.50, by seeking approval to collect at a higher rate. For airports that have fully committed their PFCs until 2030 but have not yet committed their post-2030 revenues, accessing those future revenues to undertake infrastructure projects today would require airports to borrow against the future revenue stream and incur associated financing costs.

Among the nation's 30 large-hub airports (all but one of which charges a PFC of $4.50), 18 have fully committed their PFC revenues until at least 2030, and six of these airports have fully committed their revenues until 2040 or later (FAA, 2019g). No large-hub airport has a PFC collection expiration date prior to 2023, meaning that *all* PFC revenues at *all* large-hub airports are committed through 2022 (with the exception of the one large-hub airport that could access more PFC revenues before then by increasing its PFC to the $4.50 cap). Medium hubs are less likely to have expiration dates well into the future. Among the 31 medium-hub airports (again, all but one of which charges a PFC of $4.50), ten have expiration dates in 2030 or later, while about half (14 airports) have expiration dates in 2025 or sooner. Figure 6.9 plots the distribution of PFC expiration dates across all 131 hub airports (large, medium, and small) charging a PFC, with bars corresponding to the number of airports that have fully committed their PFC revenues until each set of years. The figure shows that small and medium hubs are more likely to be able to tap additional PFC revenues for yet-to-be-approved projects in the 2020s, while most large-hub airports are fully committed until 2030 or later. A handful of authorizations span past the year 2050, and there is no limitation on how far out an airport can be authorized to collect a PFC if it has sufficient PFC-eligible projects.

We can show the extent to which potential future PFC revenues are already committed versus how much potential revenue is available for yet-to-be-approved projects, according to the current expiration dates for charge authorizations. Figures 6.10 and 6.11 combine PFC authorization data (as of August 31, 2019) with the most recent Terminal Area Forecast (TAF) data, which projects enplanements through 2045. The figures also look backward to show how PFC revenues have ramped up since 1992. The dashed line shows the maximum potential PFC revenue ($3 per enplanement until 2001 and $4.50 since) while the solid line estimates revenues committed using actual and TAF-projected enplanements data and PFC charges in place or authorized to be in place in the future.[20] Figure 6.10 includes all hub airports while

---

[19] In the event that an airport reaches its authorized PFC collection amount prior to the anticipated PFC expiration date (i.e., if enplanements are higher than expected at the time of PFC approval), the authorization to collect would lapse unless the airport submits an additional request to continue to collect for additional PFC-eligible projects. In contrast, if it takes longer to collect the authorized amount than anticipated, the airport may collect until such date that it collects the approved amount.

[20] We make several simplifying assumptions in our analysis. We assume that 10 percent of domestic enplanements and 4 percent of international enplanements are not charged a PFC, consistent with GAO, 2014c, pp. 38–39. We calculate an average PFC per year by averaging the PFC for each month and apply that value to enplanements; this method does not account for variation in enplanements across the months of the year. These values are applied to past enplanement data and future projections, which results in the solid line for past PFC collections differing from actual historical collections. In this analysis, we assume that the PFC will be held at $4.50 through 2045 and that enplanements are fixed at TAF projections and do not respond to changes in the PFC. All dollars are nominal.

Figure 6.9
Dates Through Which Future PFC Revenues Are Fully Committed for Small-, Medium-, and Large-Hub Airports, by Five-Year Period

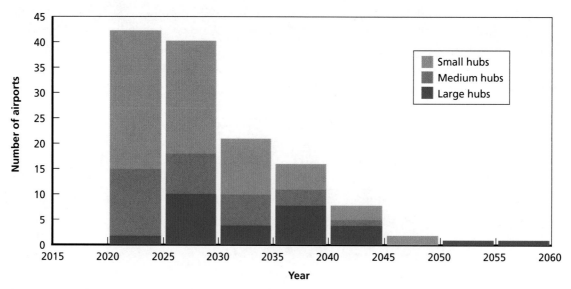

SOURCE: FAA, 2019g.
NOTE: Includes large-, medium-, and small-hub airports, using NPIAS hub definitions. Data are current as of June 2019. One airport in each size category currently charges a PFC of less than $4.50 and could access additional revenue before the date its current authorization expires by seeking to raise its PFC to $4.50. In addition, four small hubs currently do not charge a PFC at all.

Figure 6.11 is restricted to large-hub airports, which collect and spend the vast majority of all PFCs.[21]

Across all hubs, and especially for large hubs, the vast majority of PFC collections over the next decade are already committed (i.e., the area between the dashed and solid lines is small relative to the area between the solid line and the x-axis, at least until 2030). In Figure 6.10, we see that a small portion of potential PFC revenues from 2020 to 2023 is not currently committed (across all hubs); in Figure 6.11, we see that large-hub PFC revenues are virtually entirely committed through 2023 (i.e., the dashed and solid lines essentially overlap). Although large-hub airports could borrow against revenues expected to be received further into the future (though, to reiterate, many large hubs are fully locked up well past the mid-2020s), there is no additional capacity to fund projects without borrowing until 2023 at all but one large-hub airport, with the existing $4.50 cap (again, with the exception of the one that does not charge a $4.50 PFC).

It is important to note that our analysis is unable to incorporate projects that are in early planning stages—with PFC revenues expected to be used—but for which the PFC application and approval process is yet to be completed (i.e., the airport's long-term plan includes using PFC revenues for a given project, but the airport has not yet applied to the FAA to do so). Judging by the very small distance between the dashed (potential) and solid (committed or

---

[21] Of the total of $107.4 billion in approved PFC collections as of August 31, 2019, $81.0 billion (75 percent) are at large-hub airports and $104.5 billion (97 percent) are at small-, medium-, or large-hub airports. We exclude non-hub and nonprimary commercial service airports from the potential PFC revenues analysis because these airports collect a small share of PFCs (3 percent) and PFCs are a small share of their sources for infrastructure financing.

Figure 6.10
PFC Revenues Committed Versus Potential PFC Revenues for All Hub Airports, 1992–2045

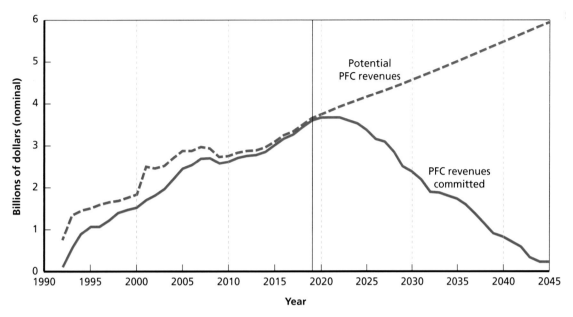

SOURCES: FAA, 2019g; enplanement data from FAA, 2018b.
NOTE: Includes large-, medium-, and small-hub airports, using NPIAS hub definitions. PFC data are current as of August 31, 2019. Yearly average PFC is calculated as an average of the PFC level authorized for each month and applied to actual or projected enplanements. Revenue calculations use GAO, 2014c, assumptions on the share of enplanements that are not charged a PFC, for both past and future enplanements.

Figure 6.11
PFC Revenues Committed Versus Potential PFC Revenues for Large-Hub Airports, 1992–2045

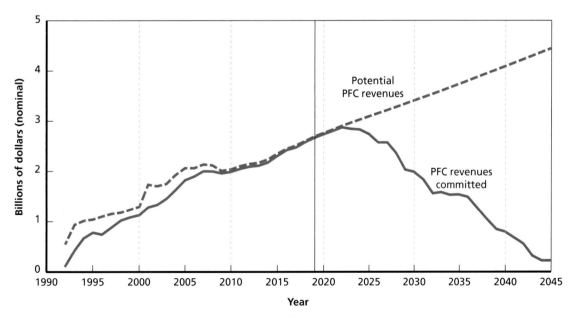

SOURCES: FAA, 2019g; enplanement data from FAA, 2018b.
NOTE: Includes large-, medium-, and small-hub airports, using NPIAS hub definitions. PFC data are current as of August 31, 2019. Yearly average PFC is calculated as an average of the PFC level authorized for each month and applied to actual or projected enplanements. Revenue calculations use GAO, 2014c, assumptions on the share of enplanements that are not charged a PFC, for both past and future enplanements.

collected) lines in past years in Figures 6.10 and 6.11, there is little reason to believe that hub airports will not plan and seek approval for projects that authorize them to collect essentially the maximum potential PFC revenue in future years as well.

For the 2020s, we estimate that 86 percent of large-hub PFC revenues are tied up, while about $4.2 billion could be earned over that period to fund as-yet-unapproved projects, without increasing the PFC cap above $4.50. The values for hub airports overall (large, medium, and small) are 80 percent committed, and $8.1 billion is available for projects in the 2020s. A larger share of future revenues remains uncommitted when looking out to 2045. We estimate that 47 percent of potential PFC revenues at large-hub airports over the 2020 to 2045 period are already accounted for, compared with 30 percent and 17 percent of medium- and small-hub potential PFC revenues, respectively. This equates to nearly $50 billion in potential PFC revenues that large-hub airports could access over that period and about $72 billion across all hub airports.

However, these large numbers require two key points of context. First, as noted above, the vast majority of this potential revenue does not free up until 2030 or beyond, which means that to use it to meet today's infrastructure needs, airports would need to take on additional long-term debt and dedicate a portion of the future PFC revenues to financing rather than project costs, resulting in higher total costs. Second, although tens of billions of dollars might be accessible (albeit by incurring financing costs), estimates of the cost of infrastructure needs are large in magnitude as well. As noted in Chapter Four, large-hub airports reported capital expenditures in 2017 of $8.7 billion. Total capital expenditures in 2017 among all 403 NPIAS airports reporting to CATS was $12.8 billion.[22]

Despite large-hub airports having largely committed future PFC revenue, the percentage of committed future PFC revenue was lower in 2018 than it was ten years prior. As of the end of 2018, 87 percent of potential large-hub PFC revenues over the next ten years and about 50 percent over the next 25 years are already committed to approved projects. As of the end of 2008, 95 percent of revenues over the following ten years and 79 percent of revenues over the following 25 years were already committed to approved projects. Figure 6.12, which depicts PFC revenues committed as of the end of 2008, shows that many of the projects currently set to be funded (with PFC authorizations set to lapse) by the 2020s were already in place in 2008. Although large-hub airports today have booked much of their future PFCs, they are not committing as much future PFC revenue as they have in the past. This could be because many airports are seeking to use PFCs to reduce borrowing costs by paying off debts faster, rather than taking on additional debt. Paying off debt requires obtaining additional revenue today, rather than committing future revenue.

Although the information and charts in this chapter can inform the discussion surrounding the adequacy of the existing maximum allowable PFC, there are limitations to this analysis. In addition to an inability to account for projects in early planning stages, this analysis does not indicate whether airports lack sufficient funds to implement additional critical projects today.

---

[22] ACI-NA identifies $81 billion of potential projects at large-hub airports between 2019 and 2023 and $128 billion of potential projects across airports of all sizes over that period.

Figure 6.12
PFC Revenues Committed Versus Potential PFC Revenues for Large-Hub Airports, 1992–2045 (as of December 2008)

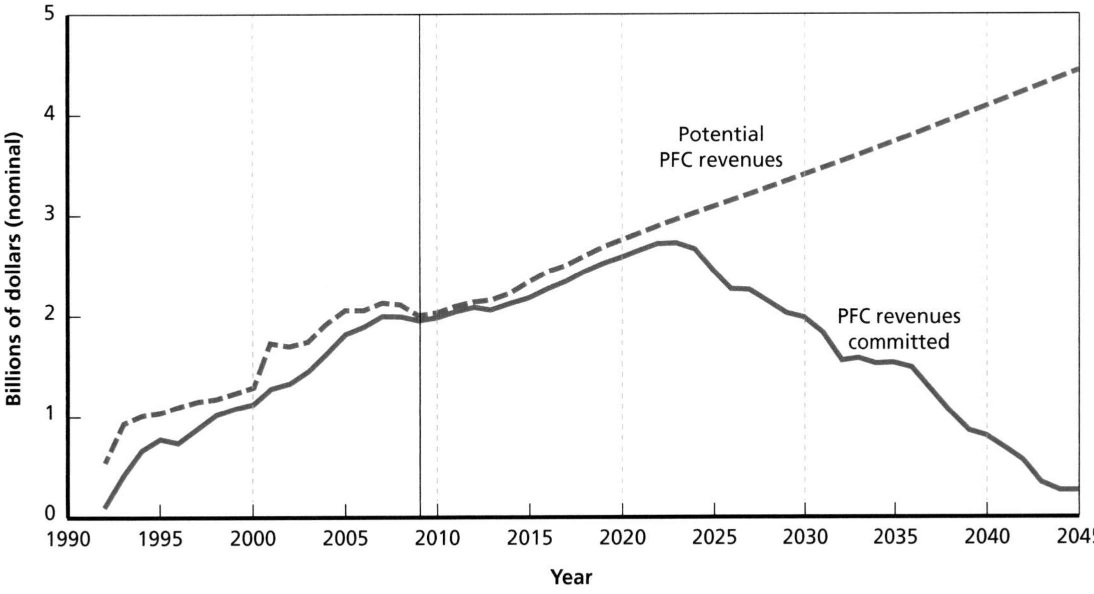

SOURCES: FAA, 2019g; enplanement data from FAA, 2018b.
NOTE: Includes large-hub airports, using NPIAS hub definitions. PFC data are current as of August 31, 2019, and reflect authorizations that had been in place as of December 31, 2008. Yearly average PFC is calculated as an average of the PFC level authorized for each month and applied to actual or projected enplanements. Revenue calculations use GAO, 2014c, assumptions on the share of enplanements that are not charged a PFC, for both past and future enplanements. The 2008–2018 enplanement numbers are actuals, not historical projections.

Effect of PFCs on Promoting Competition and Ticket Prices

One of the five primary objectives that Congress set for PFCs is to enhance competition. Increasing competition is important because many studies suggest that air travel is more expensive when competition is lower (e.g., FAA/OST Task Force, 1999; Kwoka and Shumilkina, 2010) and that competition affects the variation in prices (Gerardi and Shapiro, 2009; Gaggero and Piga, 2011; Dai, Liu, and Serfes, 2014). Incumbent airlines might use limit pricing[23] or their authority under the agreements discussed in Chapter Three to keep new entrants from entering their fortress hubs, allowing the airline to maintain higher prices and therefore higher profits at that airport. PFCs were intended to give airports a tool for protecting themselves from monopolization by airlines. FAA/OST Task Force, 1999, p. 54, explains,

> Congress clearly understood that PFCs could be important for enhancing competition at airports. During congressional hearings leading to passage of the PFC statute, statements by the Secretary of Transportation and others frequently referred to the competitive benefits of PFCs. For instance, GAO testified that PFCs would shift more control over airport expansion decisions from airlines back to airports by reducing airports' need for airline

---

[23] *Limit pricing* occurs when an incumbent temporarily reduces prices to deter the entry of competitors. Although this strategy reduces profits in the short term, it enables the incumbent to charge prices that are higher than competitive market rates in the future, once the threat of competition is gone. In some cases, the incumbent's ability to engage in limit pricing should a competitor attempt to enter the market could be sufficient to deter potential competition.

approval of capital projects. Further, a PFC would be especially useful at airports where one or two airlines control most of the traffic or most of the gates and other essential facilities through restrictive leases.

Because airline approval is not required for PFC-funded projects, airports can use PFCs to fund projects that would not normally be supported by incumbent airlines, such as terminal expansions that provide gates for new airline entrants. Further, any facility funded with PFCs cannot be leased on an exclusive-use basis. There has been a significant trend away from exclusive-use leases over the past several decades. We do not know whether PFCs initiated the decline in exclusive-use leases, but this systemwide trend might have weakened or eliminated a mechanism that airlines previously had available for keeping out competition.

We are not aware of any analysis that estimates the effect of PFCs on competition or prices at airports or city markets.[24] In this section, we provide such an analysis by looking at how PFCs, particularly those targeted at enhancing competition, have affected the HHI and ticket prices of the individual airports and markets that use them. We emphasize that this analysis is unable to address the systemwide impact of the decline in exclusive-use leases; we only measure the average impact of individual projects.

Data and Methodology

Since the inception of PFCs in 1991, 16,343 projects have been approved. Each project is matched to one of the five PFC objectives: competition, capacity, noise, safety, or security. Approximately 55 percent of projects (8,981) are for capacity improvements, and another 36 percent (5,826) are for safety improvements. Only 1 percent of PFC projects (181) have competition as their objective; 165 of these had been completed as of 2018. However, according to project descriptions and conversations with staff at the FAA and airports, we understand that a single project can achieve multiple objectives and that airports may label projects at their discretion so long as the label matches an objective of the project. Projects such as terminal expansions are thus interchangeably labeled as being for competition or capacity. Because of this overlap, we examine both competition and capacity projects, although we specifically focus on those capacity projects identified as "enhancing" capacity, as opposed to "preserving" it.[25] The 3,156 projects that potentially enhance competition provide the baseline data for this analysis.

Interviews with stakeholders yielded differing points of view on whether airlines sometimes press airports to use up their PFC funds on projects not related to competition. The data provide mixed evidence on this point. Medium-hub and non-hub airports with less competition (i.e., above-average HHI) are indeed less likely to use PFCs for enhancing competition.

---

[24] The only related estimate we are aware of is a finding regarding exclusive-use and preferential-use leases from Morrison and Winston, 2000, p. 32, which states that "[f]ares are $3.8 billion [in 1998 Q4 dollars] higher annually because of the limited availability of gates at many major and midsize airports." This value is based on a cross-sectional comparison of fares for the 1,000 most heavily traveled routes in 1998 and is, at best, correlational and not causal. The authors only observe gate lease agreements for 41 airports; their assumption that there are zero exclusive–use lease gates at other airports in their sample likely biases the estimate. Despite these concerns, this statistic remains widely cited, including in recent congressional testimony.

[25] Out of the 8,981 projects with a designated objective of capacity, 2,975 (33.13 percent) are labeled as "enhancing" capacity.

However, this pattern does not appear to hold among small-hub and large-hub airports. Additional analysis on this point can be found in Appendix K.

Figure 6.13 provides an example of the data used in the analysis. Figure 6.13 presents the aggregate HHI for airports in four markets: Detroit, Michigan;[26] Pittsburgh, Pennsylvania; Chicago, Illinois; and Atlanta, Georgia. Vertical red lines mark points in time in which at least one potentially competition-enhancing project was completed.[27] Numerous projects have been completed in the Detroit market that potentially enhance competition, as is the case for many other markets (e.g., San Francisco, California; New Orleans, Louisiana; and Chicago, Illinois). In all, for the period between 1993 and 2018, there are 398 distinct markets.

As discussed in Chapter Two, we chose to analyze competition at the market level because airlines serving the same market are often competing for the same passengers, even if they are operating out of different airports. Therefore, an expansion at one airport in a market has the potential to affect airline pricing at another airport in the market.

We used a basic linear regression framework to estimate the effect of PFC competition-enhancing projects on competition (as measured by the HHI) and average ticket fares. With this approach, we compare the HHI and average ticket fares in markets at several time inter-

Figure 6.13
Herfindahl-Hirschman Index and Potentially Competition-Enhancing PFC Projects in Four Markets

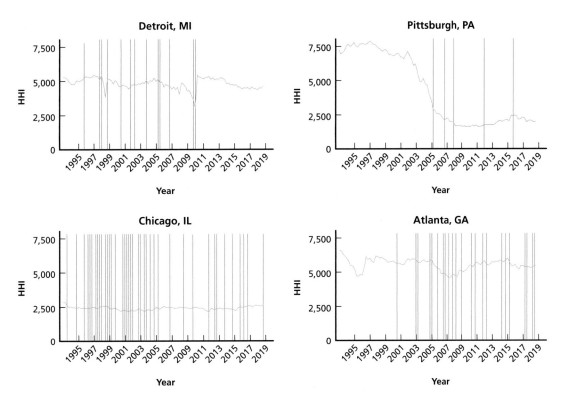

SOURCE: RAND analysis of BTS, 2019c, and PFC project data provided by the FAA.

---

[26] The airports in the Detroit, Michigan, market include Detroit Metro Wayne County, Coleman A. Young Municipal, and Willow Run.

[27] There are instances in which multiple projects are completed in the same quarter.

vals before and after the completion of their PFC projects to the HII and average ticket fares in markets that have not recently completed PFC projects. We make this comparison for five windows of time within a four-year period on either side of project completion:

- seven to 16 quarters before project completion
- two to six quarters before project completion
- one quarter before to one quarter after project completion
- two to six quarters after project completion
- seven to 16 quarters after project completion.

These windows allow us to get a sense of whether and how PFC projects change the HHI and ticket fares over time. Because the scale of PFC projects varies widely, we make this comparison for two sizes of projects: (1) projects with a cost between the 25th and 75th percentile of the distribution of costs among all PFC competition and capacity-expansion project costs, and (2) projects with a cost above the 75th percentile of the distribution.[28] A detailed description of the statistical methodology can be found in Appendix K.

Results

Overall, our analysis cannot determine whether an individual PFC project affects competition and prices. However, we can conclude that any effects of individual PFC projects are, on average, small relative to other factors, such as local economic conditions and airline hubbing decisions. Tables and figures documenting the results are provided in Appendix K.

Our estimates suggest that, for both moderately sized and large projects, a market's HHI might be slightly lower (i.e., the market is more competitive) two to six quarters after the project is completed and might be slightly higher (i.e., the market is less competitive) seven to 16 quarters after the project is completed. However, neither of these estimates is statistically different from zero. No single PFC project is likely to significantly alter the competitive landscape in an individual market, although it is possible that several PFC projects over time could build up to a larger aggregate effect. Relatively rapid increases or decreases in competition at airports are usually associated with consolidation and changes in airline hubbing decisions. For example, the steep decline in the HHI in Pittsburgh seen in Figure 6.13 occurs before any potentially competition-enhancing PFC projects are completed. That decline in the HHI reflects USAir's decision to cease using Pittsburgh as a hub, which is discussed further in Chapter Eight.

Our conclusions regarding the effects of PFC projects on prices are similar. Overall, the range of uncertainty is relatively large. None of the estimates are statistically different from zero, nor are there clear trends in prices over time before or after PFC project completion. The only clear conclusion is that no single PFC project is likely to significantly alter prices in a particular market.

---

[28] In all cases, we account for other factors that may make the HHI unusually high or low in certain years or in certain markets.

Perspectives on Changes in the PFC Program

Policymakers have proposed several possible changes to the PFC cap in recent years. Options include a fixed increase, indexing to inflation, and removing the cap entirely. The Obama administration's FYs 2014 through 2017 budgets proposed increasing the maximum allowable PFC to $8 (USDOT, 2016). An early version of the Senate's FY 2018 appropriations bill for the USDOT would have increased the cap to $8.50 (S. 1655). Legislation introduced in 2019 (H.R. 3791), with bipartisan cosponsors, would eliminate the PFC cap entirely. The same legislation also was introduced in 2017 (H.R. 1265).[29] All of these proposed changes would have been made in tandem with eliminating AIP entitlement funding for large-hub airports. Both the Obama administration proposal and H.R. 3791 would reduce the AIP obligation limitation to less than $3 billion per year, though the latter would do so while simultaneously reducing the trigger level that doubles AIP passenger entitlements, resulting in substantially less AIP money available for discretionary grants.

At a congressional hearing in March 2019, a representative of an airport trade association called for raising the PFC cap to $8.50 and indexing it to inflation (McGraw, 2019).[30] This proposal was opposed in written testimony submitted for the same hearing by an airline trade association (A4A, 2019).[31] One of the considerations of this study is "the impact to passengers and airports of indexing the [PFC] for inflation." We consider the impact of indexing the PFC cap to inflation, increasing the cap along with or instead of indexing, or eliminating the cap altogether. We describe the decisions that would determine the ultimate impacts of any change in more detail below. In general, a higher PFC cap means more potential PFC revenues available to be used for infrastructure projects, greater potential for airport-level variation in PFC levels, and larger possible impacts on passengers.

Policymaker Decisions

The effects of raising the PFC cap would depend on exactly what policymakers do. They could set a higher cap without indexing this cap to inflation moving forward. They could set a higher cap and index that cap to inflation. They could index to inflation from the current $4.50 cap. Or they could eliminate the PFC cap altogether and allow airports to decide how much to charge (though, assuming other PFC requirements are not altered, airports would still need to seek FAA approval for projects that would be funded with these PFC revenues in order to impose a PFC). Another possibility is to set the cap at where it would be if the $4.50 cap had been indexed to inflation when it was first established in 2000, and then continue the indexing in future years.

If policymakers chose to index to inflation, they would need to determine which measure of inflation. In past analyses of potential PFC changes, the GAO has used the CPI, calling it a "federal inflation index standard" (GAO, 2014c, p. 9). Using the CPI would hold constant

---

[29] Rep. Peter DeFazio, the current chairman of the House Transportation and Infrastructure Committee and a cosponsor of H.R. 1265 in the 115th Congress, was not a cosponsor of H.R. 3791 as of September 2019.

[30] Although airport support for lifting the PFC cap is widespread, it is not universal. Officials we spoke with at one airport expressed concerns that lifting the cap could negatively affect smaller airports. Many small-hub airports have a large portion of their flights go to a small number of larger airports, and increases in PFCs at those large hubs could increase the cost of flying out of the smaller airport, even if that smaller airport does not impose a higher PFC.

[31] A4A represents most, but not all, major air carriers in the United States. Delta is not a member.

the real-dollar impact to passengers. However, to the extent that increases in costs for infrastructure projects increase faster than general consumer price inflation, indexing to the CPI could nonetheless result in eroding the purchasing power of the maximum PFC, from an airport standpoint. As noted earlier, had the $4.50 PFC cap been indexed to inflation starting in 2000, it would have risen by 2018 to $6.72 if indexed to the CPI and to $7.44 if indexed to a construction materials index.

In addition, policymakers would need to decide whether to make any corresponding changes to the AIP, as have been proposed in the past alongside PFC cap increases. If, for example, the PFC cap were raised or eliminated in tandem with eliminating AIP entitlements for a class of airports (e.g., large or medium hubs) or eliminating AIP eligibility entirely for these airports (entitlement or discretionary), that would affect airports differently than PFC cap increases that do not alter AIP eligibility standards. For example, airports might increase their PFC rates higher and faster if they are losing AIP grant funds in the process. Moreover, if policymakers were to decrease the excise tax levels that generate revenue to the AATF in tandem with authorizing higher PFC levels, this could offset some of the impacts on passengers.

Finally, raising or eliminating the PFC cap could come in tandem with changes to the amount of each PFC retained by the airlines. This level is currently $0.11 per PFC collection plus retained interest, which is where it has been since 2004, when a rulemaking process that was initiated following passage of the 2000 FAA reauthorization was completed (USDOT, 2004b).

Potential Reactions by Airports, Airlines, and Passengers
Once the policy is set, airports would need to decide where to set their PFC and decide the pace of any increases. History suggests that airport-level PFCs will tend to rise to the maximum allowable level (as shown in Figure 6.2) but that this increase could occur over a period of years. This is what occurred when the cap was raised from $3 to $4.50 starting in 2001. Currently, just one large-hub airport (CLT) does not charge $4.50. A GAO analysis of potential PFC increases to $8 and $8.50 assumed that airports that currently charge a PFC would increase their PFC to the new cap in short order, "based on near universal adoption of the current maximum by nearly all of the largest airports" (GAO, 2014c, p. 12). Airport representatives we spoke with disagree with the assumption that PFC rates will automatically rise to the highest allowed level, emphasizing that any increases would need to be connected to PFC-eligible projects and be approved by the FAA.

Waiving the PFC cap entirely would be more likely to lead to airport-level variation in PFC charges and could involve airports competing with each other on the basis of their PFCs to attract passengers and airlines. This competitive force would be most relevant for attracting layover traffic and for competition between airports that are in close enough proximity that airlines or travelers could substitute one for the other to reach a given destination. By contrast, airports that are the only airport in the market, especially if it is a market with substantial origin and destination (O&D) traffic, might have more leverage to increase their PFCs while maintaining airline demand to fly from them.

In an uncapped PFC scenario, airport-level competition, along with a continued need for the FAA to approve the projects toward which the additional PFC revenues would go, would serve as the brake on PFC increases, rather than a federally set cap. We note that Canada currently does not cap the levels at which airports may set their airport improvement fees, which are broadly similar to the U.S. PFC. In Canada, though, these charges are typically limited to originating (not connecting) passengers (Air Canada, undated). Per-passenger airport improvement fees at some airports exceed 25 Canadian dollars (or a little less than 20 U.S. dollars as of this writing), and some observers believe that these fees are deterring air travel or causing passengers in close enough proximity to travel by car to the United States in search of lower airfares (Moreau, 2018; Pallini, 2019). An uncapped PFC could have similar consequences if market forces were inadequate to hold down the rate that airports charge.

There is a large amount of literature on how price changes might affect passenger demand for air travel. In its past work, the GAO has used a demand elasticity estimate of –0.8 for its baseline estimate of the impact on travel of a PFC increase, meaning a 1 percent increase of the total cost of a ticket would decrease the number of travelers by 0.8 percent (GAO, 2014c). Increases at a single airport or for a single route might result in a larger decrease in the number of travelers for that airport or route than if there was an equal increase in price across all airports and routes. The GAO models a range of elasticity estimates from –0.65 to –1.122 (GAO, 2014c). Some observers who shared their views with us pointed to the rising number of enplanements despite airlines' use of baggage fees and other ancillary fees. They argued that the most reasonable demand elasticity assumption is that there will be no negative impact at all. We note, however, that enplanements increasing as ancillary fees are imposed does not mean that there was not an impact; enplanements might have increased faster in the absence of the fees, and separating out ancillary fees does not necessarily imply a change in total ticket price.[32]

Although disentangling the numerous moving pieces is challenging, and it is not certain that prices that passengers see would increase at precisely the same rate as a potential PFC increase (just as they have not increased dollar-for-dollar with ancillary fees), we expect that, all else being equal, a higher PFC would deter some travelers at the margin. In general, the literature suggests that business travelers would be less responsive to price changes than leisure travelers and that demand for long-haul flights would drop off less than for short flights (InterVISTAS Consulting Inc., 2007). Notably, the same increase in dollar terms would constitute a different increase in percentage terms depending on the price of the ticket. This means that flights with lower-priced tickets (e.g., those of LCCs) might have a larger passenger response in terms of a decrease in demand for travel. Passengers with connections also would be hit harder by a PFC increase than travelers with nonstop flights, since the charge is imposed on each leg of a two-flight trip. These larger effects on connecting passengers could be mitigated if policymakers were to preserve the existing PFC cap for connecting flights and only allow the PFC at an airport of origin to increase.[33]

---

[32] Passengers may be less sensitive to changes in ancillary fees (e.g., baggage charges) in part because these costs are less salient than mandatory fees or costs included in the initially advertised fare (such as the PFC). For example, see the discussion in Bradley and Feldman, 2018, on how a change that required mandatory taxes and fees to be included in the initially advertised fare affected tax incidence.

[33] Such a policy would reduce the additional value of a cap increase for airports that serve an especially high share of connecting passengers. However, origin passengers make up the majority of passengers at most airports. In 2018, origin passengers made up more than 90 percent of passengers at most medium-, small-, and non-hub airports. Large hubs have more layover passengers. In 2018, more than 80 percent of all passengers were origin passengers at half of the large-hub airports, and more than 50 percent of all passengers were origin passengers at all but three airports of any size. The exceptions were CLT (30 percent origin passengers), Hartsfield-Jackson Atlanta International (41 percent origin passengers), and Dallas/Fort Worth International (48 percent origin passengers). Estimates are based on RAND analysis of BTS, 2019d.

By contrast, if increased PFCs are used to successfully improve the quality of the air travel experience at that airport, it is possible this use could potentially mitigate or offset the extent to which higher prices dissuade passengers from air travel. To that end, it is important to keep in mind that a demand elasticity reflects the impact of a change in price assuming quality is unchanged. If quality improves in tandem with a price increase, the demand response could be lower. Survey findings on passenger views on a potential increase in fees to fund airport infrastructure are mixed, with variation likely stemming in part from the precise language used. One survey by a travel association found that 58 percent of passengers "are willing to pay up to $4 more per ticket to fund airport improvements projects that would enable airports to accommodate more airlines, modernize facilities or reduce delays in and around the airport" (U.S. Travel Association, 2015). Another survey conducted on behalf of an airline association found that 80 percent of U.S. voters "oppose increasing the PFC tax" and that 65 percent "are satisfied with the quality of the country's airports" (Whitman Insight Strategies, 2019). As with all surveys, the way in which the same questions are framed and anchored can have a large effect on the response.

Another possibility is that a higher PFC cap could allow airports to draw more on PFC revenue rather than other revenue to fund projects, potentially resulting in airports reducing rates and charges for airlines and other tenants. Airlines and other tenants could then pass on these savings or otherwise reduce their costs to avoid losing customers. However, these changes are less likely in a noncompetitive market. The significant lack of competition noted in Chapter Two makes such pass-through savings unlikely.

How Much Additional PFC Revenue Could an Increase in the PFC Cap Yield?

To be clear, how much more PFC revenue airports could collect if the PFC cap were increased, indexed to inflation, or eliminated depends on the complex chain of decisions described in the previous sections. There is uncertainty with respect to when, or if, all airports that could raise their PFCs to a new, higher cap would do so (with FAA approval and assuming sufficient PFC-eligible projects toward which the new revenues would go). There is a range of elasticity estimates of how traveler demand would respond to an increase in the PFC. And it is unclear whether a PFC increase would allow for a decrease in rates and charges that might be passed on partially to passengers or whether a PFC cap increase might be enacted in tandem with a reduction in the rates of excise taxes funding the AATF to mitigate the effect on passengers of the PFC increase.

However, we can estimate the increase in potential PFC revenues over the next five years (2020 to 2024) by making some assumptions.[34] Specifically, we assume that the PFC cap is increased immediately (effective January 1, 2020) and that all hub airports could immediately increase their PFC to the new, higher cap. We consider this increase while holding all else equal and therefore assume that the increase translates dollar-for-dollar to higher ticket prices for passengers. For simplicity, we assume that each enplanement (i.e., each leg of a trip that involves a plane change) costs $150,[35] such that a per-enplanement PFC increase of $1 would be a 0.67 percent increase in the price to travel that leg of the trip. We recognize that this simpli-

[34] For this analysis, as with the discussion on potential PFC revenues earlier, we limit the scope to hub airports (small, medium, and large).

[35] In Chapter Two, we noted that the average round-trip domestic airfare (in the contiguous United States) was $432 in 2018. Assuming an equal mix of nonstop and one-connection itineraries yields an average per-leg cost of $144.

fication ignores important differences in prices for and effects on nonstop and connecting passengers, with connecting passengers paying multiple PFCs, but it is important for modeling the demand response. Specifically, applying a demand elasticity of –0.8 (the baseline value used by GAO, 2014c)[36] means that a $1 increase in the PFC would result in enplanements being lower than they otherwise would be by a factor of 0.67 × 0.8, or about 0.54 percent. If the cost per enplanement (i.e., per leg) was lower than $150, the demand response would be larger (i.e., the difference between the number of enplanements with and without the PFC increase would be larger), and vice versa.

We then apply these assumptions to the TAF data we used to generate the estimates of potential PFC revenues under the existing $4.50 cap presented earlier.[37] We assume that enplanements will be 0.54 percent lower than the TAF estimates if the PFC cap is increased by $1 because of the passenger demand response. We also present estimates for a cap increase of $4 (up to $8.50), again assuming that all hub airports can immediately increase their PFCs to this level beginning in 2020. We assume that this $4 PFC increase will make each enplanement 2.67 percent more expensive and reduce enplanements by 2.67 × 0.8, or 2.14 percent, from the level they would be in the absence of the PFC increase.

Under these assumptions, we estimate that an increase in the PFC cap of $1 would enable hub airports to collect up to $810 million in additional potential PFC revenue in 2020 ($597 million just at large hubs) and up to $4.2 billion over the 2020 to 2024 period ($3.1 billion at large hubs). We estimate that an increase in the cap of $4 (to $8.50) would enable hub airports to collect up to $3.2 billion in additional potential PFC revenue in 2020 ($2.3 billion just at large hubs) and up to $16.7 billion over the 2020 to 2024 period ($12.3 billion at large hubs). For context, hub airports in 2018 collected about $3.4 billion in PFCs and spent about $13.5 billion on capital expenditures.

As Table 6.2 shows, these estimates are sensitive to the demand elasticity assumptions, with additional potential PFC revenue across all hubs over the five-year period ranging from $16.2 billion (with a –1.25 elasticity) to $17.5 billion in additional potential revenues (with no assumed demand response).

Summary of Findings

The PFC is an important complement to AIP grants and other sources of funding for airport infrastructure. Although the AIP is designed to funnel resources to smaller airports, these airports earn little revenue from PFCs, and noncommercial airports have no ability to collect

---

[36] We recognize that the demand response will vary by category of passenger (i.e., business travelers will have a less elastic response than leisure passengers) and by route (i.e., the response is less elastic for long-haul flights than for short-haul flights, with greater ability to substitute other forms of travel). We use demand elasticities that do not distinguish between these categories for this analysis for two reasons. First, the elasticity estimates from InterVISTAS Consulting Inc., 2007, and those included in the GAO, 2014c, analysis reflect the overall demand response, accounting for differential effects across categories of passengers and routes. Second, the TAF does not separate among categories of travelers or the distance of routes when estimating enplanements, meaning that we would need to make additional assumptions to separately estimate the effects on future travel.

[37] We apply the same assumptions as in the commitments analysis earlier to map from TAF estimates of enplanements to enplanements that are charged a PFC. Specifically, we assume that 10 percent of domestic enplanements and 4 percent of international enplanements are not charged a PFC, consistent with GAO, 2014c.

Table 6.2
Additional Potential PFC Revenue with $1 and $4 PFC Cap Increases for Small-, Medium-, and Large-Hub Airports, 2020 and 2020–2024 (billions)

Assumed Elasticity of Demand	All Hub Airports		Large-Hub Airports	
	2020	2020–2024	2020	2020–2024
$1 PFC Increase				
None	$0.8	$4.4	$0.6	$3.2
−0.65	$0.8	$4.3	$0.6	$3.1
−0.80	$0.8	$4.2	$0.6	$3.1
−1.25	$0.8	$4.2	$0.6	$3.1
$4 PFC Increase				
None	$3.3	$17.5	$2.5	$12.9
−0.65	$3.2	$16.8	$2.4	$12.4
−0.80	$3.2	$16.7	$2.3	$12.3
−1.25	$3.1	$16.2	$2.3	$12.0

SOURCE: RAND calculations using TAF data (FAA, 2019b).
NOTE: We assume that airports could immediately raise their PFC by the specified amount, effective January 1, 2020, and that the entirety of the increase is passed through to passengers, holding all else equal. Revenue calculations use GAO, 2014c, assumptions on the share of enplanements not charged a PFC. Additional potential PFC revenue is calculated by taking the estimated PFC revenue under a $5.50 or $8.50 cap (with a passenger demand response) and subtracting potential PFC revenue under the existing $4.50 cap, which assumes enplanements will be as projected in the TAF. We estimate additional PFC revenue with three demand elasticity assumptions: −0.65, −0.80, and −1.25, roughly corresponding to the range and baseline values used by GAO, 2014c. We also show the values for an elasticity of zero.

PFCs at all. By contrast, the PFC program has proved to be extremely popular among larger airports, not only because they can earn vastly more by collecting PFCs than they forgo in AIP grants by doing so, but also because of the greater flexibilities that airports have when using PFCs (e.g., PFCs can be used to pay debt service). All medium- and large-hub airports currently charge a PFC and all but one in each category charge at the maximum allowable rate of $4.50 per enplanement. PFC revenues reached their highest level in 2018, both in nominal dollars and adjusted for inflation using the CPI. A combination of factors contributed to this growth over time: an increase in airports charging a PFC, an increase in the share charging at $4.50, and an increase in enplanements at these airports.

However, the purchasing power of a dollar of PFC revenues has eroded because of inflation. To have the same purchasing power as in 2000, the per-enplanement cap would need to be about $6.70 today if adjusted for inflation using the CPI, or about $7.50 if adjusted using an index for construction materials. Therefore, although the aggregate amount of PFC revenues across all airports collecting them is higher than it has ever been, there are also more passengers traveling through those airports than ever before, and each dollar of PFC revenues contributed by those passengers buys just 60 percent to 70 percent of what it did in 2000. It is unclear whether the erosion of the PFC dollar is offset by returns to scale or outweighed by infrastructure demands, which grow with operations rather than enplanements.

Under the existing PFC cap of $4.50, all large-hub airports but one (which currently does not charge at the $4.50 cap) have committed the entirety of their PFC revenues through

2022 to already approved projects, while 18 of 30 large hubs have committed all their revenues through at least 2030. We estimate that 86 percent of potential large-hub PFC revenues are locked up in the 2020s and that a bit less than half of potential revenues are accounted for over the 2020 to 2045 period. Medium- and small-hub airports are somewhat less constrained, with about 60 percent of potential revenues over the next decade and a little more than 25 percent of potential revenues over the 2020 to 2045 period already committed. When considering commitments of future PFC revenues, it is important to keep in mind that these might be going to pay down debt on projects that are, in fact, already completed. Over the lifetime of the PFC program, more than 70 percent of approved collections have been for debt service (including principal and interest) rather than used on a pay-as-you-go basis for projects. Therefore, the degree of commitment of future revenues could understate the degree to which airports are constrained in using the PFC to fund their needs. Further, although more PFC revenues are not yet committed in the 2030s and 2040s, pulling that money forward to use for infrastructure projects in the 2020s would require borrowing against this expected revenue and incurring financing costs that cut into the amount of money available for the projects themselves.

Raising the PFC cap would provide airports with additional capacity to fund more projects on an earlier time frame, incurring lower financing costs. Some airports also might use a cap increase to pay down existing debt faster, and thus reduce their interest costs. Specifically, we estimate that raising the PFC cap by $1 would increase potential PFC revenue available to hub airports over the next five years (in total) by $4.2 billion ($3.1 billion at large hubs), while an increase in the cap to $8.50 would increase potential PFC revenue at hub airports by $16.7 billion ($12.3 billion at large hubs). Collecting these additional revenues would require that airports seek and obtain FAA approval of the projects toward which they would go. Increases in individual airport PFC levels would not be automatic and might not be universal, depending on the level at which the cap is set.

A major impetus for the establishment of the PFC program in the early 1990s was to provide airports with access to a source of funding over which they could exercise greater control. Although airports are still required to secure FAA approval to collect PFCs and spend on particular projects, they are not required to gain approval from incumbent airline tenants, who might choose to veto projects funded by other sources by exercising MII provisions in their airport-airline agreements. One goal of the PFC legislation, and an allowable project objective, is to enhance airline competition, such as through terminal expansion projects that provide gates for new airline entrants. Competition is intended to benefit the traveling public through more choice and lower fares. We attempted to estimate the effect of PFC projects on competition, but our analysis does not reach a conclusion as to whether a particular PFC project can have an impact on competition or prices at an individual airport. Relatively rapid increases or decreases in competition at airports are usually associated with consolidation through mergers, acquisitions, and bankruptcies, or with changes in airline hubbing decisions.

CHAPTER SEVEN

Role of Bond Markets in Airport Infrastructure Funding

One of the financial tools available to airports for infrastructure projects is debt financing. Bonds are used to finance large capital-intensive projects, allowing airports to pay for the cost of the project upfront and then pay bondholders back (with interest) over a long period. Collectively, bond proceeds and other forms of debt have been the largest sources of funding for airport capital projects for many years (Nichol, 2007). In 2017, total bond proceeds to the NPIAS commercial service airports were $9.5 billion. For comparison, the total revenue from PFCs in 2017 was $3.3 billion, and the total in grants received from the AIP and other sources was $2.1 billion (FAA, undated c).

In this chapter, we describe the types of bonds used by airports and their issuers, how bond proceeds are used and repaid, and how the credit rating agencies rate the risks associated with airport bonds. Note that nearly all airports are operating in the municipal (tax-exempt) bond market, although there are a few exceptions of airports using taxable bonds instead.

Bond Issuers

The issuer of an airport bond depends on the oversight structure of the airport. The most common type of oversight structure is an airport authority, typically composed of board members who have been appointed by the top public official of the jurisdiction. Most airport authorities have been given the right to borrow by their respective local or state government sponsor. If a municipal government is the oversight entity of an airport, the municipal government can issue bonds to operate the airport and finance infrastructure needs. The type of bond being issued depends on the type of issuer. For example, general obligation (GO) bonds are issued by state and local governments and therefore are backed by the full faith and credit of the issuing government. Special facility bonds typically are issued by private companies for construction of non-aeronautical facilities, such as parking lots. The private issuer will then retain some or all of the revenue generated from such facilities.

Types of Bonds

Four major types of bonds are used for airport infrastructure: general airport revenue bonds (GARBs), PFC bonds, GO bonds, and special facility bonds. The first two types of bonds are backed by the revenue generated by the issuing airports, whereas the other two types are issued by external parties, such as municipal governments and development companies. Different types of bonds have different purposes and conditions, explained below in detail.

General Airport Revenue Bonds

GARBs are bonds issued by airport operators and backed by the revenues generated by the airports. Revenue bonds are the most frequently used type of bonds for airport infrastructure projects. Airports with annual enplanements of 500,000 or more prefer issuing revenue bonds over GO bonds. In these cases, the airport authority is the issuer of the GARB and has more autonomy in the process. Larger airports also generally have more-stable revenue streams, a significant factor that credit rating agencies and bond buyers consider when determining the creditworthiness of the issuer. For these reasons, GARBs are more frequently used by larger airports than smaller airports.

The covenants of individual GARBs specify the projects for which the proceeds of the bond can be spent. The types of projects can be broad and include terminal and airway construction, purchase, renovation, and installation. Other than funding for infrastructure and capital improvement projects, GARBs also can be used to pay down other debt obligations and can be deposited to interest-bearing accounts and later applied to future interest payments. Because of the long-term nature of airport infrastructure projects, GARBs are issued with maturity dates in increments of 10, 20, and 30 years.

Similar to the usage of the proceeds, the covenants of the GARBs specify the sources of revenue that can be used for repayment of the debt.[1] *Revenue* is often defined broadly to include all aeronautical and non-aeronautical revenues derived from the operation and management of the airport. However, specifications as to what is included and excluded as revenue changes from bond to bond. Some bonds exclude PFCs, AIP grants, and other grants as payable sources; others might include them. Similarly, a bond can add a revenue source, such as an aviation fuel tax.

Passenger Facility Charge Bonds

PFC bonds are backed by the PFC revenues collected by the airport operator, with FAA approval. Because the total amount that can be collected with PFCs is directly related to the number of enplanements, larger airports are considered more favorable in the bond market for PFC issuance. When PFCs were first introduced, the bond market had concerns about them being a viable source of revenue.[2] Over time, PFCs have proven to be stable, and the financial industry has come to accept them as a source of revenue that can be used to back bonds.

PFC bonds can take two forms. First is a stand-alone *single-barrel* PFC bond, which is repaid exclusively with PFC revenues. However, this type of PFC bond is rarely used. The second and more frequent form is a *double-barrel* bond, which is repaid using some combination of PFC and other airport revenues and is considered to be a GARB. As such, PFCs are typically used as one of several revenue sources backing a GARB. For large, complex projects, such as terminal expansions, restrictions on PFC use mean that only certain portions of the project can be covered by PFCs, and the fraction of costs that PFCs can cover must be determined before issuing the bond.

---

[1]   See examples of such conditions in Port of Portland, 2017; SFO, 2005; and State of Hawaii, 2010.

[2]   Interview with an airport bond industry expert, June 12, 2019.

The covenants of the individual PFC bonds dictate how the proceeds of the bonds can be used.[3] PFC bonds are used to fund various types of infrastructure projects, from construction to capital improvements of terminals and airways, in conjunction with GARBs. PFC bonds are also used as refunding bonds to pay outstanding balances of other bonds.

Issuance of PFC bonds by an airport operator, in general, does not require airline MII approval (see the section on MII provisions in Chapter Three). However, consultation between the airport and the airlines would have already taken place through the PFC application process for the relevant project. PFCs allow more autonomy and flexibility for airport operators in how the bond proceeds are used.[4] Single-barrel PFC bonds are issued by airport operators for projects that require less consultation from the airlines. For either single- or double-barrel bonds, airports must track the components of the bond proceeds to the specific projects that have been approved for PFC uses.

General Obligation Bonds

GO bonds are typically issued by a state or local government and thus are backed by the taxing power of the government. Therefore, GO bonds usually bear lower interest than GARB bonds. GO bonds for airports can be issued specifically for infrastructure projects for an airport or airports within the issuing government's jurisdiction or as part of a package of other public projects, including but not limited to projects such as installation of traffic signals, construction of playgrounds, and maintenance of public facilities. Because airport operators are not the issuers of GO bonds, they are not included on the balance sheets of airport operators.[5]

However, only a small percentage of commercial service airports rely on GO bonds issued on behalf of the airports. Therefore, it is important to note that GO bonds do not represent a potential, untapped resource for off–balance-sheet financing.[6] Airports with high enplanements have sufficient revenue streams to issue bonds directly or through their respective public authority. Smaller airports that have fewer enplanements do not have direct access to the market. Instead, these airports have their borrowing needs included in general obligation bonds issued by their controlling governmental bodies.

Special Facility Bonds

Special facility bonds are backed by the revenue from the facilities that are being financed by the bonds and that have been designated as special facilities. The revenue generated from the special facilities is excluded from the source of revenue for the repayment of GARBs.

---

[3]   For examples, see Port of Seattle, 2010, and Gallatin Airport Authority, 2009.

[4]   Interview with an airport bond industry expert, June 12, 2019.

[5]   An example of the language governing the legal obligations of a municipal government–issued GO bond is as follows:

> The Bonds are direct and general obligations of the City and shall be payable, as to principal and interest, from any moneys revenues, receipts, income, assets or funds of the City legally available for such purpose, including, but not limited to, the proceeds of a direct annual tax levied by the City in the Bond Ordinance upon all taxable property located in the City sufficient to pay the principal of and interest on the Bonds (City of Chicago, 2014).

[6]   An airport authority might have the authority to levy an ad valorem tax on properties within its jurisdictions, although this is highly uncommon. In such cases, airport authorities can be the issuer of GO bonds, and the bonds are payable through the tax levied. In these cases, the special GO bonds are reported on the airport operators' balance sheets because they are the issuers of the bonds.

Such facilities include rental car centers, terminals, and other leased infrastructure outside the normal fee structures of airports (Hazel et al., 2011). Because of the source of repayments, the usage of proceeds from special facility bonds is limited to construction and improvement of the specific facilities that generate the fees for repayment. One example of a special facility bond is a CFC revenue bond, backed by fees earned from rental car users.

Although airport operators can be issuers of such bonds, third-party conduits, such as development corporations and finance authorities, typically issue special facility bonds. Unless the issuer is the airport operator, these types of bonds are not on the balance sheets of the airport operators. Also, special facility bond covenants state that the lessees of the facilities have the obligation to pay both the principal and interest of the bonds. The covenants exclusively state that the bonds are only secured and payable from the revenue earned or fees generated by the lessees from the specific special facilities for which the bonds are being issued and are not secured by any other source of revenue at the airports (and this is generally higher risk, and lower rated, than a GARB pledge). The conduits are used to access the municipal markets and, in most cases, qualify for tax-exempt financing.

Private Activity Bonds

In the municipal bond market, a bond is considered a private activity bond if more than 10 percent of the bond proceeds are to be used for private entities and if at least the same percentage of the principal and interest payments are backed by the property used by the private entities (IRS, 2018). Many airport bonds, although issued by public entities (such as municipal governments and airport authorities), are considered private activity bonds because the infrastructure development funded by the bonds is for private entities, such as airlines, to use and profit from (Tang, 2019). An example of such a bond is a bond issued to fund the infrastructure to connect passengers from terminals to other transportation facilities, such as parking lots, car rentals, and rail transportation. However, airport bonds are typically classified as qualified private activity bonds because of the extent to which the infrastructure development is for facilities used by the public. As qualified private activity bonds, these airport bonds are subject to special tax treatment and therefore are frequently used by the market. This point is discussed in more detail in the following section.

Tax Treatment

The tax treatment of the interest earned from holding a bond plays a significant role in the interest rate offered by the bond issuer. The average difference between yields offered by AAA-grade corporate bonds and tax-exempt bonds of comparable grade from 2006 to 2016 is 0.65 percentage points (Maguire and Hughes, 2018). Even though tax-exempt bonds offer lower interest rates than taxable bonds, they can be attractive to many investors because the earned interest income is exempt from certain federal taxes.[7] At the same time, the issuer of

---

[7] Two types of tax exemptions are common in airport-related bonds. One is the exemption from the federal income tax. Although most airport bonds are issued by governments and public authorities, including airport operators, they are considered private activity bonds because some of the proceeds benefit private entities, such as airlines, and a portion of the revenues generated by the project may go directly or indirectly to the private entities (Tang, 2019). However, the federal tax exemption is allowed for bonds issued with the purpose of using 95 percent of the net proceeds for airports (26 U.S.C. § 142). The second type of tax exemption is related to the alternative minimum tax (AMT). The AMT is a

the bond is able to lower its cost of borrowing by tapping into the tax-exempt bond market. In effect, U.S. taxpayers are subsidizing the borrowing costs of tax-exempt bond issuers, and as such, these bonds are another form of federal support for airport development.[8]

Capital Market Acceptability and Credit Ratings

In the municipal bond market, the vast majority of airport bonds are rated as investment-grade bonds. A bond is rated as *investment grade* by the credit rating agencies when the risk of default is low. Investment-grade bonds are those bonds that have bond ratings, from one or more of the major credit rating agencies, that are higher than Baa3 for Moody's, BBB– for Standard and Poor's, and BBB– for Fitch. With a lower risk of default, the issuers of investment-grade bonds are able to issue bonds at lower interest rates and still generate demand in the bond market. Therefore, the cost of debt is considered to be lower than it is for the non–investment-grade issuers.

Of the 8,054 municipal bonds that include the word "airport" in the bond description (as of June 2019) in the Electronic Municipal Market Access (EMMA) database of the Municipal Securities Rulemaking Board (MSRB),[9] only 25 bonds were rated below investment grade by one of the three major credit agencies: Moody's, Standard and Poor's, and Fitch (MSRB, undated). Also, in Fitch's database of more than 70 U.S. airports rated by the agency, only one airport rated below investment grade.

Credit rating agencies and the market assess the creditworthiness of airport bonds using a variety of measures.[10] These measures include airport-specific factors, such as the issuing airport's ability to generate revenue compared with its annual debt service requirement, the level of enplanements compared with the amount of indebtedness, the ratio of annual revenue generated to total indebtedness, and the quality of the airlines that operate in the airport. Other factors include the issuing airport's debt structure and its infrastructure project plans. Regional economic factors, such as the outlook for the regional economy and the demand for airport services from the region, are also important and are analyzed when rating an airport bond. The market has a tendency to favor O&D airports over hub airports because the demand from the regional economy is considered more stable than the demand created from the designation of a hub-and-spoke network.[11]

---

provision of the tax code that ensures individuals pay a minimum level of tax above what might have resulted from various deductions and exemptions under standard federal income tax rules (Maguire and Hughes, 2018). Interest earned from airport-related private activity bonds, even when considered to be exempt from federal income tax, can be subject to the AMT. However, some private activities, such as projects by nonprofit organizations, may be further qualified to be AMT-exempt (26 U.S.C. § 501[c][3]). The bonds for these private activities have "Non-AMT" in the title of the bond. The same tax treatment and yield relationship applies to AMT and non-AMT bonds, the former providing higher yield (O'Leary, 2019).

[8]   The debate over the current structure of the tax-exempt bond market is long and spirited. For background on the origins and arguments for and against municipal bonds as currently structured, see Greenberg, 2016.

[9]   According to the MSRB EMMA website, the board is "the self-regulatory organization charged by Congress with promoting a fair and efficient municipal security market" (MSRB, undated).

[10]   Key rating drivers include revenue risk by volume, revenue risk by price, infrastructure development/renewal, debt structure, and financial profile (Fitch Ratings, 2018).

[11]   Interview with an airport bond industry expert, June 12, 2019.

Experience has shown that bonds issued by airport operators with sufficient demand to participate in the bond market have been welcomed by investors. According to Standard and Poor's Municipal Bond Airport Index and Municipal Bond Index, airport bonds outperformed the overall municipal bond market from 2012 to 2017 in all years except for 2016 (DiCicco and Given, 2019). Historically, airport bonds have had very low default rates (Shine, 2018), and they have proven to be safe even in the event of a series of defaults by commercial airline companies (Schoenberger, 2003; ACI, 2015).

Bond Proceeds Compared with Other Financing Sources

Airports use bond and other borrowing mechanisms to access future revenue today. Interest is the cost that airports pay to access their future revenue. The ability to borrow helps an airport pay for projects whose costs exceed what the airport could pay for with a single year's revenue. Throughout this report, we do not consider bond proceeds to be revenue because this would double-count revenue (today's bond proceeds are borrowed from tomorrow's revenue).

Comparing current revenue with bond proceeds shows how much of airports' future revenue they access today. Figure 7.1 shows comparisons across airport sizes between total bond proceeds and all sources of revenue, including PFCs and AIP and other grants. Note that the vertical scales differ across the graphs to capture the different magnitudes of airports' budgets. Larger airports are more likely to use the bond market to access their future revenue than smaller airports are, which is consistent with observations in Chapter Four. The ability to borrow from the bond market helps large airports finance expensive infrastructure projects. Smaller airports tend to rely more on grants from government entities to finance expensive infrastructure projects.

For large-hub primary airports, bond proceeds accounted for an average of 28.6 percent of total funding (all revenue sources and bond proceeds) from 2009 to 2017. This share is more than non-aeronautical operating revenue, which averaged 24.4 percent, but less than aeronautical operating revenue, which averaged 32.8 percent. However, as the size of an airport decreases, bond proceeds play a less important role in terms of funding. For example, bond proceeds only accounted for an average of 6 percent of total funding for non-hub primary airports and 3 percent for nonprimary airports from 2009 to 2017.

The total bond proceeds from the 403 commercial service airports that had reported their 2017 financials to CATS as of January 2019 generated $9.5 billion in bond proceeds in 2017.[12] As shown in Table 7.1, large-hub airports accounted for $58.3 billion of the $69.9 billion of bond proceeds generated from 2009 to 2017. Also, the data show that smaller airports have been issuing fewer bonds, whereas larger airports have been issuing more bonds.

The trend of larger airports issuing more bonds is also shown in the trend of larger total indebtedness—i.e., the total amount of debt owed—at year-end. As shown in Figure 7.2, large-

---

[12] Of the 403 airports that had submitted 2017 financial reports as of January 2019, 139 airports reported zero indebtedness at year-end: two large-hub primary airports, one medium-hub primary airports, 14 small-hub primary airports, 75 non-hub primary airports, and 47 nonprimary commercial service airports. Some of these airports, because of special accounting exceptions granted to the airport operator, may not report indebtedness at the individual airport level. For example, the Port Authority of New York and New Jersey, which is the operator of LGA and JFK, does not report the debt related to the two airports when reporting its financials to the FAA. Therefore, the bond proceeds and debt services in this report exclude such airports.

Figure 7.1
Bond Proceeds and Revenue, by Airport Size, 2009–2017

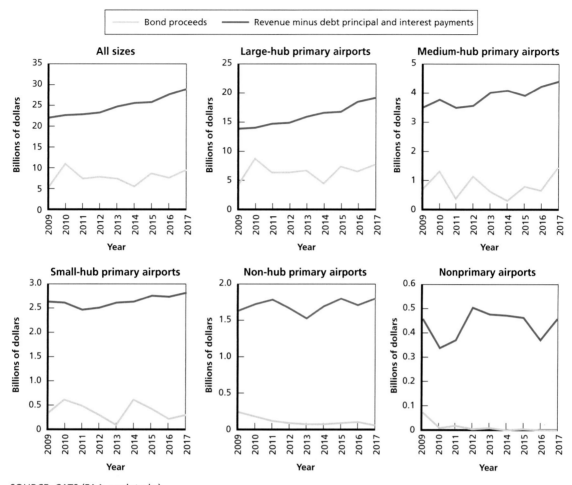

SOURCE: CATS (FAA, undated c).

Table 7.1
Bond Proceeds, by Airport Size, 2009–2017 (millions of dollars)

Airport Type	2009	2010	2011	2012	2013	2014	2015	2016	2017	Total
Large hub	4,073.4	8,722.7	6,324.7	6,285.6	6,668.3	4,505.3	7,441.1	6,569.3	7,734.1	58,324.5
Medium hub	659.2	1,289.6	350.2	1,122.4	597.1	287.7	768.5	625.9	1,447.5	7,148.1
Small hub	320.1	616.2	477.4	306.6	94.4	611.5	414.6	211.8	306.2	3,358.8
Non-hub	229.3	172.3	117.1	81.3	71.8	73.6	83.1	98.6	45.6	972.7
Nonprimary commercial service	72.7	6.9	16.2	4.0	7.5	0.6	3.0	0.4	0.1	111.4
Total	5,354.7	10,807.6	7,285.7	7,800.0	7,439.1	5,478.8	8,710.3	7,505.9	9,533.5	69,915.6

SOURCE: CATS (FAA, undated c).

Figure 7.2
Total Indebtedness at Year End, 2009–2017

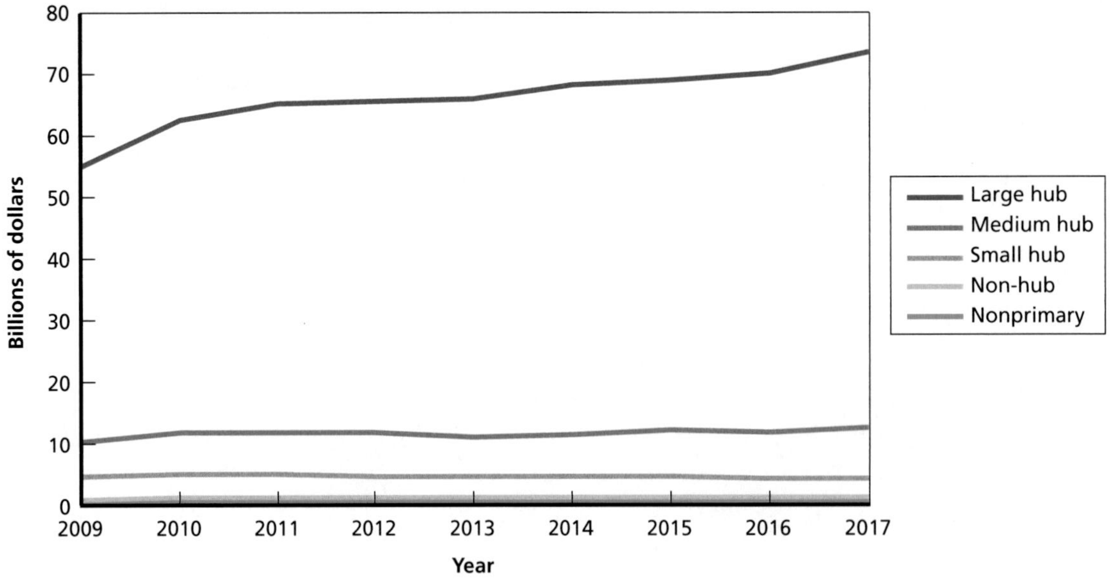

SOURCE: CATS (FAA, undated c).

hub airports are issuing more debt, and their indebtedness consistently increased from 2009 to 2017. The indebtedness of medium-hub, small-hub, and non-hub primary airports and nonprimary airports was generally constant.

The debt-to-revenue ratio is the more appropriate metric for considering the significance of debt levels. Large-hub airports are taking on more debt, but they are also generating more revenue than before. As shown in Figure 7.3, for the airports that have reported both revenue and indebtedness at year-end to the FAA, the average debt-to-revenue ratio for large-hub airports decreased, from 4.12 in 2009 to 3.99 in 2017. The trend is the same for other airport sizes, except for nonprimary airports. The debt-to-revenue ratio for nonprimary airports marginally increased, from 0.72 in 2009 to 0.74 in 2017.

Summary of Findings

The bond market has proven to be a stable source of capital over time for commercial service airports and is likely to remain so, barring changes in the tax code or major market disruptions. Airports that participate in the municipal bond market are considered by the rating agencies to offer investment-grade opportunities with a low risk of default. This fact has allowed airports to leverage the bond market to meet many of their infrastructure needs. However, not all airports participate in the bond market; larger airports have more access to the market than do smaller airports. Because larger airports tend to generate significant and stable amounts of operating revenue, these airports are able to issue bonds backed by revenue on their own. Smaller airports, which generate less operating revenue at less stable rates, are less likely to be attractive to the bond market. Therefore, smaller airports generally depend on local and state governments to gain access to the bond market.

Figure 7.3
Trends in Average Debt-to-Revenue Ratios, 2009–2017

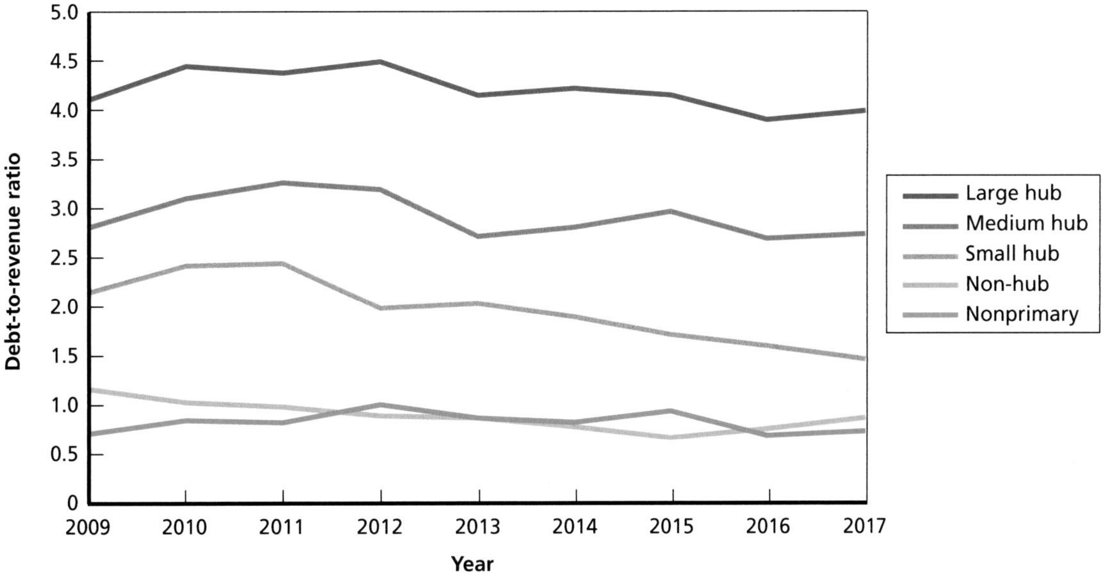

SOURCE: CATS (FAA, undated c).
NOTE: AIP and other grants have been excluded from revenue for this calculation because they cannot be used for repayment of bonds (Tang, 2019, p. 14; 49 U.S.C. § 40117).

From 2009 to 2017, the amount of debt at year-end for large-hub airports consistently increased, whereas the indebtedness of medium-hub, small-hub, and non-hub airports and nonprimary airports was generally constant. However, the revenue generated by large-hub primary airports increased more than their debt at year-end, meaning that their average debt-to-revenue ratio decreased over the period. There is no evidence to suggest that capital flows to airports have declined in recent years or are in jeopardy in the near term. Investment in airport infrastructure at airports with sufficient revenues remains a highly desirable proposition.

CHAPTER EIGHT

Assessing Future Demand and Capacity Constraints

Over the past several decades, the aviation system as a whole has seen larger planes, more flights, and more travelers, as noted in Chapter Two. Individual airports face manifestations of these national trends, but in general, changes in the number of travelers, the number of flights, and the size of planes have spurred airports to adapt and invest in modified or new infrastructure to accommodate these changing market conditions.

One of the core questions that this report is intended to answer is whether current infrastructure and the financial resources that support infrastructure investment are sufficient to "meet future demand." Meeting future demand is typically envisioned as a supply-side endeavor: providing air transportation services at affordable fares and reasonable levels of quality to travelers, businesses, and aviators that are anticipated to use these services in the future. As complements or alternatives to supply-side measures, demand-side management strategies can be employed to reduce demand and potentially reduce the need for capacity expansion. Many factors can influence both supply and demand, including the cost of fuel, technological change, security, and environmental concerns. Airlines and airports respond to demand from travelers as well as shape it. In turn, travelers respond to price, quality, and availability of services when deciding when and where to travel and the price at which they are willing to do so.

Decisions about where and how to spend resources to meet future demand are not made by airlines and airports in isolation. The FAA plays a pivotal role in distributing AIP grants among airports to ensure demand is met across the national system. In sum, the relationship between the forces of supply and demand is highly dynamic. For example, increasing supply in the form of terminal and runway capacity expansion can alleviate congestion and bottlenecks in the system and, at the same time, induce greater demand for air travel.

Given the challenge of nailing down a credible estimate of the future infrastructure investment needed to meet future demand, we instead seek to identify where infrastructure-related air travel delays are currently occurring and ask whether resources are available to make investments in capacity expansion that could reduce these delays, both at the delay-causing individual airport and for the NAS as a whole. As we discuss later, not all delays can be mitigated through investment in more or different infrastructure, nor are airports solely responsible for delays. Infrastructure investment, however, is at least part of the solution to reducing delay.

The aim of this chapter is to emphasize the dynamic nature of the supply and demand relationship and to understand how funding programs and policies can be enablers or barriers to meeting future demand.

Growing and Changing Use of Airport Infrastructure

Changes in the number of enplanements, the size of planes, and the number of operations all affect airports' infrastructure needs. Although the declining number of operations puts less pressure on some elements of airport infrastructure, the increase in the size of planes and the number of enplanements has changed airports' infrastructure needs. Airports of different sizes are affected by these changing conditions in different ways.

Figure 8.1 shows that the number of enplanements grew rapidly from 1990 to 2018 across the different sizes of primary airports. Large hubs experienced the greatest increase in enplanements, serving twice as many passengers in 2018 as in 1990. For comparison, the U.S. population grew by only 30 percent over this same period. The FAA's TAF suggests this growth will continue. Medium-, small-, and non-hub airports are all expected to see enplanements grow by 20–30 percent from 2018 to 2030; large hubs are forecast to see an even steeper increase. By 2040, the current large-hub airports are forecast to be serving more than triple the number of travelers than were served in 1990 (FAA, 2019b).

As noted in Chapter Two, the increase in passengers has not been accompanied by a comparable increase in the number of operations. Figure 8.2 shows that, from 1990 to 2018, the number of departures from large hubs increased by approximately 50 percent, from 4 million flights to 6 million flights, while the number of passengers increased by approximately 100 percent over the same period. Medium-, small-, and non-hub airports have seen essentially no change in the total number of flights, on average.[1] The large increase in passengers was

Figure 8.1
Average Growth in the Number of Passengers at Primary Airports Since 1990, by 2018 Hub Status

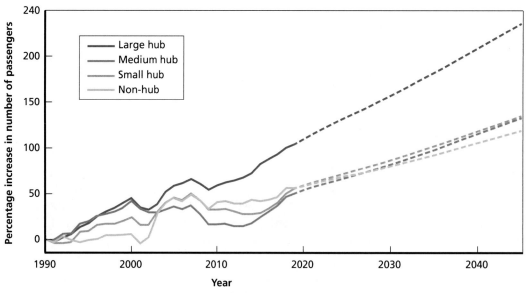

SOURCES: RAND analysis of T-100 segment data (BTS, 2019c) and TAF data (FAA, 2019b).
NOTE: To ensure that the composition of the hub groups is consistent across years, (1) airports are grouped according to 2018 hub status, rather than airport hub status in each year, and (2) airports that began service after 1990 are not included because a change since 1990 cannot be calculated for those airports.

---

[1] The increase in 2002 is due to a reporting change in the T-100 data. As of October 2002, small certificated and commuter air carriers began filing Schedule T-100 nonstop segment and on-flight market data. Before October 2002, flight statistics from these carriers were reported in Form 298-C A-1, E-1, and T-1 and were not included in Schedule T-100 data.

accommodated in part by increasing numbers of flights, but also through larger planes and fewer empty seats. The steady shift to larger planes has required airports to make changes in the capacity and configuration of their infrastructure. Some smaller airports wishing to grow can have a particularly difficult time under these conditions. They might need to expand their runways to attract more travelers, but securing the funding for expansion can require demonstrating their ability to attract higher demand.

According to the TAF, enplanements are expected to continue to outgrow operations in the near term. From 2018 to 2030, the TAF predicts enplanements to grow by roughly 30 percent at large-hub airports, whereas operations are expected to grow only by 19 percent over the same period.[2] As noted in Chapter Two, airlines have been moving toward use of larger planes to meet demand without a comparable increase in operations, and this trend is anticipated to continue. However, the relatively mild growth in the number of operations does not necessarily translate to diminished infrastructure requirements. Instead, larger planes carrying more passengers produce different operational pressures, such as more crowded terminals and the need for longer runways. If the trends of larger aircraft and increasing passenger demand continue as forecast, these infrastructure demands will likely increase accordingly.

Forecasting Future Enplanements

One of the biggest challenges for all stakeholders in the NAS is forecasting future enplanements. Airports, airlines, plane manufacturers, and a wide variety of other stakeholders must

Figure 8.2
Total Number of Departures at Primary Airports, by 2018 Hub Status

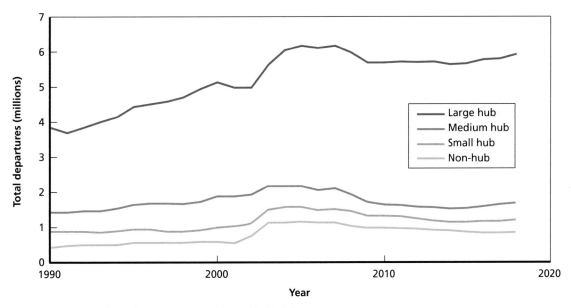

SOURCE: RAND analysis of T-100 segment data (BTS, 2019c).

---

[2]   Figure 8.2 does not include a forecast of commercial departures. The TAF forecast is based on operations, which include arrivals and departures as well as noncommercial flights, rather than only departures and commercial flights. From 2018 to 2030, operations at medium hubs are forecast to grow by 16.55 percent, small hubs by 9.66 percent, and non-hubs by 5.67 percent.

make investments now that can accommodate a variety of possible futures. Stakeholder associations, such as the International Air Transport Association (IATA) and the ACI, and corporations, such as Boeing, provide national and global projections of projected changes in total airline passengers (IATA, undated; ACI, 2018; Boeing, 2019). These projections, as well as projections of operations, freight traffic, and other metrics, are used by airports, airlines, and others to forecast revenue and make decisions about infrastructure and other business investments.

National and global projections are useful for understanding the status of the air travel industry as a whole, but each airport needs to consider how its local context and economy will change its demand projections for enplanements and operations, which will in turn drive its investment decisions. The task of making airport-specific forecasts is challenging because airports must predict local passenger demand, through-passenger demand, and cargo demand. Smaller airports must forecast and coordinate GA traffic, as well. These sources of demand are driven by many factors, including local economic conditions and the operational decisions (such as plane sizes, routing, and scheduling) of airlines, cargo companies, and other firms that airports are trying to attract. These businesses are trying to optimize in response to their own expectations of the future. Under these circumstances, forecasting demand many years into the future at an individual airport is challenging.

There are two main sources of demand forecasts for airport planners. The first is the TAF, which forecasts enplanements without consideration of capacity constraints and provides forecasts of airport operations, Terminal Radar Approach Control (TRACON) operations, and based aircraft (FAA, 2019b).[3] The most recent TAF includes historical data on total enplanements and total operations by airport beginning in 1990 and projections from the present to 2045. For large- and medium-hub airports, the TAF provides both optimistic and pessimistic scenarios in addition to its baseline forecast, as shown in Figure 8.3. These forecasts are made by aggregating O&D-level forecasts. These O&D forecasts are generated using the BTS DB1B data (a 10 percent sample of tickets) and other sources, with forecasts estimated via regression analysis using fares, fleet mix forecasts, regional demographics, and regional economic factors as predictors. For the first two years of forecasts, the TAF also incorporates airline schedules for individual airports. The FAA updates the TAF forecasts annually (FAA, 2019b).

The second main source of airport-specific forecasts is airports' master plans. Airport consultants employ techniques such as trend-line projections, regression analysis, and market-share analysis to construct individual airport forecasts contingent on local conditions. Master plan forecasts incorporate measures of the local economy, socioeconomic trends, local operating rules, and the TAF forecast, among other factors. As an example, Figure 8.4 shows the enplanement forecast from Albuquerque International Sunport's current master plan (produced in March 2015).[4] Master plans are updated much less frequently than the TAF and represent a multiyear analysis of conditions at a single airport rather than an annually updated forecast of active airports in the NPIAS.

---

[3]   *Based aircraft* are operational, airworthy, and based at an airport for a majority of the year.

[4]   As discussed previously, demand forecasting needs to encompass projections of enplanements and projections of operations (flights), the latter of which depends on the size and type of aircraft employed by the airlines as well as runway operations and competitive factors.

Figure 8.3
Baseline, Pessimistic Scenario, and Optimistic Scenario Enplanement Forecasts for Albuquerque International Sunport

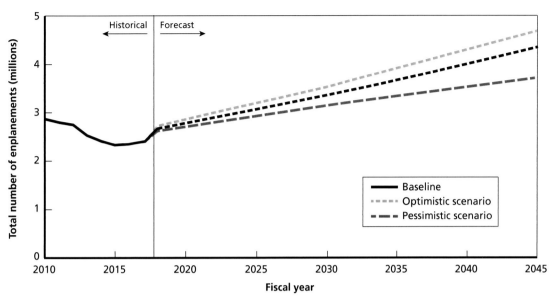

SOURCE: TAF data as of 2018 (FAA, undated a).

Figure 8.4
Enplanement Forecast from Albuquerque International Sunport's Master Plan

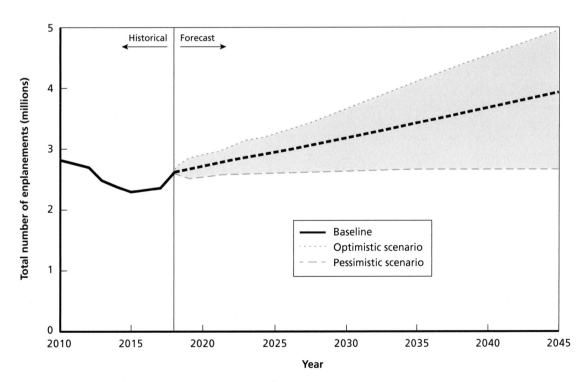

SOURCE: Adapted from Albuquerque International Sunport, 2018, p. 33.

Uncertainty and Accuracy

Forecasting future demand is difficult because airports face many sources of uncertainty. A 2012 report by the Transportation Research Board highlighted sources of uncertainty affecting decisionmaking, including

- global, regional, and local economic conditions
- airline decisions, structure, or competition
- technology change
- competition with other airports
- changes in regulatory and government policy
- shifts in societal or business attitudes toward air travel
- various disasters or disruptions (Kincaid et al., 2012).

Master plan forecasts and the TAF forecast might not always agree. Airports have expressed concern that past TAF forecasts did not sufficiently consider local conditions or recent trends, and yet GAO, 2016a, finds that the TAF consistently overestimated aviation activity. The TAF has since undergone significant methodological changes, and there is a process for communication between airports and the FAA to reconcile differences in projections between the TAF and the airports' master plans.

There are many examples of airports facing unexpected decreases and unexpected increases in enplanements and operations. Airport master plans typically include strategies for either scenario. In response to changes in market conditions, some airports have slowed down investment in new infrastructure or have even removed excess infrastructure. In other cases, airports have sped up planned investments, limited not by the availability to borrow funds to pay the upfront cost of new infrastructure but by the ability of their staff to manage the number or tempo of projects.

Capacity Constraints: Past and Future

Past events and trends across the airport system can also help inform airport planning. The analysis in this section aims to explain what changes in the system have occurred, the impact those changes have had on capacity constraints and capacity planning, and how these changes can inform future planning. For information on how capacity constraints are defined and measured, see Appendix L.

Airside Constraints

The FAA's Future Airport Capacity Task (FACT) reports provide insight into how airside constraints have evolved in the NAS over the past two decades. Published in 2004, 2007, and 2015, the FACT reports provide snapshots of airside capacity and of forecast capacity constraints at airports that were most likely to be constrained at the time of publication (FAA, 2015a). These reports rely on the TAF's forecasts of future enplanements making the assumption that airports do not face capacity constraints, forecast aircraft fleet mixes, and capacity profiles of individual airports. The FACT reports thus give insight into the evolution of airside capacity constraints as well as the inputs determining these constraints over time.

The severity of airside constraints and forecast constraints in the NAS declined substantially from the first FACT report in 2004 to the most recent report in 2015 (FAA, 2015a). As Table 8.1 demonstrates, FACT1 forecast 41 airports that could be capacity constrained by 2020, whereas FACT3 only forecast that six of that same group could be capacity constrained by 2020. Even by 2030, assuming unabated national growth in enplanements, FACT3 forecast that 12 of these airports at most would experience capacity constraints by 2030. The lower number of airports with projected capacity constraints with each successive FACT report suggests that severe airside constraints are now concentrated at a handful of airports. Capacity constraints do not appear to be a systemwide problem at this time, but FACT3's 2030 forecast indicates that capacity constraints will likely increase over time.

The decline in the number of airports that the FACT reports project could experience capacity constraints is the result of several factors. First, the FAA updated the methodology used to determine capacity-constrained airports, which might have reduced the number of projected capacity-constrained airports. Second, the number of projected airport operations decreased between the first and third FACT reports partly because of decreased demand for air travel during the Great Recession and the increasing use of larger aircraft. Fewer projected operations subsequently reduced the amount of projected airside capacity required across the NAS. Finally, additional runways and runway improvements, as well as changes to the FAA's slot allocation and demand management practices at highly constrained airports, helped to mitigate congestion at constrained airports and throughout the system (GAO, 2012b, pp. 69–70; FAA, 2015a).

Airside constraints also can occur for reasons other than inadequate infrastructure. Airlines have been the subject of complaints that they have worked in tandem to limit capacity. For example, the Department of Justice opened an investigation in 2015 into whether the four major U.S. airlines had coordinated to curb the number of available seats (McLaughlin and Sasso, 2017). The investigation was prompted by a congressional inquiry following press reports of airlines discussing "capacity discipline," or the deliberate withholding of additional seats (Blumenthal, 2015). In addition, consumers have filed lawsuits with similar allegations. Southwest and American have paid to settle these lawsuits without admitting wrongdoing (Yamanouchi, 2018), and it has been reported that the Department of Justice investigation was dropped because of lack of evidence (McLaughlin and Sasso, 2017).

The changes in projected airside capacity constraints over the past two decades contain lessons for the future of airside capacity planning. For one, external factors, such as demand for air transportation, economic conditions, and airline decisions, can significantly affect the infrastructure needs across the NAS in a relatively quick time frame. Because many large infrastructure projects can take a decade or more to plan and execute, these external factors could change airport needs to a point in which development deemed necessary at the time of planning might not be as useful by the time the project is completed. Thus, although infrastructure improvements at capacity-constrained airports can help relieve congestion, the impact of additional infrastructure is ultimately subordinate to changes in market conditions.

Landside Constraints

Neither the FAA nor the IATA nor others compile systemwide, airport-level data on landside infrastructure to assess the extent to which airports are within their target level of service or would remain within that target given projected future enplanements and operations. This information, however, is commonly available for specific airports. Airports will often work

Table 8.1
Sequence of FACT Assessments of Current and Future Capacity Constraints

Airport	FACT1			FACT2			FACT3		
	2004	2013	2020	2007	2015	2025	2011	2020	2030
ABQ		●	●						
ATL	●	○	●			●	●	●	●
BDL			●						
BHM			●						
BOS			○			○			
BUR		●	●						
BWI		○	○						
CLT		○	○		○	○			●
CVG		○	○						
DCA			○						
DEN			○						
DFW			○						
DTW			○						
EWR	●	●	●	●	●	●	●	●	●
FLL		●	○	●	○	●			○
HOU		●	●		○	○			
IAD			○			○			
IAH		○	○		○	○			●
ISP			●						
JFK		●	○		○	●	●	●	●
LAS		○	●		○	●			●
LAX		○	○			○			
LGA	●	●	●	●	●	●	●	●	●
LGB		●	●		●	●			
MDW		○	●		○	●			
MEM			○						
MIA			○						
MSP		○	○			○			
OAK		●	●		●	●			
ONT									
ORD	●	●	○	●	○	○			○

Table 8.1—Continued

Airport	FACT1			FACT2			FACT3		
	2004	2013	2020	2007	2015	2025	2011	2020	2030
PBI		●	○		○	○			
PHL	●	●	○		●	●	●	●	○
PHX		○	○			●			●
PVD			●		○	○			
SAN						●			
SAT		●	●		○	○			
SEA			○			○			
SFO						●		○	●
SLC			○						
SNA		●	●		●	●			
STL		○	○						
TUS		●	●		○	○			

SOURCE: FAA, 2015a.
NOTE: ○ = constrained in reference case, but unconstrained if planned improvements are implemented; ● = constrained even after all planned improvements are implemented, or additional capacity enhancement is needed, or constrained in base year; no symbol indicates not capacity constrained. This table lists only the airports that were identified as capacity-constrained in one of the FACT reports. Other airports that were analyzed in the FACT reports but not identified as capacity-constrained are not included. See Table C.1 in Appendix C for a list of the full airport names.

with consultants during the master planning process to quantify their landside capacity, determine when it will become constrained, and identify projects to expand.[5] We emphasize that this analysis is specific to the airport in question and is not collected on a systemwide basis. Without systemwide, empirical data on landside infrastructure, we are unable to quantify with precision the amount of landside infrastructure needed within the NAS.

Need for Adaptation

Forecasting future capacity constraints is critical to making wise long-term investments, but airports have difficulty predicting what infrastructure will be required in the presence of so many uncertainties about future market conditions and trends. For example, landside infrastructure has adapted over the past 20 years to accommodate changing technology and new security requirements. Rather than expanding ticket counter space, for instance, airports might seek to install kiosks and infrastructure needed to support them. Likewise, airports have had to adapt pickup, drop-off, and parking areas to accommodate the rise of ride-hailing services. Unforeseen events, such as the terrorist attacks on September 11, 2001, have forced airports to quickly adapt infrastructure within their terminals to meet new space or equipment requirements for security. With new technologies, such as autonomous vehicles and unmanned aerial

---

[5] For a discussion on measuring airport capacity and potential constraints, see Appendix L.

systems, and other unforeseen events on the horizon, change and adaption will continue to inject uncertainties into infrastructure planning in the future.

To illustrate how sudden changes can affect and influence airport planning, we highlight the experience of Pittsburgh International Airport (PIT). In 1992, PIT constructed a new terminal and gates to accommodate USAir, which used PIT as a primary hub and viewed the airport as "maxed out on capacity"(Marriott, 1991). However, USAir ceased using PIT as a hub in 2004. This decision was driven by factors that include PIT's close proximity to other USAir hubs (Philadelphia International and CLT) as well as USAir's inability to negotiate lower landing fees at PIT (Linares, 2015). The terminal, gates, and transportation system that had garnered PIT the title of "airport of the future" a decade earlier suddenly found the airport serving half the amount of traffic as before (Marriott, 1991; Sharkey, 2004). The underused infrastructure became a burden for PIT to maintain, and in 2017, the Allegheny Airport Authority (which operates PIT) approved a reconfiguration of the airport, including construction of a new building to accommodate modern ticketing, baggage, and security facilities and fewer gates (Belko, 2017).

Airports do their best to predict their future infrastructure requirements and plan accordingly. However, airports are aware that future infrastructure needs, as well as the revenue that pays for those investments, can change quickly. Flexibility of funding sources is of paramount concern to airports because they want and need the agility to alter plans if conditions suddenly change.

Impact of Capacity Constraints on Passengers

In this section, we focus on delays as one measure of capacity constraints, because of the availability of data on delays across airports. However, many airports, particularly the larger commercial service airports, are experiencing increasing capacity limitations that may or may not be captured in delay data. In particular, terminal and landside areas are experiencing growing challenges in terms of the number and size of gates (holdrooms), passenger circulation space and systems (such as peoplemovers), security inspection areas, curbside areas for passenger drop-off and pickup, and public access and circulation roads. These issues could be reflected in delay data in some cases, such as when terminal or landside constraints cause flight or cabin crews to be delayed or when an aircraft has landed on time but must navigate through constrained routes or wait for a gate to be available.

Regardless of whether there are changes in the policy environment, airports will continue to build infrastructure to serve their customers. Unfortunately, there is not an obvious method for determining which infrastructure will be built regardless of policy changes and which infrastructure will not be built. Some delays could be mitigated by well-conceived infrastructure investments, while others could be more operational in nature.

Reducing preventable delays to zero would be an unreasonable measure of success for "meeting future demand." For that reason, rather than assessing delays in terms of an acceptable level of performance (for which there is no consensus), we instead focus on trends in a measurable performance outcome: delays most closely associated with infrastructure shortfalls. We use this measure to assess the extent to which infrastructure is meeting demand; that is, are delays getting better, staying about the same, or getting worse? The analysis in this section identifies where capacity constraints are experienced the most by passengers, how capacity-constrained airports affect other airports in the system, and how these impacts have changed over time. This analysis provides a foundation for the subsequent section on airports' financial capacity to invest in infrastructure to address delays and meet future demand.

Types of Delays

There are several databases that contain authoritative information on airport delays. We use two sources: the USDOT's Airline Service Quality Performance (ASQP) on-time performance data and the FAA's Operations Network (OPSNET) (USDOT, 2019; FAA, undated f).[6] The ASQP database, which is maintained by the USDOT's BTS, contains arrival delay data by cause, from June 2003 to the present, for most nonstop commercial flights, as submitted by reporting carriers.[7] As shown in Figure 8.5, there are five categories of delay causes within the ASQP database: air carrier, extreme weather, national aviation system, late-arriving aircraft, and security. These categories are used to clarify which party is best able to reduce the delay.[8] In this section, we focus in particular on national aviation system delays (NAS delays).[9] Reporting carriers generally assign "NAS" to delays that occur after departure, or "pushback," at which point the aircraft is under air traffic control and subject to conditions of the NAS. Although not all NAS delays can be eliminated through corrective action, the FAA, airport operators, and the government are seen to be in the best position to reduce NAS delays.

When an NAS delay is recorded in the ASQP database, the FAA will determine the cause of the delay using data recorded within OPSNET, the FAA's database for air traffic control performance. OPSNET records departure and airborne delays of 15 minutes or more that aircraft experience while under FAA control. The FAA records the cause of a delay in OPSNET as one of five categories shown in Figure 8.5: weather, volume, equipment, runways, or other, and these categories can then be matched to flights in ASQP. Because the objective of OPSNET is to measure air traffic control performance rather than passenger delays, OPSNET data do not perfectly match the NAS delay figures reported by carriers in the ASQP. However, OPSNET remains the primary tool to determine the cause of NAS delay. Figure 8.5 shows the relationship between the ASQP and OPSNET delay categories, as well as the delay definitions of each category and its share of total delay time in 2018.

The OPSNET delay data can also be used independent of the ASQP database to assess delays at airports. The OPSNET database attributes a departure delay to the airport responsible for the delay. That is, if air traffic control holds an aircraft from take-off for more than 15 minutes in Atlanta because of equipment issues in Phoenix, OPSNET will attribute the

---

[6]   We define *delay* as any minute of delay an aircraft experiences, regardless of the total minutes of delay. The ASQP database provides records on delays less than 15 minutes. OPSNET only contains records on delays that are 15 minutes or greater in length.

[7]   In 2018, the definition of a *reportable flight* was changed to include all flights to or from any primary airport by a reporting carrier, per 14 CFR § 234.2. In the same year, the definition of a reporting carrier was expanded, from an air carrier that accounted for at least 1 percent of domestic scheduled-passenger revenue to at least 0.05 percent of domestic scheduled-passenger revenue.

[8]   An exception is that late-arriving aircraft delays are not used to identify the party best able to reduce the delay. Because late-arriving aircraft delays occur when a previous flight delayed the aircraft, causing the current flight to be delayed, the party best suited to reduce the delay depends on the cause of the initial delay. For more information, see USDOT, 2002.

[9]   The BTS uses the term *national aviation system* as a general category of delays that are attributable to a broad set of conditions, such as nonextreme weather, airport operations, heavy traffic volume, and air traffic control (USDOT, 2002). The term *NAS delay* is distinct from the FAA's definition of the *National Airspace System*.

Figure 8.5
The Relationship Between ASQP and OPSNET: Delay Causes, Share of Total Delay, and Definitions

USDOT | Airline Service Quality Performance (ASQP) on-time performance data

39.6%
Late-arriving aircraft
A previous flight with the same aircraft arrived late, causing the current flight to depart late.

30.1%
Air carrier
The cause of the cancellation or delay was due to circumstances within the airline's control.

24.5%
National aviation system (NAS delay)
Delays and cancellations attributable to the national aviation system.

FAA | The Operations Network (OPSNET)

14.0%
Weather
The presence of adverse weather conditions affecting operations.

5.1%
Volume
When the airport is in its optimum configuration and no affecting conditions have been reported when the delays were incurred. Includes compacted demand and many aircraft trying to taxi at once.

1.0%
Runway/Taxiway
Reductions in facility capacity because of runway/taxiway closure or configuration changes.

0.1%
Equipment
An equipment failure or outage causing reduced capacity.

0.4%
Other
All affecting conditions that are not otherwise attributed to weather, equipment, runway/taxiway, or volume.

3.9%
Unmatched
National aviation system delays in ASQP that did not match delays in OPSNET.

USDOT | ASQP on-time performance data

5.6%
Extreme weather
Significant meteorological conditions (actual or forecast) that, in the judgment of the carrier, delays or prevents the operation of a flight.

0.1%
Security
Delays or cancellations caused by evacuation of a terminal or concourse, reboarding of aircraft because of security breach, inoperative screening equipment, and/or long lines in excess of 29 minutes at screening areas.

delay to Phoenix. In comparison, ASQP only associates arrival delays with a flight between two airports, rather than an individual airport. The OPSNET database will assign airborne delays to TRACONs and Air Route Traffic Control Centers (ARTCCs), which are used by air traffic control when an aircraft is en route to its destination. For our analysis, we do not associate airports with their associated TRACONs in order to assess each airport individually.[10]

National Aviation System (OPSNET) Delays

NAS delays, as described above, are delays for which the FAA, airport operators, and state or local governments are in the best position to take corrective action to prevent or mitigate the delay. NAS delays thus serve as the best proxy to understand what types of delays in the system can be eliminated, at least in part, through infrastructure investment or other airport development (USDOT, 2002). NAS delays can therefore serve as a surrogate indicator of the extent to which airports' current infrastructure is inadequate to handle their current operations. Excessive NAS delay could signal that an airport is regularly capacity-constrained and requires additional infrastructure investment or changes in operations management practices to mitigate delays. Because the OPSNET database contains the subcauses of NAS delay and

Figure 8.6
Airports with the Most Hours of OPSNET Delays in 2018

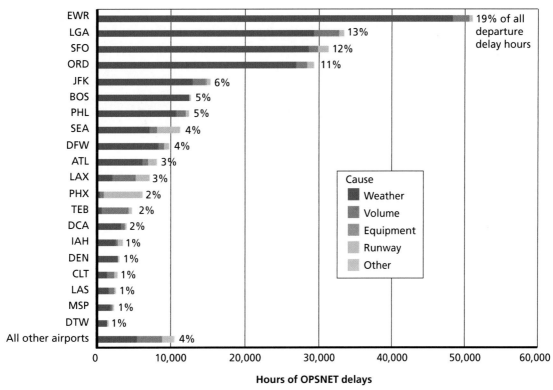

SOURCE: RAND analysis of OPSNET (FAA, undated f).
NOTE: Teterboro Airport (TEB) is a reliever airport. The 19 other airports in this figure are large-hub airports. See Table C.1 in Appendix C for a list of the full airport names.

---

[10] Several airports can share one TRACON, making it impossible to assign all airborne delays to individual airports.

attributes them to specific airports, we look at OPSNET delay data to better understand the role that infrastructure might play in NAS delay at individual airports.

Figure 8.6 shows the 20 airports with the most hours of OPSNET delay in 2018. Overall, the top 20 airports had a cumulative 250,246 hours' worth of OPSNET delays in 2018, accounting for 96 percent of the total OPSNET departure delays recorded in 2018. The top five airports alone, three of which are operated by the Port Authority of New York and New Jersey (LGA , JFK, and EWR), made up 61 percent of total OPSNET delay in 2018. The other two in the top five are SFO and ORD. In other words, OPSNET delays are not distributed evenly across the country's thousands of airports; the vast majority of OPSNET delay occurs at a handful of airports that might be frequently facing operations beyond their capacity. It is not surprising that most of the airports on this list are large hubs because, as shown in Figure 8.2, large hubs support the largest number of operations.

Notably, most OPSNET delay hours at the top airports are from weather-related delays. Each airport can face distinct weather challenges, however. San Francisco, for instance, must often deal with low ceilings because of the frequent presence of fog, whereas Denver might face snowy conditions more frequently. There are several airports where weather is not the predominant cause of delay, such as in Phoenix and Los Angeles, where the weather is frequently favorable for airport operations. Teterboro, a reliever airport in northern New Jersey also operated by the Port Authority of New York and New Jersey, had the most hours of volume delay of any airport in 2018 and is the only airport on this list that is not a large hub. Because different airports face different causes of delays, different infrastructure investments are needed. Other actions, such as further implementation of the NextGen system to improve air traffic control, might also reduce delays.

The OPSNET delays in 2018 provide a snapshot of airside capacity constraints within the system. It is also possible to analyze trends in OPSNET delay over multiple years to see whether delays are increasing or declining over time. Table 8.2 presents the top 20 airports by cumulative OPSNET delays over the ten-year period from 2009 to 2018. The color coding within the table highlights the relative change in OPSNET delay by year for each airport. Green boxes indicate years of OPSNET delays that are relatively low for that airport, while red boxes indicate years of relatively high OPSNET delays for that airport.

OPSNET delays for most airports increased from 2010 to 2018, with total delay in 2017 and 2018 being comparable to 2009 levels. Thirteen of the 20 airports with the most delays from 2009 to 2018 experienced higher OPSNET delays in 2017 and 2018 than in previous years. However, there is also significant variance across airports and time. Hartsfield-Jackson Atlanta International Airport (ATL), for example, had the second most hours of OPSNET delay in 2009 but has substantially and consistently reduced its OPSNET delays since that time. In contrast, Seattle-Tacoma International Airport (SEA) had virtually no OPSNET delays until 2015, correlated with large increases in enplanements and operations. There is also systemwide variance. In 2017, for instance, reported OPSNET delay increased by 37 percent, half of which was specifically attributable to weather delays. But even with this variance, several airports stand out as the largest contributors. Nearly a third of the increase in delays in 2017 was attributable to EWR, which operated without slot controls for the first time in a decade, and JFK, which had major runway construction that year.

Delay numbers over time are likely influenced by the number of operations an airport experiences. To account for changes in operations at an airport across years, Table 8.3 presents the top 20 airports by average minutes of OPSNET delay per operation. Similar to the results

Table 8.2
Airports with the Most Hours of OPSNET Delay, 2009–2018

Airport	2009	2010	2011	2012	2013	2014	2015	2016	2017	2018	Grand Total	Ten-Year Trend
EWR (L)	60,089	29,173	34,877	33,570	31,983	27,454	18,810	24,280	54,144	50,848	365,230	
LGA (L)	35,457	23,964	29,478	22,002	31,911	29,349	30,041	35,804	38,874	33,451	310,331	
ORD (L)	24,785	30,161	37,203	20,169	33,456	35,036	20,342	21,536	16,137	29,147	267,972	
SFO (L)	18,304	24,836	22,454	31,174	25,191	26,752	17,696	28,167	40,110	31,265	265,947	
JFK (L)	20,013	12,306	13,142	7,150	13,896	13,271	17,142	12,664	26,628	15,415	151,627	
PHL (L)	26,808	12,327	18,808	13,125	20,637	15,794	13,220	7,643	10,232	12,353	150,947	
ATL (L)	43,665	24,812	9,816	6,536	12,008	5,136	6,736	4,155	4,864	8,157	125,885	
BOS (L)	9,133	7,313	10,789	2,914	4,741	5,812	6,389	6,866	16,811	12,585	83,352	
LAX (L)	146	328	1,019	1,119	1,881	2,460	9,739	10,375	23,019	7,099	57,186	
DFW (L)	4,075	2,817	2,085	1,822	2,187	3,672	3,732	7,021	5,322	9,631	42,363	
IAH (L)	5,781	3,061	2,212	3,239	1,235	3,467	4,299	4,368	2,775	3,441	33,878	
DEN (L)	2,603	1,977	2,022	1,822	5,343	4,334	3,884	1,974	3,334	2,839	30,130	
LAS (L)	3,028	1,897	828	1,480	3,842	3,231	3,206	5,190	4,722	2,425	29,848	
TEB (R)	1,773	2,502	1,802	1,252	1,876	2,775	3,117	3,057	6,684	4,810	29,647	
CLT (L)	6,351	2,632	2,609	1,829	3,351	1,921	2,353	2,252	2,546	2,537	28,382	
MSP (L)	8,552	2,144	2,047	693	1,322	1,834	3,367	3,662	1,080	2,149	26,849	
DCA (L)	733	790	1,523	2,413	2,872	2,300	3,730	3,974	3,192	3,984	25,511	
SEA (L)	310	444	38	68	87	129	1,857	3,711	7,239	11,127	25,010	
PHX (L)	1,635	2,430	873	2,384	858	1,050	2,115	3,789	1,195	5,998	22,328	
DTW (L)	1,526	1,514	1,779	1,305	2,257	1,713	1,279	1,323	1,449	1,447	15,592	
All other airports	7,582	7,462	9,587	8,446	9,467	10,796	6,765	7,825	8,399	10,613	86,943	
All airports	358,814	253,421	266,984	214,065	270,431	265,490	240,762	263,284	361,072	345,157	2,839,480	

High ⬛⬜ Low

By airport

SOURCE: RAND analysis of OPSNET (FAA, undated f).
NOTE: The total for all airports for each year includes associated TRACONs and ARTCCs that cannot be assigned to a specific airport. (L) = large hub and (R) = reliever. See Table C.1 in Appendix C for a list of the full airport names.

Table 8.3
Average Minutes of OPSNET Delay per Operation at the Most-Delayed Airports, 2009–2018

Airport	2009	2010	2011	2012	2013	2014	2015	2016	2017	2018	Average	Ten-Year Trend
EWR (L)	8.7	4.3	5.0	4.8	4.6	4.1	2.7	3.4	7.3	6.7	5.2	
LGA (L)	6.0	3.9	4.8	3.5	5.1	4.8	4.9	5.7	6.4	5.4	5.0	
SFO (L)	2.9	3.8	3.3	4.4	3.6	3.7	2.5	3.8	5.2	4.0	3.7	
PHL (L)	3.4	1.6	2.5	1.8	2.9	2.3	1.9	1.2	1.7	2.0	2.1	
JFK (L)	2.8	1.8	1.9	1.0	2.0	1.8	2.3	1.7	3.5	2.0	2.1	
ORD (L)	1.8	2.1	2.5	1.4	2.3	2.4	1.4	1.5	1.1	1.9	1.8	
BOS (L)	1.5	1.2	1.7	0.5	0.8	0.9	1.0	1.0	2.5	1.8	1.3	
TEB (R)	0.7	0.9	0.7	0.5	0.7	1.0	1.1	1.0	2.2	1.7	1.1	
ATL (L)	2.7	1.6	0.6	0.4	0.8	0.4	0.5	0.3	0.3	0.5	0.8	
DCA (L)	0.2	0.2	0.3	0.5	0.6	0.5	0.8	0.8	0.6	0.8	0.5	
LAX (L)	0.0	0.0	0.1	0.1	0.2	0.2	0.9	0.9	2.0	0.6	0.5	
ASE (N)	0.0	0.1	0.1	0.1	0.6	0.6	0.5	0.5	0.9	0.8	0.4	
IAH (L)	0.6	0.3	0.3	0.4	0.1	0.4	0.5	0.6	0.4	0.4	0.4	
DFW (L)	0.4	0.3	0.2	0.2	0.2	0.3	0.3	0.6	0.5	0.9	0.4	
MSP (L)	1.2	0.3	0.3	0.1	0.2	0.3	0.5	0.5	0.2	0.3	0.4	
SEA (L)	0.1	0.1	0.0	0.0	0.0	0.0	0.3	0.5	1.0	1.5	0.4	
LAS (L)	0.4	0.2	0.1	0.2	0.4	0.4	0.4	0.6	0.5	0.3	0.3	
CLT (L)	0.7	0.3	0.3	0.2	0.4	0.2	0.3	0.2	0.3	0.3	0.3	
DEN (L)	0.3	0.2	0.2	0.2	0.5	0.5	0.4	0.2	0.3	0.3	0.3	
PHX (L)	0.2	0.3	0.1	0.3	0.1	0.1	0.3	0.5	0.2	0.8	0.3	
All other airports	0.01	0.01	0.01	0.01	0.01	0.01	0.01	0.01	0.01	0.01	0.01	
All airports	0.1	0.1	0.1	0.0	0.1	0.1	0.1	0.1	0.1	0.1	0.1	

High — By airport — Low

SOURCE: RAND analysis of OPSNET (FAA, undated f).
NOTE: Operations are defined as all arrivals and departures from an airport and are pulled from OPSNET. The average for all airports for each year does not include associated TRACONs and ARTCCs. (L) = large hub, (R) = reliever, and (N) = non-hub. ASE = Aspen/Pitkin County Airport. See Table C.1 in Appendix C for a list of the full airport names.

in Table 8.2, average delay time per operation was higher from 2017 to 2018 than during the eight years prior at 15 airports. Even when controlling for the number of operations, we find that more airports are beginning to experience more delays. A smaller number of airports have been able to decrease their average delay per operation relative to prior years, such as ATL and Minneapolis–Saint Paul International Airport (MSP). Notably, the airports with the most significant decline in delay time per operation also had declining operations over the same period, and the airports with the most significant increase in delay time per operation had an increasing number of operations. In other words, a change in operations has an outsized impact on delay time, making future operations an important planning consideration.

OPSNET delays are useful in understanding which airports are facing airside capacity constraints, but there are limits to their significance to infrastructure. Not all OPSNET delays are the result of infrastructure shortfalls, nor can they all be eliminated with additional infrastructure investment. During times of peak demand, one delayed flight can cause numerous others to be delayed. Additional capacity, at least at those airports able to expand, can reduce the probability that volume delays will occur when airlines schedule many flights at the same time, but it is unlikely to eliminate all congestion at peak times. Likewise, improved infrastructure, such as larger holding pads and more gates, might reduce some weather delays, but not all weather delays can be efficiently prevented via infrastructure investment. And it could be the case that increased success in reducing delays lets airlines more confidently schedule more flights during windows of time that passengers would most prefer to travel. Consequently, we only view NAS delays, or OPSNET delays, as metrics for understanding where capacity constraints may exist and where additional infrastructure investments may serve as part of the solution to reducing delays.

Propagated Delays

Propagated delays occur when an initial delay of one aircraft at an airport causes subsequent flights for that aircraft to be delayed. Delays such as NAS delays therefore affect passengers at airports other than where the delays originated. Accordingly, we seek to understand how much propagated delay in the system is tied to NAS delays at individual airports to measure the total impact of NAS delays on passengers throughout the airport system. To measure this impact, we use the ASQP database, which contains the amount of NAS and late-arriving aircraft delay by flight.

Figure 8.7 provides an example of how the initial NAS delay from the first flight passes through to each subsequent route, using a hypothetical flight sequence between LGA and ORD. The first flight from LGA to ORD had 12 minutes of NAS delay. To calculate propagated NAS delay, we assume that if the flight had not arrived at ORD 12 minutes late, it would have been able to depart ORD up to 12 minutes earlier, but it would not have left earlier than planned. In our example, the second flight from ORD back to LGA ultimately was ten minutes late (the airplane made up two minutes of delay in the air); we assume these ten minutes of delay would have been avoided if the original NAS delay had not occurred, and we call these ten minutes of delay "propagated NAS delay." In this example, the third flight from LGA back to ORD was five minutes late (this flight made up five minutes of delay in the air). We assume these five minutes of delay would have been avoided if the second flight had not been ten minutes late, which in turn would have been avoided if the initial NAS delay had not occurred. Similarly, the fourth flight from ORD to LGA was two minutes late, which we also assume would have been avoided if not for the original NAS delay. In this example, if the

Figure 8.7
NAS Delay and Propagated NAS Delay for a Hypothetical Flight Sequence

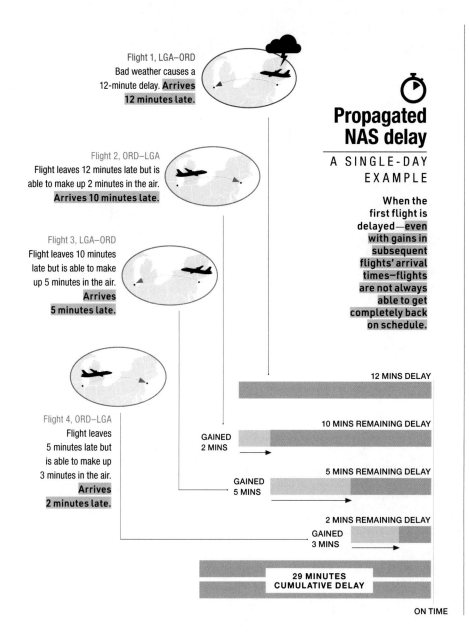

Flight 1, LGA–ORD
Bad weather causes a 12-minute delay. **Arrives 12 minutes late.**

Flight 2, ORD–LGA
Flight leaves 12 minutes late but is able to make up 2 minutes in the air. **Arrives 10 minutes late.**

Flight 3, LGA–ORD
Flight leaves 10 minutes late but is able to make up 5 minutes in the air. **Arrives 5 minutes late.**

Flight 4, ORD–LGA
Flight leaves 5 minutes late but is able to make up 3 minutes in the air. **Arrives 2 minutes late.**

Propagated NAS delay

A SINGLE-DAY EXAMPLE

When the first flight is delayed—even with gains in subsequent flights' arrival times—flights are not always able to get completely back on schedule.

12 MINS DELAY

GAINED 2 MINS — 10 MINS REMAINING DELAY

GAINED 5 MINS — 5 MINS REMAINING DELAY

GAINED 3 MINS — 2 MINS REMAINING DELAY

29 MINUTES CUMULATIVE DELAY

ON TIME

Total NAS delay

ONE-YEAR STATISTICS, 2018
Total NAS delay per flight segment

Flight 1
358,141 hours

Flight 2
123,969 hours

Flight 3
42,983 hours

Flight 4 plus subsequent flights
20,899 hours

545,992 hours total NAS delay for 2018

initial 12 minutes of NAS delay had been eliminated, it would have removed an additional 17 minutes of propagated delay on subsequent flights.[11] Although it is impossible to reduce all initial NAS delay, propagated delay as calculated here shows the broader benefits of reducing NAS delay. Note that this definition of propagated delay does not consider additional delays created by the holding of other flights to accommodate late-arriving passengers or flight crew from delayed flights.

The right side of Figure 8.7 also shows the total amount of initial and propagated NAS delays throughout the system in 2018. There were 358,141 hours of initial NAS delay recorded in 2018. Second flights carried over 123,969 hours of propagated NAS delay from the initial flight, third flights carried over 42,983 hours, and fourth flights and beyond carried over 20,899 hours of NAS delay from the initial NAS flight delay. Together, there were 187,851 hours of propagated NAS delay, or 52 percent of the initial NAS delay. This total is similar to the figure found in the FAA's On-Time NAS Report, which measures how many flights would be on time if NAS delays and late arrival delays that had been prorated for the NAS delay's share of non–late-arriving delay were the only causes of delay (FAA, undated b). Combining initial and propagated NAS delays results in approximately 546,000 hours of NAS delay throughout the system in 2018. This flight-based measure of propagated delay might undercount the total amount of propagated delay experienced by travelers for two reasons. First, late-arriving passengers who need to change planes might miss their subsequent flight. Second, late-arriving flight crews who need to change planes could delay the departure of other flights.

Because of the structure of the data, initial and propagated NAS delays must be calculated by route rather than by airport.[12] Consequently, this measure of total NAS delay cannot be attributed to an individual airport. As an example of how total delay is calculated, Table 8.4 provides the top 13 O&D pairs that produce the most total NAS delay. These 13 O&D pairs represent 5 percent of cumulative NAS delay in the system. In fact, the majority of NAS delays are produced within a small number of O&D pairs. Figure 8.8 charts the number of O&D pairs against the cumulative percentage of NAS delay that these pairs generate. It shows that just 572 O&D pairs, or 9 percent of all pairs, are responsible for 50 percent of the cumulative NAS delay. Perhaps unsurprisingly, the airports that appear most frequently within these pairs are also many of the large hubs identified earlier as having the most attributable OPSNET delay. Systemwide delays are thus not created evenly across the system. Rather, a small number of capacity-constrained airports and airport pairs appears to be responsible for delays throughout the system.

Changes in National Aviation System Delay over Time
One way to assess whether airports are successfully resolving these delays on their own is to examine whether national aviation system–related delays are increasing or decreasing. Figure 8.9 displays the total initial delay (Flight 1) and the propagated delay (Flights 2 through

[11] More generally, we compute propagated delays in the system by taking the minimum between a flight's late-arriving aircraft delay and the NAS delay of the previous flights. In other words, the propagated NAS delay of an initial flight is equal to the reduction in the following flights' overall delay that would have occurred if the initial flight had no NAS delay. We applied this algorithm to all subsequent flights of a single flight, which measured the magnitude and duration of propagated delays for each flight.

[12] The ASQP database only provides the cause of delay for arrival delays. Destination airports are typically responsible for arrival delays; however, both the origin and the destination airport can share responsibility (Hao et al., 2014, p. 248).

Table 8.4
Origin and Destination Pairs with the Most Associated NAS Delays

O&D Pair	Initial Hours of NAS Delay	Propagated Hours of NAS Delay	Total Hours of NAS Delay
ORD–LGA	2,321	1,228	3,550
LAX–SFO	1,713	1,029	2,742
LGA–ORD	1,773	893	2,666
MCO–EWR	1,635	555	2,190
ATL–EWR	1,439	662	2,101
BOS–LGA	1,105	996	2,101
FLL–EWR	1,376	543	1,920
SAN–SFO	1,120	696	1,816
BOS–EWR	1,118	685	1,803
SEA–SFO	1,170	527	1,697
SFO–LAX	1,019	678	1,697
LAS–SFO	1,067	547	1,614
DTW–EWR	1,032	493	1,525

SOURCE: RAND analysis of ASPQ data (USDOT, 2019).

NOTE: See Table C.1 in Appendix C for a list of the full airport names

Figure 8.8
A Small Percentage of Origin and Destination Pairs Are Responsible for Most NAS Delays

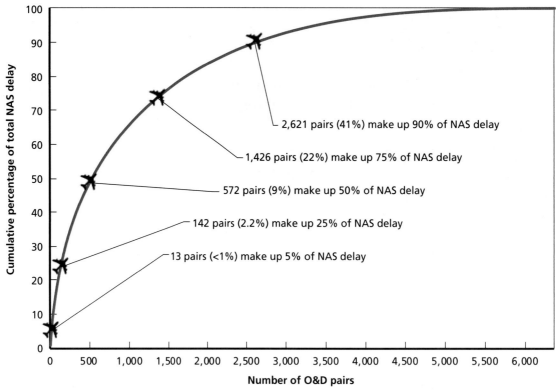

SOURCE: RAND analysis of ASPQ data (USDOT, 2019).

Figure 8.9
Changes in NAS Delays over Time

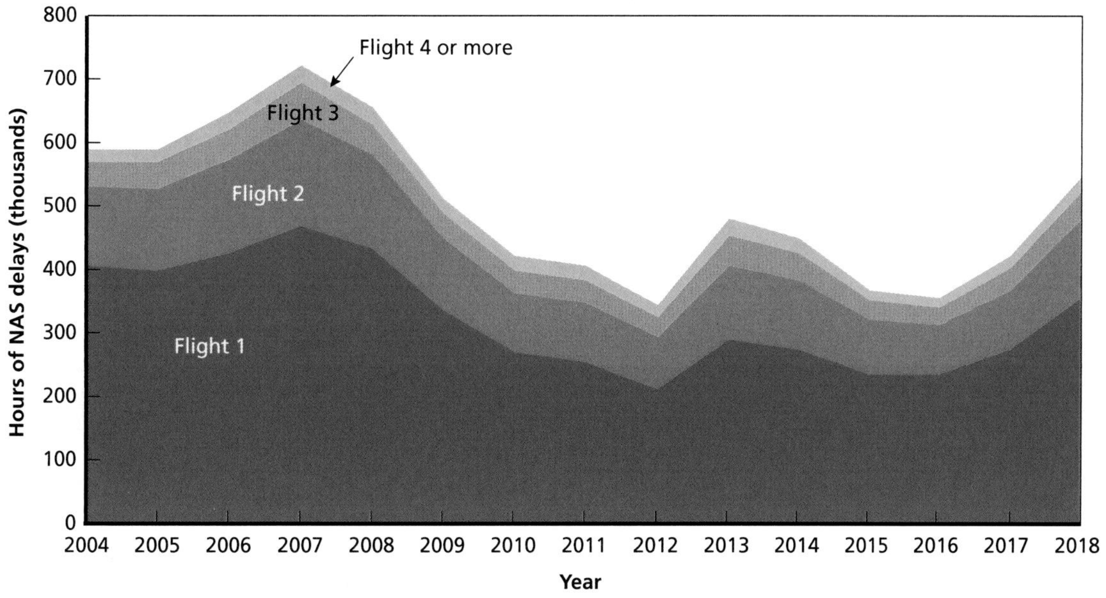

SOURCE: RAND analysis of ASPQ data (USDOT, 2019).

4 or more) across the entire system by year, from 2004 to 2018. Hours of total annual NAS delays fell by almost 50 percent in the years following the Great Recession and have oscillated around 400,000 hours of delay since 2010. The spike in 2018 is misleading because a change in reporting requirements increased the number of carriers required to report flight data, as explained earlier in this chapter. Overall, it is difficult to conclude from past trends whether NAS-related delays are likely to increase or decrease in the future. The results suggest that NAS delays are not spiraling out of control, but neither are they steadily being reduced through infrastructure investments or other airport decisions.

Airports' Financial Capacity to Reduce Capacity Constraints

As we have shown in this chapter, capacity constraints are concentrated at a small but growing number of airports. However, the effects of these capacity-constrained airports (specifically, delays) spill over to other airports and affect the entire system. The 545,992 hours of NAS delays that come from these capacity-constrained airports can be mitigated, at least in part, through infrastructure investment. Whether additional financial resources are necessary to make those investments depends on whether these airports have the financial capacity to resolve these delays on their own.

Airports are nonprofit entities but maintain unrestricted cash reserves and restricted reserves to continue covering operating expenses and debt service in the event of a decline in revenue or to save for future projects. If an airport's annual revenue can be thought of as its salary, then an airport's reserves can be thought of as the amount of money in its saving account. A strong level of reserves is required to receive favorable treatment in the bond market because it shows that the airport can weather a temporary decline in revenue. Bond rating agencies offer different recommendations for exactly how many days of operating expenses and debt service an airport's reserves should be able to cover; this metric is commonly referred to as "days of cash on hand." The recommended amount varies depending on whether the airport or airline bears the risk of paying costs if revenues fall short.

As shown in Table 8.5, the average for large hubs falls between 500 and 650 days of cash on hand, and the average for medium hubs falls between 400 and 650 days. Staff we spoke with at one airport had a target of 500 days cash on hand but found that spending down was challenging because current interest rates are low, and the airport would prefer to spend down its cash on hand when borrowing rates are high. Staff we spoke with at another airport emphasized that days of cash on hand does not measure an airport's uncommitted financial reserves because it includes funds that the airport might have already encumbered for planned future capital projects, much like a household might set aside money for a large purchase, such as a home or a car. Airports might increase their days of cash on hand if they are saving up for a large project and might spend down their days of cash on hand to pay for projects without having to go through the slower process of borrowing funds.

Table 8.5 shows that the days of cash on hand for large airports varies considerably. Some, such as CLT and Salt Lake City International Airport, are sitting on considerably large reserves relative to their daily expenses. These airports have funds available to back large infrastructure investments without a significance increase in revenue. Others, such as SEA and Baltimore Washington International Airport, are sitting below recommended levels of cash reserves. Airports operated by the Port Authority of New York and New Jersey do not report their amount of cash on hand. Cash on hand is not the only metric the bond market looks at, but the low number of days of cash on hand suggest these airports might not have sufficient reserves to take on the debt associated with additional major infrastructure projects.

Considering an airport's capacity to invest in future infrastructure, and considering its future infrastructure needs, requires a holistic examination of the individual airport's finances. Credit rating agencies consider many aspects of an airport's financial status, including the airport's service area, traffic composition, airport competition, passenger trends and services levels, airline market share, use-and-lease provisions, capital program, debt, and finances (ACI-NA Finance Committee, 2011). Table 8.6 provides an example of some of the many factors that should be considered when determining an airport's financial context. For example, investment in infrastructure at airports with high levels of OPSNET delay could provide benefits to that airport, as well as to the NAS as a whole. The number of days of cash on hand provides one metric for measuring the airport's current financial status. Large- and medium-hub airports have seen their days of cash on hand slowly increase in recent years, although as noted above, these airports might also be saving for additional infrastructure projects to meet growing demand. Airports with low or shrinking days of cash on hand have less savings built up for future projects.

Airports with a low or shrinking debt service coverage ratio (DSCR), another possible measure, might be less able to take on additional debt to finance new infrastructure projects, while the market will be more willing to lend to airports with a high DSCR, all else being equal. Airports with the best market ratings had DSCRs that "ranged from a high of 5.98x to a low of 1.30x, with a median of 1.94x" (ACI-NA Finance Committee, 2011). The extent of future growth in enplanements and operations reflects both an airport's need for additional infrastructure and its potential for future revenue growth.

Table 8.5
Days of Cash on Hand Across Large-Hub Airports

Airport	Domestic Enplanements	Days of Cash on Hand	Rate-Setting Methodology
ATL	46,093,349	781	Compensatory
ORD	33,259,780	690	Residual
LAX	30,304,593	431	Compensatory
DEN	30,212,529	531	Hybrid
DFW	28,752,994	336	Residual
LAS	22,219,103	697	Hybrid
SEA	21,444,141	279	Compensatory
SFO	21,065,673	437	Residual
PHX	20,841,034	608	Compensatory
CLT	20,776,035	1,539	Hybrid
MCO	20,163,971	951	Compensatory
MSP	17,035,199	743	Compensatory
BOS	16,451,678	724	Compensatory
IAH	16,011,937	416	Compensatory
EWR	15,945,042	N/A	Compensatory
DTW	15,636,865	355	Residual
JFK	14,137,146	N/A	Compensatory
LGA	13,965,553	N/A	Compensatory
FLL	13,519,284	715	Residual
PHL	13,403,058	333	Residual
BWI	12,966,967	137	Compensatory
SLC	11,794,382	1,668	Hybrid
SAN	11,777,319	691	Compensatory
DCA	11,216,291	414	Hybrid
MIA	10,555,211	340	Residual
MDW	10,506,475	371	Residual
TPA	10,002,668	318	Hybrid
PDX	9,397,671	297	Compensatory
IAD	7,796,507	647	Hybrid
HNL	7,255,001	1,264	Hybrid

Table 8.5—Continued

Methodology	Average Days of Cash on Hand
All	619
Compensatory	517
Residual	574
Hybrid	634

SOURCES: RAND analysis of T-100 segment and CATS data (BTS, 2019c; FAA, undated c). Rate setting methodology is from Wu, 2017.
NOTE: See Table C.1 in Appendix C for a list of the full airport names. LGA, JFK, and EWR, all managed by the Port Authority of New York and New Jersey, reported zero unrestricted cash and investments and zero restricted debt reserves for 2018, as well as in years prior. We calculated days of cash on hand using 2018 CATS data, with the following equation:

$$\text{Days Cash} = \frac{\text{Unrestricted Cash and Investments + Restricted Debt Reserves}}{\text{Operating Expenses (excluding depreciation) + Debt Service (excluding coverage)}}$$

Table 8.6 shows that a holistic view of airports with the most OPSNET delays per operation in 2018 reveals variation and nuance in airports' status. For example CLT has relatively normal delays per operation for a large-hub airport. It has a very large amount of cash on hand and a high DSCR relative to other large-hub airports. Both enplanements and operations are forecast to grow significantly from 2018 to 2030 at CLT; according to these factors, however, CLT appears well-positioned financially to manage this growth.

SEA faces a different context. Over the past few years, OPSNET delays at SEA have increased from trivial levels to a point where this airport is one of the most delayed in the nation. Its cash on hand was below average for large hubs in 2010 and has been declining since then. Its DSCR is not significantly lower than other large-hub airports but has declined since 2009. Massive future growth in both enplanement and operations is expected. According to these factors, SEA looks like an airport that might benefit significantly from increased revenue.

In addition to these financial considerations, many airports face other nonfinancial constraints on infrastructure investment. Some airports lack the physical space in which to expand. Staff we spoke with at one airport said the airport is already expanding at the fastest pace they can responsibly manage. Combining information about the amount of and trends in delays faced by airports, airports' financial status, and airports' expected future growth can help paint a picture of which airports are in need of infrastructure investment and which are able to afford and manage that investment.

Unsurprisingly, the answer to whether airports require additional revenue is "if you've seen one airport, you've seen one airport." In other words, it depends. Some airports appear to be financially prepared to meet growing future demand. Others are struggling to keep up. Multiple interviews and dozens of recent documents from airports have made it clear that many airports would use an increase in revenue to initiate approved projects sooner and to lower borrowing costs by paying off interest expenses faster. We cannot say how savings from reduced borrowing costs will be used. In some cases, savings could be used to fund additional capital projects. In other cases, airports suggest they could pass savings back to airlines, passengers, and other stakeholders through reductions in other fees.

Table 8.6
Measures of an Airport's Financial Capacity

		2018 OPSNET Delay		Cash on Hand			Debt Service Coverage Ratio			Projected Future Growth	
Airport	**Hub Size**	**OPSNET Delay per Operation (minutes)**	**% of National OPSNET Delay**	**Days Cash on Hand 2010**	**Trend 2010–2018**	**Days Cash on Hand 2018**	**DSCR 2009**	**Trend 2009–2017**	**DSCR 2017**	**Projected Percentage Growth in Enplanements, 2018–2030**	**Projected Percentage Growth in Operations, 2018–2030**
EWR	Large hub	6.75	19	N/A		N/A	N/A		N/A	44	23
LGA	Large hub	5.44	13	N/A		N/A	N/A		N/A	30	8
SFO	Large hub	3.99	12	292.0018921		436.9431458	1.1573963		0.87914864	30	21
JFK	Large hub	2.01	6	N/A		N/A	N/A		N/A	38	27
PHL	Large hub	1.95	5	181.6531372		333.1800842	1.804785722		1.60533197	27	16
ORD	Large hub	1.94	11	68.36309814		688.9406738	0.071737587		0.70224447	30	4
BOS	Large hub	1.76	5	257.1665344		723.3652954	1.862422141		2.26166683	34	27
TEB	Reliever	1.65	2	N/A		N/A	N/A		N/A	16	8
SEA	Large hub	1.52	4	391.8338928		278.5472412	1.855813452		1.52525321	38	36
DFW	Large hub	0.87	4	357.3208313		335.3744202	1.092117714		1.22924694	29	18
PHX	Large hub	0.83	2	86.23265839		607.552063	0.203719243		1.99380368	25	21
DCA	Large hub	0.80	2	166.5322876		413.3347778	1.574631609		2.17973263	34	4
ASE	Non-hub	0.79	0	N/A		N/A	N/A		N/A	10	10
LAX	Large hub	0.60	3	436.6620483		430.3193359	11.18921318		2.87975066	29	24
ATL	Large hub	0.55	3	595.5045166		780.1002197	N/A		1.63250881	27	19
IAH	Large hub	0.44	1	243.9391479		415.3152771	N/A		2.29556382	33	14
SUN	Non-hub	0.42	0	N/A		407.4380798	N/A		N/A	20	8
AGS	Non-hub	0.39	0	965.2310181		450.1483765	N/A		N/A	21	16
MSP	Large hub	0.32	1	745.9819946		742.7874146	1.858295793		2.52490346	21	12
DEN	Large hub	0.28	1	576.7400513		530.6394043	1.086849949		1.56405689	30	14
CLT	Large hub	0.28	1	889.7783813		1537.280762	1.015640316		2.73352892	28	24

NOTE: SUN = Friedman Memorial Airport; AGS = Augusta Regional Airport. See Table C.1 in Appendix C for a full list of the airport names. The OPSNET delay reported in this table does not include TRACONs and ARTCCs.

Summary of Findings

Airports have needed to adapt their infrastructure as the number of passengers and size of planes has changed. Infrastructure investments are expensive and can take years to complete, so airports, as well as other stakeholders, put considerable energy into forecasting future usage rates of airport infrastructure. Regardless of these efforts, the future remains uncertain. This irreducible uncertainty has made it difficult to accurately forecast capacity constraints in the NAS over time. The outlook for systemwide, airside capacity constraints has improved over the past two decades because of adjusted forecasts, changing economic conditions, the transition to larger commercial aircraft, and additional infrastructure. At the same time, the number of airports facing severe airside capacity constraints, while limited now, is likely to increase over time. On the landside, a lack of systemwide data to measure landside capacity across airports limits any type of empirical assessment of national-level capacity needs over time. In sum, for both landside and airside infrastructure, an uncertain future and the uncertain effects of external factors (e.g., economic conditions and airline decisions) make airport planning difficult. This is one reason why airports find flexibility in funding desirable.

Capacity constraints can manifest themselves in several ways throughout the system but most visibly affect passengers through delays. In practice, a small number of airports are the source of most delays, and some of these delays could be reduced by infrastructure investments. Moreover, these airports produce substantial propagated delays that affect airports systemwide. Infrastructure investment cannot mitigate or prevent all of these delays but could be part of a portfolio of strategies to reduce congestion if tailored to address the capacity issues at specific airports.

A key question is whether delays that could be in part reduced by infrastructure are increasing or decreasing over time. Although NAS delays, as recorded in OPSNET, have been getting more severe in recent years at the most capacity-constrained airports, NAS delays overall are not getting substantially worse, nor are they being reduced through new infrastructure investments. Importantly, the persistence of delays at the capacity-constrained airports is not perfectly correlated with the ability or inability of an airport to borrow funds to invest in additional capacity.

An airport's financial status is based on a wide variety of factors, including the airport's service area, traffic composition, airport competition, passenger trends and services levels, airline market share, use-and-lease provisions, capital program, debt, and finances (ACI-NA Finance Committee, 2011). Some airports appear well-positioned financially to manage future growth, while others appear to be in need of additional revenue to manage their anticipated future growth.

CHAPTER NINE

Key Findings and Recommendations

In this chapter, we synthesize our findings from the previous chapters, discuss relevant policy options, and make recommendations directed to both Congress and the FAA. In shaping our recommendations, we were guided by our findings and the following vision of what funding and financing policies in support of an effective NAS should look like, informed by our analysis and consultations with experts and stakeholders:

- Airports are able to draw on sufficient and stable sources of revenue, in conjunction with funding from capital markets, to maintain existing capacity, accommodate growth, and support a safe and sustainable NAS in the coming decades.
- Federal funding is effectively, efficiently, and flexibly deployed to address needs in the NAS that are of national significance and benefit.
- Airports of all sizes run safe, efficient, and sustainable operations for the betterment of their communities and the NAS as a whole.

The challenge for Congress in considering changes to federal policy and programs is to ensure that there is coherence in its overall strategy, either with the vision above or an alternative vision, and a willingness to adapt federal programs and resources to align with that overall strategy.

We begin this chapter by presenting our findings on the core challenges faced by airports and the NAS regarding the funding and financing of airport infrastructure. We then present a portfolio of recommendations designed to address those challenges and help achieve the vision described above. Finally, we identify issues that warrant further consideration but for which we do not make recommendations, either because they are beyond our scope or because sufficient data are unavailable.

Key Findings

In this section, we provide a broader perspective on the core challenges faced by airports and the NAS regarding the funding and financing of airport infrastructure. These summaries draw on the detailed findings described throughout the rest of the report and illuminate the base of evidence on which our recommendations are founded.

Finding 1: The Color—and Control—of Money Matters

Federal law requires commercial service airports, all of which are publicly owned, to operate in a businesslike way: Revenues generated from activities on airport property combined with federal or state grants are supposed to be sufficient to cover the airport's operating and capital expenses. Airports cannot generate profits, but they maintain financially prudent reserves for managing annual variability in revenue generation, major capital needs, and emergencies. Large airports are generally able to borrow from capital markets at favorable interest rates because of a history of financial responsibility, their proven capability to weather temporary economic downturns, and federal law that prohibits all but a handful of the public authorities that own airports from diverting airport revenues to nonairport uses. For those airports that borrow capital funds through bond markets, discipline on airport spending is further imposed through the forces of the marketplace and credit rating agencies.

Running an airport is complicated. The patchwork system of federally authorized funding mechanisms that have accreted over the past 50 years makes running an airport even more complicated. Airports draw revenue from a wide variety of sources, each of which comes with different rules and restrictions on how funds can be spent, as well as different conditions regarding which entities must approve planned projects. As a consequence, airport operators consider more than whether sufficient dollars are available to fund an infrastructure project. They also carefully consider whether and how much funding can come from different sources.

Control of funding decisions is an important determinant in an airport's funding preferences. Depending on the "color of money," airports might be required to line up approvals from the appropriate combination of federal regulators, local governments, state governments, and airlines before making investments in airport infrastructure. Decisions made by airports can have significant ramifications for these stakeholders. As a result of these complexities, investing in airport infrastructure is a far more complex and time-consuming process than simply tallying up whether sufficient dollars are available.

Further, airports are operating under a variety of public ownership models that require them to compete with other local or regional public priorities. Navigating these demands further complicates airport investment decisions.

Finding 2: If You've Seen One Airport, You've Seen One Airport

Although airports across the nation face many of the same challenges, the financial capabilities and local context of each airport can vary widely. All commercial service airports face the same broad industry trends, such as growing demand for air travel, increasing plane sizes, and the vulnerability of airport business models to disruptive technologies, such as ride-hailing services, self-driving vehicles, and the use of drones. Airports also face the same federal rules and regulations on funding, safety, security, and other issues. Most airports have managed to sustain sufficient investment in runways, terminals, and other services while maintaining strong credit ratings.

However, other factors affecting airports' financial capacities vary widely from airport to airport. Some airports appear better positioned financially to manage future growth than others. The prospect of growth in demand is closely tied to local economic conditions, which can inject a significant amount of uncertainty into airports' financial plans. With the exception of a few large-hub airports that serve as key airline hubs, most enplanements are from local passengers rather than those passing through. Further, how financial risks are distributed between airports and airlines depends on the particulars of use-and-lease agreements between individual airports and their tenant airlines. Differences in local governance arrangements and physical assets shape airports' opportunities for raising capital. Airports also have widely varying cash reserves, airline competition, and infrastructure-related delays, some of which reflect limitations on land availability or disagreements over local land-use policy and public priorities. These differences underscore the benefit to airports of maintaining some flexibility in federal policies.

Finding 3: There Are Known Areas in Which Infrastructure Investment Is Needed

Airport runways are generally in good repair. In 2013, 97.5 percent of NPIAS runways were rated excellent, good, or fair; at commercial service airports generally, 98 percent of runways were rated excellent, good, or fair. This reflects the priority given to airside infrastructure in federal grants provided under the AIP and the effectiveness of funding from all sources to meet airside needs. However, terminals and control towers are widely viewed as being in need of modernization, repair, or replacement. The growth in the number of enplanements has led to more crowded terminals at some airports, and many aging control towers and other air traffic control facilities require rehabilitation and upgrading. Smaller airports, which are almost wholly reliant on federal grants, struggle to generate sufficient revenues for spending on landside infrastructure for the processing of passengers, ground transportation vehicles, and other purposes.

These infrastructure limitations are one of several factors contributing to delays in the NAS, and these infrastructure-related delays are thus not spread evenly across the system. Rather, a small number of capacity-constrained airports and airport pairs appear to be responsible for delays that could be partially (but not fully) addressed by sound infrastructure investment. Twenty airports (19 large hubs and one reliever) accounted for 96 percent of delays measured by the FAA's OPSNET in 2018. The top five airports alone, three of which are operated by the Port Authority of New York and New Jersey (LGA, JFK, and EWR), accounted for 61 percent of delays. These delays propagate through the NAS: A flight delayed in arriving at its initial destination might be late departing for its next destination. On average, each hour of national aviation system delay at a capacity-constrained airport results in 30 more minutes of delay for subsequent flights at other airports. Some of this congestion could be addressed in part through sound investments in reconfiguring or expanding infrastructure on both the airside and the landside.

Finding 4: Easing Revenue Restrictions on the Passenger Facility Charge Would Reduce Airports' Borrowing Costs but Likely Would Increase Ticket Prices

Airports will need to make significant investments in the coming years to sustain existing capacity and services and to accommodate growth in enplanements and commercial operations. The larger commercial service airports are likely to find ways to make the investments they deem to be critical, but increased access to higher revenue streams in the near term would enable these airports to complete approved priority projects sooner and at lower borrowing costs.

One proposed method for allowing commercial service airports to raise additional revenue is to change the cap on the fee that passengers are charged for their use of airport infrastructure at airports that choose to participate in the federally authorized PFC program. With reference to the color of money in Finding 1, airlines cannot veto FAA-approved PFC-funded projects. The cap on PFCs has been set at $4.50 per passenger since the 2000 FAA Reauthorization Act. Since that time, the purchasing power of a dollar of PFC revenues has eroded because of inflation; each dollar of PFC revenue buys only 60 percent of the construction materials it did in 2000. Increasing enplanements have increased capital investment needs at many airports. It is also true that aggregate PFC revenues have grown because of increased nationwide enplanements, the increased number of airports using PFCs, and the increase of the PFC cap from $3.00 to $4.50. The eroding per-passenger value of the PFC could be partially offset by returns to scale as the number of passengers increases or by infrastructure demands that grow with operations rather than enplanements, but the degree of offset is difficult to quantify with precision.

In most cases, airports of all sizes are already maximizing their revenue from all available sources under current policies. Revenue from landing fees and concession contracts are governed by long-term contracts; increasing these fees would require renegotiation with those parties and, like any price increase, would risk the loss of those customers. PFC revenues at all large-hub airports but one are committed through 2022, 18 of 30 large hubs have fully committed their PFC revenues until at least 2030, and six large hubs are committed until at least 2040. Among the 31 medium hubs, ten have fully committed their PFC revenues until at least 2030, while 14 will have new revenues available by 2025. These airports are effectively unable to tap additional PFC revenue in the near future.

Increasing the PFC cap above the current level of $4.50 would enable those airports that seek additional PFC revenue to initiate their approved projects sooner and pay them off more quickly, lowering costs. In the aggregate, costs for some passengers are likely to increase as a consequence of the higher PFC. However, the impacts of a PFC increase on ticket prices at a particular airport may vary depending on both airport and airline decisions

Finding 5: Small Airports in Small Markets Have Limited Opportunities for Revenue Generation and Rely Primarily on Grants

Smaller airports by definition have a smaller user base that offers fewer opportunities for raising revenue and are therefore more reliant on federal (and to a much lesser extent, state) grants than larger airports for paying the high fixed costs related to runways, taxiways, aprons, safety, and security. Expanding airports' revenue base to include the taxing of nonairport local businesses and residents is unattractive to local governments and would increase the costs of local goods and services unrelated to air travel. GA airports are not eligible to collect PFCs, a mechanism that Congress authorized exclusively for use by commercial service airports, nor do GA airports have sufficient passenger volume to support such a user fee. Instead, GA and nonprimary commercial service airports rely on AIP funding, which is redistributive by design; smaller airports receive a larger share of AIP dollars than they generate in excise tax revenues to the AATF, which funds the AIP and many other FAA programs. Airports must be included in the NPIAS to be eligible to receive AIP funds.

There are two general types of AIP grants: entitlements and discretionary. The FAA uses discretionary grants to target specific projects at individual airports according to need and the benefit to the system as a whole. The FAA awards entitlement grants to most airports in the NPIAS, although airports that receive approval for PFC-funded projects forgo a portion of their entitlement. Under current congressionally mandated funding formulas, GA and nonprimary commercial service airports are each eligible to receive entitlement grants of up to $150,000 per year, an amount too small to support airport construction of any consequence. Airports, however, are permitted to defer their annual entitlements over several years to accumulate sufficient funds to undertake a project.

Finding 6: The Airport and Airway Trust Fund Has a Large and Growing Uncommitted Balance

The AATF, which funds many FAA programs (including the AIP), took in $750 million more in excise tax revenues than it spent in FY 2018, ending the year with an uncommitted balance of $6.1 billion. An uncommitted balance refers to funds that have not yet been obligated for spending. The AATF's uncommitted balance is projected to grow to $18.8 billion by the end of FY 2023, assuming passenger enplanements (and associated excise tax revenues) continue to rise. Several of the excise taxes that fund the AATF are pegged to inflation, and all of them relate to the volume of air infrastructure utilization.

Congress has the authority to obligate AATF funds for AIP grants to airports and a wide array of other underfunded capital needs. Currently, the FAA Reauthorization Act of 2018 holds the authorized level of AATF-funded AIP grants constant at $3.35 billion over the FY 2019 to FY 2023 period, and outlays from the AATF for other FAA purposes are assumed to grow only with inflation.

Finding 7: Revenue Diversion Is Still an Issue

Revenue diversion is the use of airport operating revenues for expenditures that are either not on airport property or do not directly serve aviation purposes. Because of the historical precedent that is discussed in Chapter Three, revenue diversion comes in two forms that are treated differently in policy. Both are a problem. In the first form, 12 airport sponsors—the cities or other public entities that own one or more airports—were grandfathered in when Congress mandated an end to such revenue diversion practices in 1982. Airports operated by these airport sponsors are legally allowed to divert airport operating revenue, up to a statutory limit. The second form encompasses revenue diversion by any other airport sponsor, which most frequently takes the form of state or local governments diverting revenue from aviation fuel taxes to nonaviation purposes.

The argument for grandfathering was that accounting and spending practices at these airports made a clean separation of revenue between airport and nonairport uses difficult. Correcting this challenge is not impossible because the grandfathering provision has been removed for three of the 12 airport sponsors. The amount of funds being diverted is not trivial; a 2018 USDOT Inspector General's report found that "[f]rom 1995 to 2015, grandfathered sponsors have reported over $10 billion in grandfathered payments in 2015 inflation-adjusted dollars, including over $1.2 billion in 2015" (USDOT, Office of Inspector General, 2018, pp. 1–2). The full extent of revenue collected and diverted is difficult to quantify by outside observers, including the FAA. The USDOT Inspector General's report found that both the FAA and sponsors made errors in reporting grandfathered payments, and that the State of Hawaii had exceeded its statutory limit. The Port Authority of New York and New Jersey might have also exceeded its statutory limits.

The FAA has effective enforcement options available for discouraging the second form of revenue diversion, but the FAA's existing enforcement mechanisms are largely unable to prevent grandfathered airports from exceeding their statutory limit. When a grandfathered airport diverts more revenue than allowed by its cap, the FAA can and does use that airport's noncompliant status as a factor in determining whether to grant discretionary funds, but these airports may not request discretionary funds. The FAA can also deny future PFC applications, but it cannot withhold PFC funds that have already been approved, as is often the case. Unlike other forms of revenue diversion, the FAA cannot withhold USDOT funding from grandfathered airports with excess revenue, and sponsors are not subject to financial damages. As a result, the FAA is largely unable to prevent grandfathered airports from exceeding their statutory limit.

Mapping of Section 122 Findings to Report Chapters

Section 122 of the FAA Reauthorization Act of 2018 requested that the independent organization conducting this study address 21 issues. These issues are addressed throughout the report, but not necessarily in the order in which they are listed in Section 122. Therefore, Table 9.1 provides a guide to the findings associated with each issue and their location within the report.

Recommendations

We recommend a portfolio of complementary changes to the PFC program, the AIP, the AATF, and to policies and procedures regarding revenue diversion, as indicated in Figure 9.1. The interrelated nature of these funding programs and policies makes it important to consider

Figure 9.1
Recommended Portfolio of Policy Options

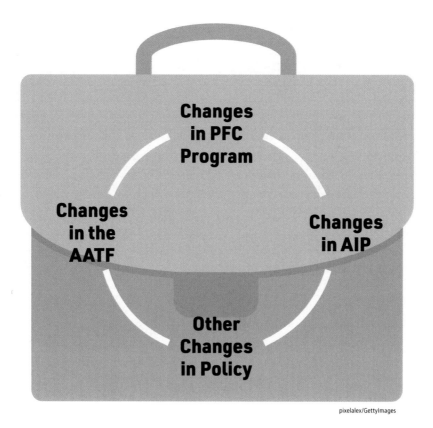

pixelalex/GettyImages

Table 9.1
Summary of Responses to Section 122 Issues

Subsection of Section 122	Issue	Summary of Findings	Chapter in Report
All Commercial Service Airports			
(c)(1)	Ability of airport infrastructure to meet current and projected passenger volumes	Twenty airports (19 large hubs and one reliever) account for 96 percent of delays measured by the FAA's Operations Network (OPSNET). Delays at most of these airports, as well as the National Airspace System (NAS) as a whole, had been declining since 2009 but have been increasing over the past three years as enplanements have increased. Some of these delays could be partially reduced by appropriate infrastructure investments.	Chapter Eight
(c)(2)	Available financial tools and resources for airports of different sizes	Airports of all sizes draw on multiple sources of funding. Larger airports tend to generate most of their revenues from their operations and take advantage of the municipal bond market. In contrast, smaller airports rely on Airport Improvement Program (AIP) and other grants for funding and have limited access to the bond market.	Chapters Four and Seven
(c)(3)	Available financing tools and resources for airports in rural areas	Rural airports, which are predominantly smaller airports, rely heavily on AIP and other grants as their major source of revenue, with these grants accounting for more than 50 percent of their revenue on average. Rural airports are less likely to participate in the bond market.	Chapter Four
(c)(4)	Current debt held by airports and its impact on future construction and capacity needs	Over the last ten years, large-hub airports have increased their debt by 34 percent, to $73.6 billion in 2017, but their debt-to-revenue ratio has remained relatively stable. Debt and debt-to-revenue ratios across commercial service airports of all other sizes have generally held steady over the past two decades. Airports' ability to finance future construction and capacity needs will depend on their financial status, regional and local economic conditions, and other factors.	Chapter Seven
(c)(5)	Impact of capacity constraints on passengers and ticket prices	As noted in (c)(1), 20 airports account for 96 percent of delays measured by the FAA's OPSNET. These airports create delays for passengers that propagate throughout the NAS.	Chapter Eight
		Separately, the average inflation-adjusted domestic ticket price fell from $630 in 1993 to $432 in 2018. Competition and market conditions are the primary determinants of ticket prices. We do not find evidence that capacity-enhancing projects significantly affect ticket prices.	Chapters Two and Six
(c)(6)	Purchasing power of the passenger facility charge (PFC) from the last increase in 2000 to the year of enactment of this Act	The purchasing power of the maximum per-enplanement PFC has declined, from $4.50 in 2000 to $2.72 in 2018, expressed in year 2000 dollars indexed to construction prices.	Chapter Six
(c)(7)	Impact to passengers and airports of indexing the PFC for inflation	If the $4.50 PFC cap had been indexed to inflation in construction prices in 2000, the current cap on passengers would be $7.44. If the cap were indexed to inflation moving forward, this would prevent further erosion of its purchasing power. According to historical precedent, airports' adoption of higher PFCs likely would become widespread over time.	Chapter Six
(c)(8)	How long airports are constrained with current PFC collections	PFC revenues at all large-hub airports but one are fully committed to FAA-approved projects through 2022. Eighteen of 30 large hubs have fully committed their PFC revenues until at least 2030, and six are committed until at least 2040. Among the 31 medium hubs, ten have fully committed their PFC revenues until at least 2030, while 14 will have new revenues available by 2025.	Chapter Six

Table 9.1—Continued

Subsection of Section 122	Issue	Summary of Findings	Chapter in Report
(c)(9)	Impact of PFCs on promoting competition	Analysis of existing data does not provide conclusive evidence of whether individual PFC projects have had impacts on competition. Facilities funded with PFCs may not be leased on an exclusive-use basis, and that policy element of the PFC program might support competition. Airline hubbing decisions and local economic conditions are more likely to drive significant changes in competition.	Chapter Six
(c)(10)	Additional resources or options to fund terminal construction projects	Airports typically combine funds from multiple sources to fund terminal construction projects. Many funds come from airport revenue. PFC funds can be used for non–revenue-generating portions of terminals, while AIP grants are generally focused on airside infrastructure. Expanding airports' revenue bases to include the taxing of nonairport local businesses and residents is unattractive to local governments and would increase the cost of local goods and services unrelated to air travel. Privatization is possible but rarely pursued; the Airport Investment Partnership Program, established in 1997, allows airports to explore privatization but has had few takers.	Chapters Four through Seven
(c)(11)	Resources eligible for use toward noise reduction and emission reduction projects	AIP grants and PFCs can be applied to noise reduction and emission reduction projects. We found no evidence that resources for these purposes are insufficient to meet current noise and emissions requirements.	Chapter Three
(c)(12)	Gap between the cost of projects eligible for the AIP and the annual federal funding provided	Airports consult with FAA regional staff to determine which AIP-eligible projects to submit, given program funds and priorities. This consultation process makes identifying the magnitude of a funding gap difficult in practice. The FAA's list of AIP-eligible projects exceeds annual AIP funding, but airports can and do use other funds to pay for AIP-eligible projects.	Chapters Five and Eight
(c)(13)	Impact of regulatory requirements on airport infrastructure financing needs	Airports draw revenue from a wide variety of sources, each of which comes with its own rules and restrictions on how funds can be spent and who has approval authority. A benefit of regulatory processes is that they provide an opportunity for the public to voice concerns or support for specific projects. Effects on project completion timelines and cost are likely to vary depending on local context. We were unable to estimate cumulative impacts.	Chapters Three and Four
(c)(14)	Airline competition	Over the past few decades, mergers and bankruptcies in the airline industry have led to fewer overall airlines, with four airlines currently responsible for 73 percent of available seat miles and 80 percent of enplanements. National average fares have fallen 36 percent since 1993, but fares on individual routes fluctuate. Markets with fewer passengers are likely to be served by fewer airlines.	Chapter Two
(c)(15)	Airline ancillary fees and their impact on ticket pricing and taxable revenue	Some airlines have separated ancillary fees, such as fees for baggage and reserved seats, from their base fares. Ancillary fees that have been separated from base fares are exempt from the 7.5 percent excise tax that helps fund the Airport and Airway Trust Fund (AATF). If the $4.9 billion in baggage fees collected by airlines in 2018 had been subject to the 7.5 percent tax, AATF revenues would have been about $367 million higher, all other factors being equal.	Chapter Five
(c)(16)	Ability of airports to finance necessary safety, security, and capacity projects	To date, airports have been able to finance necessary safety, security, capacity, and environmental projects identified in capital improvement plans. Their financial ability to continue doing so in a timely manner varies. Policy changes that increase revenue would enable some airports to initiate projects sooner and at a lower borrowing cost than they could otherwise but would likely increase passenger ticket prices.	Chapter Eight

Table 9.1—Continued

Subsection of Section 122	Issue	Summary of Findings	Chapter in Report
Large-Hub Airports			
(d)(1)	Analyze the current and future capacity constraints of large-hub airports	Nineteen large-hub airports account for 94 percent of delays measured by FAA's OPSNET. Delays at most of these airports, as well as the NAS as a whole, had been declining since 2009 but have been increasing over the past three years as enplanements have increased. Some of these delays could be partially reduced by appropriate infrastructure investments.	Chapter Eight
(d)(2)	Quantify large-hub airports' infrastructure requirements, including terminal, landside, and airside infrastructure	Infrastructure at large-hub airports served 534,507,475 domestic commercial enplanements and 11,893,110 operations in 2018. As noted in (d)(3), this use of airport infrastructure is expected to grow. We cannot say how to convert these activity levels to credible estimates of specific infrastructure requirements, because this depends largely on the flexibility of airports' current configuration, local context, market forces, and changes in technology.	Chapter Two
(d)(3)	Quantify the percentage growth in infrastructure requirements of the large-hub airports relative to other commercial service airports	The FAA's Terminal Area Forecast (TAF) suggests that large-hub airports' operations will increase by 19 percent and enplanements will increase by 30 percent from 2018 to 2030. Over the same period, operations at medium hubs are forecast to grow by 17 percent, small hubs by 10 percent, and non-hubs by 6 percent. This growth will likely lead to increased infrastructure requirements, but local circumstances will determine whether changes are required and, if so, their associated costs.	Chapter Eight
(d)(4)	Analyze how much funding from the AIP has gone to meet the requirements of large-hub airports over the past ten years	In total, large hubs received about $6 billion in AIP grants from FYs 2009 to 2018. This was 17 percent of all AIP grant dollars over that period. The percentage of large hubs' capital expenditures that comes from AIP grants has declined, down to 5 percent in FY 2018 from approximately 10 percent to 15 percent between FYs 2009 and 2015. Under present policies, large- and medium-hub airports forgo much of their AIP primary entitlement grants when imposing PFCs but retain access to other AIP grants.	Chapter Five
(d)(5)	Project how much AIP funding would be available to meet the requirements of large-hub airports in the next five years if funding levels are held constant	If appropriations, statutory entitlements, and the distribution of discretionary funds that goes to large hubs were all to remain the same as they have over the past ten years, then about $3 billion of AIP funding would be available for large hubs over the next five years. This would represent 17 percent of the total AIP funding that would be available over this five-year period.	Chapter Five

these recommendations as a whole rather than in isolation. Taken together, these changes have the potential to help airports of all sizes maintain safe, efficient, and sustainable operations.

The vision and findings presented at the beginning of this chapter provide the basis for our recommendations. The vision underlies all of our recommendations, and Table 9.2 shows how our recommendations are connected to the preceding findings. Our findings are in turn supported by the details presented in this report.

Changes to the PFC Program

Congress has several options regarding changes to the PFC program. We present and discuss four policy options, illustrated in Figure 9.2: (A) index the current cap to inflation, (B) increase the flexibility of airport revenue but do not increase cumulative revenue, (C) raise but do not remove the PFC cap, and (D) remove the PFC cap entirely. We recommend that Congress pursue Option C by increasing, but not removing, the PFC cap.

Option A: Index to Inflation

- Index the current PFC cap to inflation.
- Make no other changes.

Option A would index the current PFC cap to inflation but make no other changes to the program. To ensure that airports have sufficient and stable sources of revenue commensurate with present and future capital needs, the PFC cap should be indexed to inflation, regardless of whether the PFC cap is otherwise changed. Indexing the PFC to a construction index, such as the Producer Price Index for construction materials, would stabilize the parity of purchasing power at the current cap or at a new cap set by Congress for airports making infrastructure investments. Indexing to the CPI would hold constant the effect of PFC increases on passenger ticket prices. PFC collections in the aggregate have increased without indexing because of

Table 9.2
Connection Between Recommendations and Findings

Finding	Changes to the PFC	Changes to the AIP	Changes to the AATF	Changes to revenue diversion
Finding 1: The color—and control—of money matters.	■			■
Finding 2: If you've seen one airport, you've seen one airport.	■			■
Finding 3: There are known areas in which infrastructure investment is needed.	■			
Finding 4: Easing revenue restrictions on the PFC would reduce airports' borrowing costs but likely would increase ticket prices.	■			
Finding 5: Small airports in small markets have limited opportunities for revenue generation and rely primarily on grants.		■		
Finding 6: The AATF has a large and growing uncommitted balance.			■	
Finding 7: Revenue diversion is still an issue.				■

NOTE: Shaded boxes identify the findings that provide evidentiary support for the recommendation.

increasing nationwide enplanements, increases in the number of airports using PFCs, and the increase in the PFC cap from $3.00 to $4.50. At the same time, increases in enplanements and operations will likely lead to increased infrastructure requirements.

Under current policy, larger airports are generally able to raise funds for critical projects and are meeting their debt obligations. Some airports, such as CLT, appear to be financially well-positioned to meet growing future demand. However, other airports, such as SEA, appear to be to be struggling to keep up with growing demand under existing policies. We do not recommend this option because it does not improve the ability of constrained airports to meet growing needs in the near term.

Option B: Increase Airport's Flexibility with Minimal Changes in Revenue
- Raise the PFC cap from $4.50 to $4.75.
- Index the new PFC cap to inflation.
- Reduce statutory AIP entitlements per passenger by $1.00 at those airports that choose to raise their PFC to $4.75.

Option B generally does not offer airports additional revenue but does convert more-restrictive AIP grant funds into more-flexible PFC revenues. Increased flexibility would enable airports to better match available funds to areas of need. As with Option A, Option B would not help those airports that have demonstrated needs to raise additional revenue to meet higher demand.

This option could be structured to tie higher PFC revenues to corresponding reductions in AIP primary entitlements. These entitlements—like PFC revenues—are calculated based

Figure 9.2
Policy Options for the PFC Cap

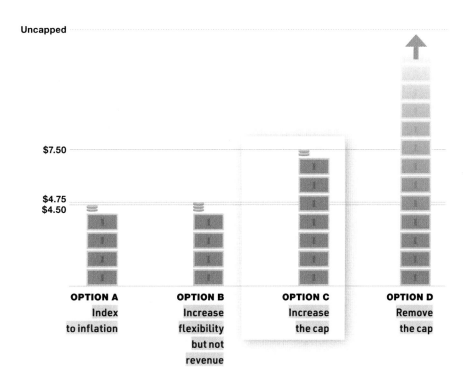

on the number of enplanements. So long as the annual appropriation for the AIP is at least $3.2 billion, statutory AIP primary entitlements per passenger are $1.00 after the first 1 million enplanements. However, airports that charge a $4.50 PFC already give up 75 percent of this entitlement, so they only receive $0.25 per passenger in practice for enplanements above 1 million, up to a statutory cap on primary entitlements.[1]

Therefore, in this option, airports that increase their PFC to $4.75 and reduce their statutory AIP primary entitlements by $1.00 per passenger would simply be converting $0.25 per passenger of AIP funds into $0.25 per passenger of PFC funds, until they reach the number of enplanements that would result in hitting the statutory cap on primary entitlements (22,975,000). Airports with enplanements below this number but above 1 million enplanements would still ultimately receive $757,500 in entitlement funds on their first 1 million passengers.[2] After that, they could continue to give back $0.25 in entitlements per enplanement (to offset the additional $0.25 in PFC they are collecting) until they forgo their primary entitlements entirely. The largest airports, with more than about 26 million enplanements, would be more than made whole by the ability to keep collecting at the higher PFC level after forgoing their primary entitlements.

Option C: Increase the Cap
- Raise the current PFC cap of $4.50 to approximately $7.50 for origin passengers only.
- Index the new PFC cap to inflation.
- Eliminate 100 percent of AIP primary entitlements for medium- and large-hub airports that choose to raise their PFC above $4.50.

Option C would give airports the ability to raise additional revenue, when necessary, by increasing the PFC cap beyond Options A or B. This option would improve airports' ability to make timely and efficient capital investments to meet growing future demand, while leaving in place FAA oversight of project justification and costs on passengers.

We are not aware of compelling evidence or data justifying a particular level for a new cap. Any number could be chosen, but we note that if the $4.50 cap had been indexed to inflation in 2000 using the Producer Price Index for construction materials, it would now be set at $7.44. For this reason, we suggest that the cap in this option be around this value, perhaps rounded up to $7.50, although other levels could be chosen. Although an increase in the PFC cap would likely result in higher ticket prices for passengers traveling through airports that raised their PFC collections, there remains in place a set of guardrails to weigh the public benefits of PFC-funded projects relative to the costs imposed on passengers. Airports will continue to be required to justify the net benefits of projects proposed for PFC funding to the FAA, and the FAA retains its discretion to approve or disapprove applications for these projects. Further, airports will still need to be responsive to comments from airlines and other stakeholders when requesting a PFC increase.

---

[1]   The statutory cap on primary entitlements is $26 million, or $6.5 million after forgoing 75 percent, when the AIP appropriation is at least $3.2 billion. This threshold is reached at 22,975,000 enplanements.

[2]   See Table 5.2. Reducing the entitlements per enplanement by $1.00 would cause airports with 1 million or more passengers to receive, at most, $3,030,000 in entitlements. Current rules require airports with a PFC of $4.50 to give up 75 percent of their entitlements, leaving them with $757,500 in entitlements.

Not all airports will choose to seek an immediate or longer-term PFC increase. To increase transparency regarding the intentions of airports in maintaining cash reserves beyond those required by bond rating agencies, we suggest that the FAA consider an airport's cash reserves and broader financial status when determining whether to approve the airport's request for an increase in its PFC.

We recommend that large- and medium-hub airports that raise their PFC above $4.50, indexed to inflation, should forgo their AIP primary entitlements dollar-for-dollar for each dollar of PFCs they collect, up to 100 percent of these entitlements. Instead, that money could more efficiently achieve the redistributive purpose of the AIP by being either focused on the needs of national significance among smaller airports or directed to other priorities affecting the safety and sustainability of the NAS. Airports that raise their PFC above $4.50 would remain eligible for other categories of AIP funding, including cargo entitlements and discretionary awards.

We recommend that any increase in the PFC cap apply only to passengers who originate at that airport, while the PFC for layover passengers remains capped at $4.50, indexed to inflation. The rationale for restricting future PFC increases to origin passengers only is to ensure that airports that increase their PFCs do so at their own expense, rather than at the expense of other airports. Under current law, passengers with one or more layovers must pay two PFCs: one to the origin airport and one to the first layover airport. If an airport's PFC increase applies to layover passengers, demand for flights that have layovers at that airport would decrease. This would be particularly problematic for small airports, where almost all routes go through one or two larger "feeder" airports to connect their community to the national and international system. Because origin passengers represent the majority of passengers at most airports, and because layover passengers can still be charged PFCs at currently approved rates, all commercial service airports would still receive a meaningful increase in their ability to raise revenue through PFCs.

Having a separate cap for origin and layover passengers will require some changes in implementation but would be manageable. The FAA should be given time to update its systems and conduct a study of the most efficient way to implement this recommendation as well as of infrastructure use by origin passengers versus layover passengers to determine the appropriate cap for layover passengers.[3]

Option D: Remove the Cap
- Remove the PFC cap for origin flights only.
- Index the current $4.50 PFC cap for layovers to inflation.
- Eliminate 100 percent of AIP entitlements for airports that raise their PFC above $4.50.

Removing the PFC cap entirely would provide airports with the most flexibility, but it is worth noting that we are not aware of any airports advocating this option. Having said that, the concern with this option is that airports would burden their customers and airlines' passengers with the cost of unnecessary projects. There are two main checks against airports increasing the PFC to inappropriately high levels. The first is that the PFC application process requires

---

[3] Until such a study is completed, airports should not be allowed to charge layover passengers a PFC of less than 50 percent of the origin PFC. This would prevent airports from lowering their layover PFC to $0 to attract layover traffic and only charge origin passengers for infrastructure use.

airports to consult with stakeholders and reply to their concerns when requesting the FAA's approval. As discussed in Chapter Six, the PFC request must be related to specific projects, and those projects must support one or more approved objectives. The FAA does consider whether the scope of each project is justified with respect to existing statute, but the FAA is not responsible for conducting a cost-benefit analysis or any market-based assessment of need. The second check against excessive PFC increases is market-based. Airports that raise their PFC will face decreased demand from travelers and therefore will face decreased business from airlines. An airport that raises its PFC too high could actually lose revenue for this reason.

Despite these checks, there remains a small risk that airports would raise their PFC to excessive levels. Although some cities have multiple small-, medium-, or large-hub airports, many cities have only one major airport. Travelers could either choose to pay the higher PFC or drive many hours out of their way to avoid it, and thus decrease demand at the high-PFC airport. As experience over the past two decades showed, virtually all airports raised their PFC to the cap over time. However, we do not see a rationale or signs of demand for entirely removing the cap. If Congress were to choose this option, we would recommend maintaining an inflation-indexed cap on layover passengers and having airports that exceed a PFC of $4.50 forgo AIP primary entitlements dollar-for-dollar, up to 100 percent of these entitlements, for all the same reasons outlined in Option C.

Changes to the Airport Improvement Program
Congress Should Remove the Automatic Doubling of Airport Improvement Program Primary Entitlements

Under current law, whenever Congress appropriates at least $3.2 billion to the AIP, primary entitlements per passenger double (subject to a cap), with those increases resulting in less money available for other AIP funds, including discretionary grants. As a consequence of this policy, annual AIP funding is spread across all primary airports according to their enplanements, and the FAA has less discretion to effectively direct funds to current high-priority projects at specific airports.

We recommend that Congress remove the triggered primary entitlement increase that occurs when Congress appropriates at least at $3.2 billion to the AIP. Those airports not voluntarily forgoing AIP entitlements in return for the ability to collect PFCs could still receive comparable levels of AIP funding over time, but the timing and magnitude of annual grants would be better aligned with the timing and magnitude of needs. Airports could compete to receive more funds in the form of larger grants from the pool of discretionary funding, when needed, but would receive fewer guaranteed funds in the form of annual entitlements.

Congress Should Consider Removing Nonprimary Entitlements

As with primary entitlements, under current law, whenever Congress appropriates at least $3.2 billion to the AIP, each nonprimary airport in the NPIAS receives an entitlement of up to $150,000 instead of those funds going to more-flexible state apportionments for nonprimary airports. This amount is insufficient for major construction projects, and the existing state apportionment mechanism is both better suited to meet nonprimary airports' needs and has sufficient oversight mechanisms in place. We recommend that Congress eliminate nonprimary entitlements that occur under current law when the AIP appropriation is at least $3.2 billion. As with the previous recommendation, airports could still compete to receive comparable levels of funding over time, but the timing and magnitude of individual distributions would be better aligned with the timing and magnitude of needs.

Changes to the Airport and Airway Trust Fund
Congress Should Avoid the Accumulation of Large Uncommitted Airport and Airway Trust Fund Balances, While Still Maintaining a "Rainy Day" Reserve Fund
Existing spending guarantee mechanisms in statute are designed to prevent the accumulation of a large uncommitted balance in the AATF and to ensure excise tax revenues are spent on aviation system priorities. In practice, the enforcement mechanism is weak and is regularly ignored by Congress. Under excise tax levels set in current law, a large uncommitted balance is projected to materialize. Congress should take advantage of the existing uncommitted balance to establish and maintain a "rainy day" fund to ensure funding levels can remain stable over time. In years that experience unusually low demand for air travel, such as 2002 and 2009, actual revenues to the AATF can fall approximately $2 billion below projected revenues. A rainy day fund containing $4 billion to $6 billion would be sufficient to ensure that AATF outflows, for all purposes, can remain stable even in the face of two to three years of severe revenue shortfalls. However, after seeding the rainy day fund, additional revenues should be appropriated to meet clearly identified needs, as determined by the FAA.

Congress Should Include Ancillary Fees in the Domestic Passenger Ticket Tax
Ancillary fees are charges for airline-provided services or products that some airlines sell separately from tickets, such as checked baggage, advance seat assignments, and priority boarding. These fees are excluded from the 7.5 percent Domestic Passenger Ticket Tax that helps fund the AATF. This policy favors airlines that separate ancillary fees from their base ticket price over those that do not. Airlines should be free to separate ancillary fees if they wish, but the Domestic Passenger Ticket Tax should not incentivize one business model over another by taxing ancillary services differently from bundled ticket prices. However, Congress should not be collecting additional AATF revenue without a commitment to spend it, as noted in the preceding recommendation. For this reason, we recommend that Congress ask the FAA to help determine the level of reduction in the Domestic Passenger Ticket Tax that would make the taxation of ancillary fees revenue-neutral.

Changes to Enforcement of Prohibitions on Revenue Diversion
The FAA Should Increase Enforcement of Existing Rules
Revenue diversion refers to the practice of airport sponsors spending aviation-related revenue on nonaviation purposes, a practice generally prohibited by law. Revenue diversion remains a significant problem, even though the FAA has sought to clarify its rules regarding the disposition of state-based fuel taxes in recent years. Generally, the pressure to divert revenue comes from other local interests and not airport management, which has every interest in retaining the revenues generated by airport operations. Thus, withholding AIP grants as a punishment for revenue diversion is not a well-targeted deterrence strategy. Under current law, the USDOT, if triggered by FAA enforcement action, has the authority to withhold other USDOT grants from airport sponsors (as opposed to withholding FAA grants from airport management) that remain out of compliance with revenue diversion rules. This withholding rarely occurs, but the FAA should pursue this path when compliance is not swift.

Congress Should Phase Out Grandfathering

Twelve airport sponsors were originally granted waivers in 1982 from prohibitions on revenue diversion because of their particularly complicated arrangements for mingling revenues and expenditures across multiple public assets under their jurisdiction. The grandfathering provision has already been removed for three of these airport sponsors, proving that ending this exception is possible. Ending this exception also is important for supporting good governance at the local level.

Issues for Further Analysis

Many Airports and Routes Lack a Healthy Level of Competition

Many airports, cities, and routes are served by only one or two airlines. Lack of competition among airlines at a given airport can result in higher costs for travelers. An objective of the PFC program is to enhance competition by giving airports a stream of revenue that can be spent independently from airline influence. Our analysis in Chapter Six finds that available data do not provide conclusive evidence as to whether individual PFC projects have had an effect on competition. Facilities funded with PFCs may not be leased on an exclusive-use basis, and that policy element of the PFC program might support competition. In practice, PFC projects provide airports with a means of accommodating new entrants without a veto by legacy carriers, but competition cannot be enhanced solely through changes in infrastructure finance policy.

Competition challenges are not limited solely to airlines. Under current law, airport sponsors that manage multiple airports can use PFC funds collected at one of their airports to pay for projects at another of their airports.[4] This occurs rarely, but it challenges the notion that PFCs are a user fee.

In both cases, broader economic issues and trade-offs are in play that require a more comprehensive assessment.

Impacts of Regulations and Requirements Are Uncertain

As previously noted, airports draw revenue from a wide variety of sources, each of which comes with its own rules and restrictions on how funds can be spent and who has approval authority. Control of funding decisions is an important determinant in shaping an airport's funding preferences, but in nearly all cases, the FAA plays an important oversight role in maintaining discipline in spending at commercial service airports. In addition to regulations applying to project eligibility, recipients of AIP grants must meet a long list of labor, environmental, health, safety, and security regulations and other requirements. Many anecdotes have accumulated over the years about individual projects being delayed or stopped entirely as a consequence of local opposition, whether because of cost, noise, or encroachment into neighboring communities. But projects being halted or delayed by regulations or requirements is not necessarily inappropriate, because impacts on other stakeholders are important considerations. This long-standing question in public policy remains a topic ripe for independent, objective, and rigorous

---

[4]   Airports in the same city are often managed by the same airport sponsor. Such regional coordination can greatly improve efficiency and urban planning but may limit the extent to which competition between airports for the same passengers encourages airports to keep costs low.

analysis to provide Congress and other decisionmakers with clearer direction on how regulations can be harmonized and streamlined to increase their effectiveness at protecting public safety, health, labor, and the environment and to enhance efficiency in their application.

Revenue-Neutral Alternatives to Fuel Taxes Will Eventually Be Needed

Fuel taxes are not the largest portion of AATF revenue. Nonetheless, progress on developing and deploying electric planes could eventually lead to declines in fuel-based tax revenues while leaving the electric planes using the same infrastructure untaxed. A comparable situation applies to the gas tax supporting the Highway Trust Fund. To ensure stability and equity of funding, Congress should authorize the FAA to conduct a study that considers transitional or alternative tax structures, such as weight-based or operations-based taxes, including alternatives that would be revenue-neutral relative to revenues generated by the current levels of fuel-based taxes.

Inventory Existing Infrastructure and Assess Infrastructure Capacity and Physical Condition

Existing inventories and assessments of airport infrastructure have significant shortcomings. There is a need for an objective and analytically rigorous national inventory of existing airport infrastructure, air traffic control towers, and other air traffic facilities, and there is a need for an assessment of their current capacity, functionality, and physical condition. An up-to-date inventory and assessment of infrastructure conditions would provide a valuable foundation for Congress to make more-informed choices in the future about the levels of investment required across the different infrastructure types. A possible model for the assessment portion of this recommendation is a 1987 study by the Transportation Research Board on measuring airport landside capacity (Transportation Research Board, 1987).

Concluding Thoughts

Airport infrastructure is funded by a wide variety of revenue sources, each of which comes with different rules and restrictions on how funds can be spent and different conditions regarding which entities must approve planned projects. Airports are constantly investing in new infrastructure to keep up with growing demand for air travel, and most airports do rather well in serving the traveling public, strengthening the economic base of their communities, and contributing to national economic well-being. Some airports appear to be financially prepared to meet growing future demand. Others are struggling to keep up.

Changes in federal policies would help ensure airports are able to draw on sufficient and stable sources of revenue, in conjunction with funding from capital markets, to maintain existing capacity and accommodate future growth. Increasing the PFC cap would help airports keep up with growing demand by initiating approved projects sooner and at lower borrowing costs. However, costs for passengers are likely to increase at airports that request and obtain increased PFC rates.

Changes in federal policies could also help ensure funds are getting to the right places. First, AIP entitlement funds are spread too thinly across too many airports to match the nature of infrastructure expenses, which are large and infrequent. These funds would be more effective if targeted at current high-priority projects at specific airports. Airports could still receive comparable levels of AIP funding over time, but the timing and magnitude of annual grants would be better aligned with the timing and magnitude of needs. Second, although airport runways are widely agreed to be well-maintained, terminals and control towers are widely viewed as being in need of modernization, repair, or replacement. These known needs in the NAS provide an opportunity to put forecast growth in AATF funds to good use. Third, revenue diversion makes the system as a whole a leaky bucket: Plugging these leaks is important for restoring good governance at the local level.

Together, these changes can help airports of all sizes run safe, efficient, and sustainable operations for the betterment of their communities and the NAS as a whole.

References

A4A—*See* Airlines for America.

ACI—*See* Airports Council International.

ACI-NA—*See* Airports Council International–North America.

Air Canada, "What Are the Additional Charges in My Fare?" webpage, undated. As of September 6, 2019:
https://www.aircanada.com/content/dam/aircanada/portal/html/dailog-box/booking-flow/surcharges_en.html

Airline Deregulation Act—*See* Public Law 95-504.

Airlines for America, "U.S. Airline Mergers and Acquisitions," webpage, undated. As of June 25, 2019:
http://airlines.org/dataset/u-s-airline-mergers-and-acquisitions/

———, "The Cost of Doing Nothing: Why Investment in Our Nation's Airports Matters," testimony presented before the Committee on Transportation and Infrastructure, U.S. House of Representatives, March 26, 2019. As of June 26, 2019:
http://airlines.org/wp-content/uploads/2019/03/A4A-Written-Testimony-For-the-Record-3-26-2019.pdf

Airports Council International, "US Publicly-Owned Airports Are an Underrated Sector," *Airport World*, July 24, 2015. As of August 5, 2019:
http://www.airport-world.com/news/general-news/
5129-us-publicly-owned-airports-are-an-underrated-sector-kroll-bond-rating-agency-kbra.html

———, *World Airport Traffic Forecasts 2018–2040*, Montreal, November 1, 2018.

Airports Council International–Europe, *The Ownership of Europe's Airports 2016*, Brussels, 2016. As of July 9, 2019:
https://www.aci-europe.org/component/downloads/downloads/5095.html

Airports Council International–North America Finance Committee, *Credit Ratings and Cash Reserves: How They Influence the Borrowing Costs of Airports: An Industry White Paper*, Washington, D.C., January 25, 2011. As of November 11, 2019:
https://airportimprovement.com/pdfs/ACI_White-Paper-final_1-25-2011.pdf

Albuquerque International Sunport, *Sustainable Airport Master Plan*, Albuquerque, New Mexico, April 2018. As of November 25, 2019:
http://thesunport.airportstudy.com/master-plan/

American Society of Civil Engineers, "Infrastructure Report Card: Aviation," 2017. As of November 11, 2019:
https://www.infrastructurereportcard.org/wp-content/uploads/2017/01/Aviation-Final.pdf

ASCE—*See* American Society of Civil Engineers.

Beckman, Howard, "Ability of Local Jurisdictions to Regulate Airport Noise," webpage, August 2, 2012. As of June 26, 2019:
http://www.airportnoiselaw.org/abate.html

Belko, Mark, "Pittsburgh International Airport's Midfield Terminal at 20: A Shell of Its Past Self," *Pittsburgh Post-Gazette*, September 30, 2012. As of June 25, 2019:
https://www.post-gazette.com/news/transportation/2012/09/30/
Pittsburgh-International-Airport-s-midfield-terminal-at-20-A-shell-of-its-past-self/stories/201209300226

———, "$1.1B Approved for Reconfiguration of Pittsburgh International, Including New Landside Terminal," *Pittsburgh Post-Gazette*, September 12, 2017. As of October 17, 2019:
https://www.post-gazette.com/business/development/2017/09/12/
Pittsburgh-International-Airport-Allegheny-County-Authority-board-vote-plan-new-landside-terminal/
stories/201709120131

Blumenthal, Richard, "Citing Unprecedented Consolidation Within Airline Industry, Blumenthal Urges DOJ to Investigate Potential Anti-Competitive, Anti-Consumer Behavior and Misuse of Market Power," press release, Washington, D.C., June 17, 2015. As of June 13, 2019:
https://www.blumenthal.senate.gov/newsroom/press/release/citing-unprecedented-consolidation-within-airline-industry-blumenthal-urges-doj-to-investigate-potential-anti-competitive-anti-consumer-behavior-and-misuse-of-market-power

Boeing, *Commercial Market Outlook: 2019–2038*, Chicago, September 2019. As of October 10, 2019:
http://www.boeing.com/resources/boeingdotcom/commercial/market/commercial-market-outlook/assets/
downloads/cmo-sept-2019-report-final.pdf

Bradley, Sebastien, and Naomi E. Feldman, *Hidden Baggage: Behavioral Responses to Changes in Airline Ticket Tax Disclosure*, Washington, D.C.: Board of Governors of the Federal Reserve System, Finance and Economics Discussion Series 2018-057, July 2018. As of September 6, 2019:
https://www.federalreserve.gov/econres/feds/files/2018057pap.pdf

Brancatelli, Joe, "Don't Believe the Airfare Spin: Cost to Travel Is Sky High," *Business Journals*, May 8, 2014. As of November 11, 2019:
https://www.bizjournals.com/bizjournals/blog/seat2B/2014/05/
don-t-believe-the-airfare-spin-cost-to-travel-is.html

BTS—*See* Bureau of Transportation Statistics.

Bureau of Labor Statistics, "Producer Price Index by Commodity for Special Indexes: Construction Materials," retrieved from FRED, Federal Reserve Bank of St. Louis, in August 2019. As of November 22, 2019:
https://fred.stlouisfed.org/series/WPUSI012011

Bureau of Transportation Statistics, "Number 261: Final Rule Changes to T-100 and T-100(F) Traffic Reporting Systems," August 27, 2002. As of September 6, 2019:
https://www.bts.gov/topics/airlines-and-airports/
number-261-final-rule-changes-t-100-and-t-100f-traffic-reporting

———, "Rural Airports," webpage, December 18, 2018. As of May 1, 2019:
https://www.bts.gov/modes/aviation/rural-airports

———, "On-Time Performance: Flight Delays at a Glance," 2019a. As of October 18, 2019:
https://www.transtats.bts.gov/HomeDrillChart.asp

———, "Air Carrier Summary Data: T1: U.S. Air Carrier Traffic and Capacity Summary by Service Class," updated March 2019b. As of June 25, 2019:
https://www.transtats.bts.gov/Tables.asp?DB_ID=130&DB_Name=Air%20Carrier%20Summary%20Data

———, "Air Carrier Statistics (Form 41 Traffic) – All Carriers, T-100 Segment," updated April 2019c. As of September 13, 2019:
https://www.transtats.bts.gov/Tables.asp?DB_ID=111&DB_Name=Air%20Carrier%20Statistics%20
%28Form%2041%20Traffic%29-%20All%20Carriers&DB_Short_Name=Air%20Carriers

———, "Airline Origin and Destination Survey (DB1B): Market," updated June 2019d. As of September 13, 2019:
https://www.transtats.bts.gov/DatabaseInfo.asp?DB_ID=125

———, "Air Carrier Summary: Schedule P-1.2, 39062 - Property - Passenger Baggage Fees," updated June 17, 2019e. As of September 6, 2019:
http://www.transtats.bts.gov/Fields.asp?Table_ID=295

———, "Baggage Fees by Airline 2019," updated June 17, 2019f. As of June 24, 2019:
https://www.bts.gov/content/baggage-fees-airline-2019

Cho, Aileen, "Old, New and JetBlue Join at New York Airport," *Engineering News-Record,* Vol. 260, No. 12, 2008, p. 12.

Ciliberto, Federico, and Jonathan W. Williams, "Limited Access to Airport Facilities and Market Power in the Airline Industry," *Journal of Law and Economics*, Vol. 53, No. 3, August 2010, pp. 467–495.

City of Chicago, *General Obligation Bonds: Project and Refunding Series 2014A and Taxable Project and Refunding Series 2014B*, Supplement to Official Statement, Chicago, Ill., March 18, 2014. As of November 22, 2019:
https://emma.msrb.org/EA590845-EA461808-EA857838.pdf

Code of Federal Regulations, Title 14, Chapter 1, Subchapter F, Part 93, Subpart S, Section 93.227, Slot Use and Loss, January 1, 2019.

Code of Federal Regulations, Title 14, Chapter 1, Subchapter G, Part 139, Certification of Airports, January 1, 2011.

Code of Federal Regulations, Title 14, Chapter 1, Subchapter I, Part 158, Subpart A, Section 158.3, Definitions, January 1, 2019.

Code of Federal Regulations, Title 14, Chapter 1, Subchapter I, Part 158, Subpart A, Section 158.15, Project Eligibility at PFC Levels of $1, $2, or $3, January 1, 2019.

Code of Federal Regulations, Title 14, Chapter 1, Subchapter I, Part 158, Subpart A, Section 158.17, Project Eligibility at PFC Levels of $4 or $4.50, January 1, 2002.

Code of Federal Regulations, Title 14, Chapter 1, Subchapter I, Part 158, Subpart C, Collection, Handling, and Remittance of PFC's.

Code of Federal Regulations, Title 14, Chapter 1, Subchapter I, Part 158, Subpart C, Section 158.53, Collection Compensation, January 1, 2019.

Code of Federal Regulations, Title 14, Chapter 1, Subchapter I, Part 158, Subpart D, Reporting, Recordkeeping and Audits.

Code of Federal Regulations, Title 49, Part 1542, Airport Security, October 1, 2018.

Coogan, Matthew A., MarketSense Consulting LLC, and Jacobs Consultancy, *Ground Access to Major Airports by Public Transportation*, Washington, D.C.: Transportation Research Board, ACRP Report 4, 2008.

Dai, Mian, Qihong Liu, and Konstantinos Serfes, "Is the Effect of Competition on Price Dispersion Nonmonotonic? Evidence from the U.S. Airline Industry," *Review of Economics and Statistics*, Vol. 96, No. 1, March 2014, pp. 161–170.

Day, Don, "Big Changes Are Coming to Boise's Airport. We Now Know More About What and When," BoiseDev, March 26, 2019. As of July 11, 2019:
https://boisedev.com/news/2019/03/26/boise-airport-expansion/

Dempsey, Paul Stephen, *Theory and Law of Airport Revenue Diversion*, Washington, D.C.: National Academies Press, ACRP Legal Research Digest 2, 2008.

DiCicco, Dennis, and Jeffrey Given, "Cleared for Takeoff: Seeking Income Opportunities in Airport Municipal Bonds," Manulife Investment Management, January 3, 2019. As of June 26, 2019:
https://www.manulifeam.com/us/Research-and-Insights/Market-Views-And-Insights/Cleared-for-takeoff-Seeking-income-opportunities-in-airport-municipal-bonds/

Dillingham, Gerald, "Airport and Airway Trust Fund: Declining Balance Raises Concerns over Ability to Meet Future Demands," testimony presented before the Committee on Finance, U.S. Senate, Washington, D.C.: Government Accountability Office, GAO-11-358T, February 3, 2011. As of June 24, 2019:
https://www.gao.gov/assets/130/125456.pdf

Dulles Corridor Metrorail Project, "Funding," webpage, undated. As of June 25, 2019:
http://www.dullesmetro.com/about-dulles-rail/funding/

Evansville Airport v. Delta Airlines, 405 U.S. 707, 1972.

FAA—*See* Federal Aviation Administration.

FAA/OST—*See* Federal Aviation Administration/Office of the Secretary of Transportation.

Faulhaber, Joseph M., Jeffrey J. Schulthess, Andrew C. Eastmond, Scott P. Lewis, and Roy W. Block, *Airport/Airline Agreements—Practices and Characteristics*, Washington, D.C.: Transportation Research Board, 2010.

Federal Aviation Administration, "2018 TAF: Optimistic and Pessimistic Forecast Scenarios," webpage, undated a. As of December 9, 2019:
https://taf.faa.gov/Downloads/TAF2018Scenarios/TAF2018Scenarios.html

———, "Airline Service Quality Performance System (ASQP)," database, undated b. As of September 11, 2019:
https://aspm.faa.gov

———, "Certification Activity Tracking System (CATS)," webpage, undated c. As of July 9, 2019:
https://cats.airports.faa.gov

———, "FY 2018 Primary Entitlements," undated d. As of June 24, 2019:
https://www.faa.gov/airports/aip/grantapportion_data/media/FY-2018-Primary-Entitlement.pdf

———, "Instructions for Preparing Attachments for PFC Application Form: Section 6 of FAA Form 5500-1," undated e. As of November 22, 2019:
https://www.faa.gov/airports/resources/forms/media/pfc_5500_1_instruct_attach_0810.pdf

———, "The Operations Network (OPSNET)," database, undated f. As of July 14, 2019:
https://aspm.faa.gov/opsnet/sys/main.asp

———, *General Aviation Airports: A National Asset*, Washington, D.C., May 2012a. As of October 17, 2019:
https://www.faa.gov/airports/planning_capacity/ga_study/

———, "Interim Guidance on Land Uses Within a Runway Protection Zone," memorandum to Regional Airports Division Managers, 610 Branch Managers, 620 Branch Managers, and ADO Managers, September 27, 2012b. As of June 25, 2019:
https://www.faa.gov/airports/planning_capacity/media/interimLandUseRPZGuidance.pdf

———, "Policy Regarding Airport Rates and Charges," *Federal Register*, Vol. 78, No. 175, September 10, 2013, pp. 55330–55336.

———, "Feedback from the Policy Regarding Airport Rates and Charges Listening Sessions," updated April 17, 2014. As of July 10, 2019:
https://www.faa.gov/airports/airport_compliance/media/Airports-Rates-Charges-Listening-Sessions-2014.pdf

———, *FACT3: Airport Capacity Needs in the National Airspace System*, Washington, D.C., January 2015a. As of June 25, 2019: https://www.faa.gov/airports/planning_capacity/media/
FACT3-Airport-Capacity-Needs-in-the-NAS.pdf

———, "Airport Noise Compatibility Planning Toolkit," webpage, updated April 14, 2015b. As of July 11, 2019:
https://www.faa.gov/about/office_org/headquarters_offices/apl/noise_emissions/planning_toolkit/

———, "Passenger Facility Charge (PFC) Program: Eligibility of Ground Access Projects Meeting Certain Criteria" *Federal Register*, Vol. 81, No. 85, May 3, 2016. As of June 25, 2019:
https://www.federalregister.gov/documents/2016/05/03/2016-10334/
passenger-facility-charge-pfc-program-eligibility-of-ground-access-projects-meeting-certain-criteria

———, *Airport Improvement Program: Fiscal Years 2014–2016*, Washington, D.C., November 1, 2017a. As of June 24, 2019:
https://www.faa.gov/airports/aip/grant_histories/annual_reports/media/
FY2014-2016-AIP-Annual-Report-to-Congress.pdf

———, "Grant Funding Authorizations, Obligation Limitations, and Obligations," APP-500, November 14, 2017b. As of June 24, 2019:
https://www.faa.gov/airports/aip/grant_histories/annual_reports/media/
grant-funding-authorizations-limitations-obligations-1982-2016.pdf

————, "Overview: What is AIP?" webpage, updated November 15, 2017c. As of June 24, 2019:
https://www.faa.gov/airports/aip/overview/#eligible_projects

————, *National Plan of Integrated Airport Systems (NPIAS): 2019–2023*, Washington, D.C., 2018a. As of October 17, 2019:
https://www.faa.gov/airports/planning_capacity/npias/reports/

————, *Terminal Area Forecast Summary: Fiscal Years 2018–2045*, Washington, D.C., 2018b. As of July 9, 2019:
https://www.faa.gov/data_research/aviation/taf/media/taf_summary_fy_2018-2045.pdf

————, "Grandfathered Airports," fact sheet, May 1, 2018c. As of September 9, 2019:
https://cats.airports.faa.gov/GrandfatheredAirports.pdf

————, "FY 2018-2020 Airport Improvement Program Supplemental Appropriation Frequently Asked Questions (FAQs)," updated July 15, 2018d. As of June 26, 2019:
https://www.faa.gov/airports/aip/aip_supplemental_appropriation/media/
Frequently-Asked-Questions-FY-2018-Supplemental-Appropriation.pdf

————, "FAA Supplemental Appropriation Grant Detail Report," September 27, 2018e. As of June 26, 2019:
https://www.faa.gov/airports/aip/aip_supplemental_appropriation/media/
AIP-Supplemental-Grants-Announced-2018-09-27.pdf

————, "Voluntary Airport Low Emissions Program (VALE)," webpage, updated November 13, 2018f. As of June 24, 2019:
https://www.faa.gov/airports/environmental/vale/

————, *Airport Improvement Program Fiscal Year 2017 Report to Congress*, Washington, D.C., February 2019a. As of August 23, 2019:
https://www.faa.gov/airports/aip/grant_histories/annual_reports/media/
FY2017-AIP-Annual-Report-to-Congress.pdf

————, "Terminal Area Forecast (TAF)," webpage, updated April 12, 2019b. As of July 9, 2019:
https://www.faa.gov/data_research/aviation/taf/

————, "Airport and Airway Trust Fund (AATF): Fact Sheet," updated May 2019c. As of July 11, 2019:
https://www.faa.gov/about/budget/aatf/media/AATF_Fact_Sheet.pdf

————, "Slot Administration," webpage, updated May 9, 2019d. As of October 16, 2019:
https://www.faa.gov/about/office_org/headquarters_offices/ato/service_units/systemops/perf_analysis/
slot_administration/

————, "FY 2018–2020 Round 2 Airport Improvement Program Supplemental Appropriation Frequently Asked Questions (FAQs)," May 15, 2019e. As of June 26, 2019:
https://www.faa.gov/airports/aip/aip_supplemental_appropriation/media/
Frequently-Asked-Questions-FY-2018-2020-Supplemental-Appropriation-Round-2.pdf

————, "Key Passenger Facility Charge Statistics," May 31, 2019f. As of June 24, 2019:
https://www.faa.gov/airports/pfc/monthly_reports/media/stats.pdf

————, *PFC Approved Locations*, spreadsheet, May 31, 2019g. As of June 24, 2019:
https://www.faa.gov/airports/pfc/monthly_reports/media/airports.xlsx

————, "Airport Improvement Program (AIP) 2018–2020 Supplemental Appropriation," updated June 13, 2019h. As of June 24, 2019:
https://www.faa.gov/airports/aip/aip_supplemental_appropriation/

————, "What Is NextGen?," webpage, updated August 8, 2019i. As of October 30, 2019:
https://www.faa.gov/nextgen/what_is_nextgen/

————, "Fact Sheet – Airport Investment Partnership Program (AIPP) – Formerly Airport Privatization Pilot Program," October 1, 2019j. As of December 9, 2019:
https://www.faa.gov/news/fact_sheets/news_story.cfm?newsId=24114

Federal Aviation Administration Advisory Circular 150/5070-6B, Change 2, *Change 2 to Airport Master Plans*, Washington, D.C.: Federal Aviation Administration, January 27, 2015. As of October 10, 2019:
https://www.faa.gov/documentLibrary/media/Advisory_Circular/AC_150_5070-6B_with_chg_1&2.pdf

Federal Aviation Administration Advisory Circular 150/5100-21, *State Block Grant Program*, Washington, D.C.: Federal Aviation Administration, October 31, 2016. As of June 24, 2019:
https://www.faa.gov/documentLibrary/media/Advisory_Circular/AC_150_5100-21.pdf

Federal Aviation Administration Advisory Circular 150/5360-13A, *Airport Terminal Planning*, Washington, D.C.: Federal Aviation Administration, July 13, 2018. As of June 25, 2019:
https://www.faa.gov/documentLibrary/media/Advisory_Circular/
AC-150-5360-13A-Airport-Terminal-Planning.pdf

Federal Aviation Administration/Office of the Secretary of Transportation Task Force, *Airport Business Practices and Their Impact on Airline Competition*, Washington, D.C., October 1999.

Federal Aviation Administration Order 5100.39A, *Airports Capital Improvement Plan*, Washington, D.C.: Federal Aviation Administration, August 22, 2000. As of June 26, 2019:
https://www.faa.gov/documentLibrary/media/Order/order-5100-39A-acip.pdf

Federal Aviation Administration Order 5500.1, *Passenger Facility Charge*, Washington, D.C.: Federal Aviation Administration, August 9, 2001. As of June 24, 2019:
https://www.faa.gov/documentLibrary/media/Order/PFC_55001.pdf

Federal Aviation Administration Order 5190.6B, *FAA Airport Compliance Manual*, Washington, D.C.: Federal Aviation Administration, last updated September 30, 2009. As of December 12, 2019:
https://www.faa.gov/airports/resources/publications/orders/compliance_5190_6/

Federal Aviation Administration Order 5100.38D, Change 1, *Airport Improvement Program Handbook*, Washington, D.C.: Federal Aviation Administration, February 26, 2019. As of June 24, 2019:
http://www.faa.gov/airports/aip/aip_handbook/

Federal Aviation Administration Order 5090.5, *Formulation of the NPIAS and ACIP*, Washington, D.C.: Federal Aviation Administration, September 3, 2019. As of November 12, 2019:
https://www.faa.gov/documentLibrary/media/Order/Order-5090-5-NPIAS-ACIP.pdf

Fitch Ratings, "Airports Rating Criteria," February 23, 2018. As of December 9, 2019:
https://www.fitchratings.com/site/re/10021613

Florida Department of Transportation, *Public Airports Revenue Use Guide*, Bartow, Fla., 2008.

Forbes, Silke Januszewksi, and Mara Lederman, *The Role of Regional Airlines in the U.S. Airline Industry*, 2006. As of August 29, 2019:
http://faculty.weatherhead.case.edu/forbes/book_chapter_oct06.pdf

Gaggero, Alberto A., and Claudio A. Piga, "Airline Market Power and Intertemporal Price Dispersion," *Journal of Industrial Economics*, Vol. 59, No. 4, December 2011, pp. 552–577.

Gallatin Airport Authority, *Airport Revenue Bonds, Series 2009*, Bozeman, Mont., October 7, 2009. As of November 22, 2019:
https://emma.msrb.org/EP332996-EP37912-EP659937.pdf

GAO—*See* Government Accountability Office.

Gentry, Jennifer, Kent Duffy, and William J. Swedish, *Airport Capacity Profiles*, Washington, D.C.: Federal Aviation Administration, July 2014. As of June 25, 2019:
https://www.faa.gov/airports/planning_capacity/profiles/media/Airport-Capacity-Profiles-2014.pdf

Gerardi, Kristopher S., and Adam Hale Shapiro, "Does Competition Reduce Price Dispersion? New Evidence from the Airline Industry," *Journal of Political Economy*, Vol. 117, No. 1, February 2009, pp. 1–37.

Gilbert, Trish, "Improving Air Traffic Control for the American People: Examining the Current System," testimony presented before the Subcommittee on Aviation and Space, Committee on Commerce, Science, and Transportation, U.S. Senate, September 24, 2019. As of October 19, 2019:
https://www.natca.org/images//NATCA_PDFs/Congressional_Testimony/
TrishGilbertSenateTestimonySept242019.pdf

Goetz, Andrew R., and Timothy M. Vowles, "The Good, the Bad, and the Ugly: 30 Years of US Airline Deregulation," *Journal of Transport Geography*, Vol. 17, No. 4, July 2009, pp. 251–263.

Goldberg, Roy, "Airline Challenges to Airport Abuses of Economic Power," *Journal of Air Law and Commerce*, Vol. 72, No. 2, 2007, pp. 351–367.

Goldenstein, Taylor, "Austin Airport's Retro-Styled South Terminal Aims to Open April 13," *Austin American-Statesman*, March 1, 2017. As of August 14, 2019:
https://www.statesman.com/news/20170301/austin-airports-retro-styled-south-terminal-aims-to-open-april-13

Gosling, Geoffrey D., Wenbin Wei, and Dennis Freeman, *Collaborative Funding to Facilitate Airport Ground Access*, San Jose, Calif.: Mineta Transportation Institute, MTI Report 11-27, June 2012.

Government Accountability Office, *Airline Competition: Passenger Facility Charges Represent a New Funding Source for Airports*, Washington, D.C., GAO-RCED-91-39, December 1990. As of June 24, 2019:
https://www.gao.gov/assets/220/213373.pdf

———, *Commercial Aviation: Consumers Could Benefit from Better Information About Airline-Imposed Fees and Refundability of Government-Imposed Taxes and Fees*, Washington, D.C., GAO-10-785, July 2010. As of June 24, 2019:
https://www.gao.gov/assets/310/307042.pdf

———, *Airport and Airway Trust Fund: Factors Affecting Revenue Forecast Accuracy and Realizing Future FAA Expenditures*, Washington, D.C., GAO-12-222, January 2012a. As of June 24, 2019:
https://www.gao.gov/assets/590/587866.pdf

———, *Slot-Controlled Airports: FAA's Rules Could Be Improved to Enhance Competition and Use of Available Capacity*, Washington, D.C., GAO-12-902, September 2012b. As of October 16, 2019:
https://www.gao.gov/products/GAO-12-902

———, *Airline Competition: The Average Number of Competitors in Markets Serving the Majority of Passengers Has Changed Little in Recent Years, but Stakeholders Voice Concerns About Competition*, Washington, D.C., GAO 14-515, June 2014a. As of June 25, 2019:
https://www.gao.gov/products/GAO-14-515

———, *Airport Privatization: Limited Interest Despite FAA's Pilot Program*, Washington, D.C., GAO-15-42, November 2014b. As of October 16, 2019:
https://www.gao.gov/products/GAO-15-42

———, *Commercial Aviation: Raising Passenger Facility Charges Would Increase Airport Funding, but Other Effects Less Certain*, Washington, D.C., GAO-15-107, December 2014c. As of June 26, 2019:
https://www.gao.gov/assets/670/667444.pdf

———, *Aviation Forecasting: FAA Should Implement Additional Risk-Management Practices in Forecasting Aviation Activity*, Washington, D.C., GAO-16-210, March 2016a. As of November 12, 2019:
https://www.gao.gov/assets/680/675679.pdf

———, *Airport and Airway Trust Fund: Less Than Half of Noncommercial Jet Fuel Tax Receipts Are Transferred*, Washington, D.C., GAO-16-746R, August 8, 2016b. As of June 24, 2019:
https://www.gao.gov/assets/680/678899.pdf

———, *Commercial Aviation: Information on Airline Fees for Optional Services*, Washington, D.C., GAO-17-756, September 2017a. As of June 24, 2019:
https://www.gao.gov/assets/690/687258.pdf

———, *Transportation Security Administration: After Oversight Lapses, Compliance with Policy Governing Special Authority Has Been Strengthened*, Washington, D.C., GAO-18-172, December 2017b. As of June 25, 2019:
https://www.gao.gov/assets/690/689138.pdf

Government Accountability Office, Office of the General Counsel, *Whether the Airport and Airway Trust Fund Was Created Solely to Finance Aviation Infrastructure*, Washington, D.C., B-281779, February 12, 1999. As of June 24, 2019:
https://www.gao.gov/decisions/archive/281779.pdf

Graham, Anne, "Understanding the Low Cost Carrier and Airport Relationship: A Critical Analysis of the Salient Issues," *Tourism Management*, Vol. 36, June 2013, pp. 66–76.

Greenberg, Scott, *Reexamining the Tax Exemption of Municipal Bond Interest*, Washington, D.C.: Tax Foundation, July 21, 2016. As of September 18, 2017:
http://taxfoundation.org/article/reexamining-tax-exemption-municipal-bond-interest

Greenville-Spartanburg Airport Commission, "Minutes," Greer, S.C., May 28, 2019. As of July 11, 2019:
https://www.gspairport.com/site/user/files/1/Greenville-Spartanburg-Airport-Commission-May-28-2019-Regular-Meeting-Minutes-20190624-Final-and-Executed.pdf

Hao, Lu, Mark Hansen, Yu Zhang, and Joseph Post, "New York, New York: Two Ways of Estimating the Delay Impact of New York Airports," *Transportation Research Part E: Logistics and Transportation Review*, Vol. 70, October 2014, pp. 245–260.

Hazel, Robert A., Jan David Blais, Thomas J. Browne, and Daniel M. Benzon, *Resource Guide to Airport Performance Indicators*, Washington, D.C.: Transportation Research Board, ACRP Report 19A, 2011.

H.R. 1265—See Investing in America: Rebuilding America's Airport Infrastructure Act, 2017.

H.R. 3791—See Investing in America: Rebuilding America's Airport Infrastructure Act, 2019.

IATA—*See* International Air Transport Association.

ICAO—*See* International Civil Aviation Organization.

Internal Revenue Service, "Private Business Use – Management Contracts," updated November 16, 2018. As of June 25, 2019:
https://www.irs.gov/tax-exempt-bonds/private-business-use-management-contracts

International Air Transport Association, "20 Year Passenger Forecast," undated. As of October 10, 2019:
https://www.iata.org/publications/store/Pages/20-year-passenger-forecast.aspx

International Civil Aviation Organization, *Operation of Aircraft: Annex 6 to the Convention on International Civil Aviation*, 9th ed., Montreal, July 2010. As of September 8, 2019:
https://www.verifavia.com/bases/ressource_pdf/299/icao-annex-6-part-i.pdf

———, *ICAO's Policies on Charges for Airports and Air Navigation Services*, 9th ed., Montreal, 2012. As of September 9, 2019:
https://www.icao.int/publications/Documents/9082_9ed_en.pdf

InterVISTAS Consulting Inc., *Estimating Air Travel Demand Elasticities*, prepared for the International Air Transport Association, December 28, 2007.

Investing in America: Rebuilding America's Airport Infrastructure Act, H.R. 1265, 115th Congress, 2017.

Investing in America: Rebuilding America's Airport Infrastructure Act, H.R. 3791, 116th Congress, 2019.

IRS—*See* Internal Revenue Service.

JCT—*See* Joint Committee on Taxation.

J. D. Power, "North American Airports Effectively Navigating Construction, Capacity Challenges, J. D. Power Finds," press release, Costa Mesa, Calif., September 21, 2017. As of July 9, 2019:
https://www.jdpower.com/business/press-releases/jd-power-2017-north-america-airport-satisfaction-study

Joint Committee on Taxation, *Overview of Selected Tax Provisions Relating to the Financing of Infrastructure*, Washington, D.C., JCX-29-11, May 13, 2011. As of June 24, 2019:
https://www.jct.gov/publications.html?func=download&id=3789&chk=3789&no_html=1

———, *Overview of Selected Internal Revenue Code Provisions Relating to the Financing of Public Infrastructure*, Washington, D.C., JCX-7-19, March 4, 2019. As of June 24, 2019:
https://www.jct.gov/publications.html?func=download&id=5168&chk=5168&no_html=1

Kaplan, Stephen H., and Eric T. Smith, "Airline Use and Lease Agreements," presentation slides for 30th Annual AAAE Basics of Airport Law Workshop and 2014 Legal Update, Atlanta, Ga., October 19–21, 2014. As of June 25, 2019:
https://www.kaplankirsch.com/portalresource/lookup/wosid/cp-base-4-5402/overrideFile.name=/
Airline_Use_and_Lease_Agreements.pdf

Karaskiewicz, Timothy R., *Legal Considerations in the Funding and Development of Intermodal Facilities at Airports*, Washington, D.C.: Transportation Research Board, ACRP Legal Research Digest 35, September 2018.

Kasper, Daniel M., and Darin Lee, *An Assessment of Competition and Consumer Choice in Today's U.S. Airline Industry*, presentation prepared for Airlines for America, June 26, 2017.

Kincaid, Ian, Michael Tretheway, Stéphane Gros, and David Lewis, *Addressing Uncertainty About Future Airport Activity Levels in Airport Decision Making*, Washington, D.C.: Transportation Research Board, ACRP Report 76, 2012.

Kirk, Robert S., *Aviation Spending Guarantee Mechanisms*, Washington, D.C.: Congressional Research Service, RL33654, March 25, 2008.

Koenig, David, and Scott Mayerowitz, "Airlines Carve US into Markets Dominated by 1 or 2 Carriers," Associated Press, July 14, 2015. As of June 14, 2019:
https://apnews.com/7f964b3e484d4b43b732424dd9df0975

Kwoka, John, and Evgenia Shumilkina, "The Price Effect of Eliminating Potential Competition: Evidence from an Airline Merger," *Journal of Industrial Economics*, Vol. 58, No. 4, December 2010, pp. 767–793.

"Lawmakers Press to Protect Perimeter Rule at DCA from Further Encroachment," InsideNoVa, April 12, 2018. As of July 11, 2019:
https://www.insidenova.com/news/arlington/lawmakers-press-to-protect-perimeter-rule-at-dca-from-further/
article_b51f5cca-3e4f-11e8-adc4-43d7a6d5e904.html

LeighFisher and Exstare Federal Services Group, *Resource Manual for Airport In-Terminal Concessions*, Washington, D.C.: Transportation Research Board, ACRP Report 54, 2011.

Linares, Luis, "Flashback Friday: A Look Back at US Airways," *Airways*, April 10, 2015. As of October 17, 2019:
https://airwaysmag.com/airchive/flashback-friday-a-look-back-at-us-airways/

Maguire, Steven, and Joseph S. Hughes, *Private Activity Bonds: An Introduction*, Washington, D.C.: Congressional Research Service, RL31457, July 13, 2018. As of June 26, 2019:
https://fas.org/sgp/crs/misc/RL31457.pdf

Mark, Rob, "ATC Privatization: Inside the Fight for Air Traffic Control's Future," *Flying*, August 2, 2017. As of July 9, 2019:
https://www.flyingmag.com/atc-privatization/

Marriott, Michael, "Pittsburgh Builds Airport of Future Now," *New York Times*, November 12, 1991. As of October 17, 2019:
https://www.nytimes.com/1991/11/12/us/pittsburgh-builds-airport-of-future-now.html

Marron, Donald B., "Financing Investment in the Air Traffic Control System," testimony before the Committee on Transportation and Infrastructure Subcommittee on Aviation, U.S. House of Representatives, September 27, 2006. As of June 24, 2019:
https://permanent.access.gpo.gov/websites/www.cbo.gov/ftpdocs/75xx/doc7597/09-27-AirTraffic.pdf

Massachusetts Institute of Technology, Airline Data Project, "Average Seat Capacity per Departure—All Aircraft," spreadsheet, undated. As of September 6, 2019:
http://web.mit.edu/airlinedata/www/Aircraft&Related.html

Mathews, J. Scott, "A Counterpoint Assessment of Vancouver International Airport as a Gateway to North America," *Thunderbird International Business Review*, Vol. 41, No. 3, May/June 1999, pp. 265–272.

McGraw, Candace S., "The Cost of Doing Nothing: Why Investment in Our Nation's Airports Matters," testimony presented before the Committee on Transportation and Infrastructure, U.S. House of Representatives, March 26, 2019. As of June 26, 2019:
https://transportation.house.gov/imo/media/doc/McGraw%20Testimony.pdf

McLaughlin, David, and Michael Sasso, "U.S. Airlines Unlikely to Face Antitrust Case on Capacity," Bloomberg News, January 11, 2017.

Metropolitan Washington Airports Authority, "DCA Reagan National - Slot & Perimeter Rules," webpage, undated. As of October 16, 2019:
https://www.flyreagan.com/dca/dca-reagan-national-slot-perimeter-rules

Miami Intermodal Center, "Finance," webpage, undated. As of June 25, 2019:
http://micdot.com/financing.html

Moreau, Alexandre, "How High Taxes and Fees Punish Canadian Air Travelers," *Globe and Mail*, June 24, 2018. As of September 6, 2019:
https://www.theglobeandmail.com/business/commentary/
article-how-high-taxes-and-fees-punish-canadian-air-travellers/

Morrison, Steven A., and Clifford Winston, "The Remaining Role for Government Policy in the Deregulated Airline Industry," in Sam Peltzman and Clifford Winston, eds., *Deregulation of Network Industries: What's Next?* Washington, D.C.: AEI-Brookings Joint Center for Regulatory Studies, 2000, pp. 1–40.

———, "Delayed! U.S. Aviation Infrastructure Policy at a Crossroads," in Clifford Winston and Ginés de Rus, eds., *Aviation Infrastructure Performance: A Study in Comparative Political Economy*, Washington, D.C.: Brookings Institution Press, 2008, pp. 7–35.

Mouawad, Jad, "The Challenge of Starting an Airline," *New York Times*, May 25, 2012. As of October 15, 2019:
https://www.nytimes.com/2012/05/26/business/start-up-airlines-face-big-obstacles.html

MSRB—*See* Municipal Securities Rulemaking Board.

Municipal Securities Rulemaking Board, Electronic Municipal Market Access, homepage, undated. As of November 22, 2019:
https://emma.msrb.org

National Association of State Aviation Officials, *NASAO State Aviation Funding and Organizational Data Report 2015*, McLean, Va., August 3, 2015. As of June 25, 2019:
http://onlinepubs.trb.org/onlinepubs/acrp/Temp/NASAOdata.pdf

National Safe Skies Alliance, *Recommended Security Guidelines for Airport Planning, Design, and Construction*, Louisville, Tenn., April 2017. As of September, 9 2019:
https://www.sskies.org/images/uploads/subpage/
PARAS_0004.Recommended_Security_Guidelines.FinalReport.v2.pdf

Nichol, Cindy, *Innovative Finance and Alternative Sources of Revenue for Airports: A Synthesis of Airport Practice*, Washington, D.C.: National Academies Press, 2007. As of November 11, 2019:
https://www.nap.edu/catalog/14041/innovative-finance-and-alternative-sources-of-revenue-for-airports

Nunes, Ashley, "Is Trump's Plan to Privatize Air-Traffic Control a Good Idea?" *The Atlantic*, June 7, 2017. As of July 9, 2019:
https://www.theatlantic.com/business/archive/2017/06/trump-privatize-air-traffic-control/529503/

Office of Management and Budget, "Historical Tables, Table 2.4—Composition of Social Insurance and Retirement Receipts and of Excise Taxes: 1940–2024," undated. As of June 24, 2019:
https://www.whitehouse.gov/omb/historical-tables/

———, OMB Circular No. A-11, Section 20, *Preparation, Submission, and Execution of the Budget*, Washington, D.C., 2016. As of October 9, 2019:
https://www.whitehouse.gov/sites/whitehouse.gov/files/omb/assets/a11_current_year/s20.pdf

———, "Supplemental Materials: Public Budget Database," March 2019. As of June 24, 2019:
https://www.whitehouse.gov/omb/supplemental-materials/

O'Leary, Shawn P., "Rx for High-SALT Investors: Municipal Bonds," Nuveen, March 4, 2019. As of December 9, 2019:
https://www.nuveen.com/en-us/thinking/municipal-bond-investing/rx-for-high-salt-investors

OMB—*See* Office of Management and Budget.

Ostrower, Jon, "Can New Airlines Make It in America?" CNN Money, February 15, 2018. As of November 11, 2019:
https://money.cnn.com/2018/02/14/news/onejet-new-airlines/index.html

Pallini, Thomas, "Crossing O'er: Why North American Travelers Trek Across International Borders for Cheaper Flights," AirlineGeeks, February 15, 2019. As of September 6, 2019:
https://airlinegeeks.com/2019/02/15/crossing-oer-why-north-american-travelers-trek-across-international-border-for-cheaper-flights/

Poirier, Florian, Jasenka Rakas, and Linda J. Perry, "Analysis of Trends in Aircraft Sizing and Fleet Mix: Implications for Airport Design," presentation at Air Transport Research Society (ATRS) World Conference, Berkeley, Calif., June 21–23, 2007. As of October 8, 2019:
http://faculty.ce.berkeley.edu/rakas/Poirier_Rakas_Perry_ATRS2007.pdf

Poole, Robert W., Jr., *Annual Privatization Report 2017: Air Transportation*, Los Angeles, Calif.: Reason Foundation, October 2017. As of September 9, 2019:
https://reason.org/wp-content/uploads/files/annual_privatization_report_2017_air_transportation.pdf

———, "Airport Policy News #126," Reason Foundation, November 14, 2018.

Port of Portland, *Official Statement: Portland International Airport Revenue Bonds, Series Twenty-Four A and Series Twenty-Four B*, Portland, Oreg., January 11, 2017. As of November 22, 2019:
https://emma.msrb.org/ER1016183-ER795431-ER1196665.pdf

Port of Seattle, *Official Statement Relating to Port of Seattle Passenger Facility Charge Revenue Refunding Bonds*, Seattle, Wash., November 9, 2010. As of November 22, 2019:
https://www.portseattle.org/sites/default/files/2018-05/Final%20Official%20Statement%20-%202010%20PFC%20bonds.pdf

Public Law 79-377, Federal Airport Act of 1946, May 13, 1946.

Public Law 91-258, Airport and Airway Development Act of 1970, May 21, 1970.

Public Law 93-44, Airport Development Acceleration Act of 1973, June 18, 1973.

Public Law 95-504, Airline Deregulation Act of 1978, October 24, 1978.

Public Law 97-248, Tax Equity and Fiscal Responsibility Act of 1982, Title V, Airport and Airway Improvement, September 3, 1982.

Public Law 100-223, Airport and Airway Safety and Capacity Expansion Act of 1987, December 30, 1987.

Public Law 101-508, Omnibus Budget Reconciliation Act of 1990, November 5, 1990.

Public Law 103-305, Federal Aviation Administration Authorization Act of 1994, August 23, 1994.

Public Law 104-264, Federal Aviation Reauthorization Act of 1996, October 9, 1996.

Public Law 106-181, Wendell H. Ford Aviation Investment and Reform Act for the 21st Century, April 5, 2000.

Public Law 109-59, Safe, Accountable, Flexible, Efficient Transportation Equity Act: A Legacy for Users, August 10, 2005.

Public Law 112-95, FAA Modernization and Reform Act of 2012, February 14, 2012.

Public Law 113-9, Reducing Flight Delays Act of 2013, May 1, 2013.

Public Law 115-141, Consolidated Appropriations Act, 2018, March 23, 2018.

Public Law 115-254, FAA Reauthorization Act of 2018, October 5, 2018.

Public Law 116-6, Consolidated Appropriations Act, 2019, February 15, 2019.

Rabinowitz, Jason, "Why Did New York's JFK Airport Struggle to Cope with Its Flight Backlog After the Bomb Cyclone?" The Points Guy, January 7, 2018. As of June 25, 2019:
https://thepointsguy.com/2018/01/why-did-jfk-struggle-flight-backlog/

Redondi, Renato, Paolo Malighetti, and Stefano Paleari, "De-Hubbing of Airports and Their Recovery Patterns," *Journal of Air Transport Management*, Vol. 18, No. 1, January 2012, pp. 1–4.

Regional Airline Association, *Annual Report 2018*, Washington, D.C., 2019. As of August 19, 2019:
https://www.raa.org/content-hub/raa-annual-reports/

Rupp, Nicholas G., and Kerry M. Tan, "Mergers and Product Quality: A Silver Lining from De-Hubbing in the U.S. Airline Industry," *Contemporary Economic Policy*, Vol. 37, No. 4, October 2019, pp. 652–672.

Russell, Edward, "Congressman Makes Show of Axing Washington National Perimeter," *FlightGlobal*, December 14, 2018. As of July 11, 2019:
https://www.flightglobal.com/news/articles/congressman-makes-show-of-axing-washington-national-454442/

S. 1655—*See* Transportation, Housing and Urban Development, and Related Agencies Appropriations Act, 2018.

San Francisco International Airport, *Official Statement: Second Series Taxable Revenue Refunding Bonds, Issue 31F*, San Francisco, Calif., January 26, 2005. As of November 22, 2019:
https://emma.msrb.org/MS230444-MS205752-MD399844.pdf

Schoenberger, Chana R., "Airport Munis," *Forbes*, June 9, 2003. As of August 5, 2019:
https://www.forbes.com/forbes/2003/0609/134.html#69dc7b604157

SFO—*See* San Francisco International Airport.

Sharkey, Joe, "Pittsburgh, Once a Showplace Hub, Feels US Airways' Woes," *New York Times*, September 14, 2004. As of October 17, 2019:
https://www.nytimes.com/1991/11/12/us/pittsburgh-builds-airport-of-future-now.html

Shine, Conor, "*DFW Airport Plans to Issue Billions in Bonds for Improvements, Possibly Including a Sixth Terminal*," *Dallas Morning News*, November 30, 2018. As of June 26, 2019:
https://www.dallasnews.com/business/dfw-airport/2018/11/30/
gates-again-dfw-airport-plans-billions-bond-sales-airfield-terminal-improvements

Smith, Eric T., *Legal Issues Relating to Airports Promoting Competition*, Washington, D.C.: Transportation Research Board, ACRP Legal Research Digest 37, June 2019.

Starostina, Tatiana, and Dafang Wu, "ACI-NA 2017–18 Business Term Survey," presentation at 2018 Business of Airports Conference, Portland, Oreg., June 11–13, 2018. As of September 6, 2019:
https://dwuconsulting.com/images/Articles/180608%20ACI-NA%20Business%20Term%20Survey.pdf

State of Hawaii, *Official Statement: Airports System Revenue Bonds Consisting of Series 2010A and Refunding Series 2010B*, Honolulu, Hawaii, March 24, 2010. As of November 22, 2019:
https://emma.msrb.org/EA377223-EA296730-EA692380.pdf

Tang, Rachel Y., *Financing Airport Improvements*, Washington, D.C.: Congressional Research Service, updated March 15, 2019. As of June 24, 2019:
https://fas.org/sgp/crs/misc/R43327.pdf

Tang, Rachel Y., and Bart Elias, *The Airport and Airway Trust Fund (AATF): An Overview*, Washington, D.C.: Congressional Research Service, R44749, January 31, 2017. As of June 24, 2019:
https://fas.org/sgp/crs/misc/R44749.pdf

Transportation, Housing and Urban Development, and Related Agencies Appropriations Act, 2018, S. 1655, 115th Congress, 2017.

Transportation Research Board, *Measuring Airport Landside Capacity*, Washington, D.C., 1987.

———, *Winds of Change: Domestic Air Transport Since Deregulation*, Washington, D.C., 1991.

———, *Entry and Competition in the U.S. Airline Industry: Issues and Opportunities*, Washington, D.C., 1999. As of July, 14, 2019:
https://www.nap.edu/catalog/25103/entry-and-competition-in-the-us-airline-industry-issues-and-opportunities

Transportation Security Administration, "Electronic Baggage Screening Program," webpage, undated. As of June 25, 2019:
https://www.tsa.gov/for-industry/electronic-baggage-screening

TSA—*See* Transportation Security Administration.

Turner & Townsend, *International Construction Market Survey 2019*, Leeds, United Kingdom, 2019. As of July 11, 2019:
http://www.infrastructure-intelligence.com/sites/default/files/article_uploads/
Turner%20Townsend%20International%20Construction%20Market%20Survey%202019.pdf

United Airlines, Inc. v. The Port Authority of New York and New Jersey – Complaint and Exhibits A to NN (16-14-13), FAA-2015-0026, posted January 8, 2015. As of June 25, 2019:
https://www.regulations.gov/document?D=FAA-2015-0026-0001

U.S. Code, Title 14, Chapter 2, Subchapter A, Part 234, Section 234.2, Definitions, January 1, 2010.

U.S. Code, Title 26, Subtitle A, Chapter 1, Subchapter B, Part IV, Subpart A, Section 142, Exempt Facility Bond, January 3, 2012.

U.S. Code, Title 26, Subtitle A, Chapter 1, Subchapter F, Part I, Section 501, Exemption from Tax on Corporations, Certain Trusts, etc., January 3, 2012.

U.S. Code, Title 49, Subtitle VII, Part A, Subpart i, Chapter 401, Section 40117, Passenger Facility Fees, January 3, 2012.

U.S. Code, Title 49, Subtitle VII, Part B, Chapter 471, Subchapter I, Section 47101, Policies, January 8, 2008.

U.S. Code, Title 49, Subtitle VII, Part B, Chapter 471, Subchapter I, Section 47102, Definitions, January 3, 2012.

U.S. Code, Title 49, Subtitle VII, Part B, Chapter 471, Subchapter I, Section 47105, Project Grant Applications, January 3, 2012.

U.S. Code, Title 49, Subtitle VII, Part B, Chapter 471, Subchapter I, Section 47106, Project Grant Application Approval Conditioned on Satisfaction of Project Requirements, January 3, 2012.

U.S. Code, Title 49, Subtitle VII, Part B, Chapter 471, Subchapter I, Section 47107, Project Grant Application Approval Conditioned on Assurances About Airport Operations, January 5, 2009.

U.S. Code, Title 49, Subtitle VII, Part B, Chapter 471, Subchapter I, Section 47114, Apportionments, January 3, 2012.

U.S. Code, Title 49, Subtitle VII, Part B, Chapter 471, Subchapter I, Section 47116, Small Airport Fund, January 8, 2008.

U.S. Code, Title 49, Subtitle VII, Part B, Chapter 475, Subchapter I, Section 47504, Noise Compatibility Programs, February 1, 2010.

U.S. Code, Title 49, Subtitle VII, Part B, Chapter 475, Subchapter I, Section 47505, Airport Noise Compatibility Planning Grants, January 3, 2012.

U.S. Code, Title 49, Subtitle VII, Part C, Chapter 481, Section 48103, Airport Planning and Development and Noise Compatibility Planning and Programs, February 1, 2010.

U.S. Department of Justice, "Herfindahl-Hirschman Index," webpage, updated July 31, 2018. As of November 12, 2019:
https://www.justice.gov/atr/herfindahl-hirschman-index

U.S. Department of Transportation, "Reporting the Causes of Airline Delays and Cancellations," Final Rule, *Federal Register*, Vol. 67, No. 227, November 25, 2002. As of October 18, 2019:
https://www.govinfo.gov/content/pkg/FR-2002-11-25/pdf/02-29910.pdf

———, "Notice of Policy Regarding the Eligibility of Airport Ground Access Transportation Projects for Funding Under the Passenger Facility Charge Program," Notice, *Federal Register*, Vol. 69, No. 27, February 10, 2004a. As of June 24, 2019:
https://www.faa.gov/airports/resources/publications/federal_register_notices/media/pfc_69fr6366.pdf

————, "Revisions to Passenger Facility Charge Rule for Compensation to Air Carriers," Final Rule, *Federal Register*, Vol. 69, No. 53, March 18, 2004b. As of June 24, 2019:
https://www.faa.gov/airports/resources/publications/federal_register_notices/media/pfc_69fr18Mr0415.pdf

————, *Transforming Communities in the 21st Century: Fiscal Year 2017 Budget Highlights*, Washington, D.C., 2016. As of June 24, 2019:
https://www.transportation.gov/sites/dot.gov/files/docs/DOT_BH2017_508%5B2%5D.pdf

————, "Essential Air Service," webpage, updated November 22, 2017. As of November 13, 2019:
https://www.transportation.gov/policy/aviation-policy/small-community-rural-air-service/essential-air-service

————, "Operating Limitations at John F. Kennedy International Airport," Extension to Order, *Federal Register*, Vol. 83, No. 180, September 17, 2018a. As of October 18, 2019:
https://www.govinfo.gov/content/pkg/FR-2018-09-17/pdf/2018-20138.pdf

————, "Operating Limitations at New York LaGuardia Airport," Extension to Order, *Federal Register*, Vol. 83, No. 181, September 18, 2018b. As of October 18, 2019:
https://www.govinfo.gov/content/pkg/FR-2018-09-18/pdf/2018-20226.pdf

————, "Airline On-Time Performance Data," database, updated August 2019. As of October 11, 2019:
https://www.transtats.bts.gov/Tables.asp?DB_ID=120&DB_Name=Airline%20On-Time%20
Performance%20Data&DB_Short_Name=On-Time

U.S. Department of Transportation, Office of Inspector General, *FAA Needs to More Accurately Account for Airport Sponsors' Grandfathered Payments*, Washington, D.C., Report No. AV2018041, April 17, 2018. As of September 6, 2019:
https://www.oig.dot.gov/sites/default/files/
FAA%20Oversight%20of%20Grandfathered%20Airports%20Final%20Report%5E4-17-18.pdf

USDOT—*See* U.S. Department of Transportation.

U.S. Travel Association, "Survey: Travelers Willing to Pay More to Improve Flying Experience," press release, Washington, D.C., March 25, 2015. As of September 6, 2019:
https://www.ustravel.org/press/survey-travelers-willing-pay-more-improve-flying-experience

Whitman Insight Strategies, "National Poll Shows Overwhelming Opposition to Proposed Increases in Airport Traveler Tax," PR Newswire, October 4, 2019. As of October 10, 2019:
https://www.prnewswire.com/news-releases/national-poll-shows-overwhelming-opposition-to-proposed-increases-in-airport-traveler-tax-300931275.html

"Why You Can't Get There from LaGuardia," editorial, *New York Times*, August 14, 2015. As of July 11, 2019:
https://www.nytimes.com/2015/08/14/opinion/why-you-cant-get-there-from-la-guardia.html

Wu, Dafang, "Classifying Airline Rates and Charges Methodologies" webpage, March 15, 2015a. As of June 25, 2019:
https://www.dwuconsulting.com/airport-finance/articles/airport-rate-methodology

————, "United States Airport Rates and Charges Regulations," webpage, March 15, 2015b. As of June 25, 2019:
https://www.dwuconsulting.com/airport-finance/articles/airport-rate-regulation

————, "Air Ticket Taxes and Fees," webpage, March 27, 2016. As of June 24, 2019:
https://dwuconsulting.com/air-traffic/articles/air-ticket-taxes-and-fees

————, Airport Finance 101," webpage, March 31, 2017. As of June 25, 2019:
https://www.dwuconsulting.com/airport-finance/articles/airport-finance-101

Yamanouchi, Kelly, "Settlements in Air Fare Collusion Suit Puts Pressure on Delta, United," *Atlanta Journal-Constitution*, June 28, 2018. As of June 25, 2019:
https://www.ajc.com/business/settlements-air-fare-collusion-suit-puts-pressure-delta-united/
J6bgHDJ4ymc995g1EDAxHI/